Surveillance Studies:
An Overview

Surveillance Studies: An Overview

DAVID LYON

polity

First published in 2007 by Polity Press

Polity Press
65 Bridge Street
Cambridge CB2 1UR, UK.

Polity Press
350 Main Street
Malden, MA 02148, USA.

ISBN-13: 978-07456-3591-0
ISBN-13: 978-07456-3592-7 (pb)

A catalogue record for this book is available from the British Library.

Typeset in 11 on 13 pt Scala
by Servis Filmsetting Ltd, Manchester
Printed and bound in Great Britain by
MPG Books Ltd, Bodmin, Cornwall

The publisher has used its best endeavours to ensure that the URLs for external websites referred to in this book are correct and active at the time of going to press. However, the publisher has no responsibility for the websites and can make no guarantee that a site will remain live or that the content is or will remain appropriate.

For further information on Polity, visit our website: www.polity.co.uk

Contents

Preface and Acknowledgements

This book offers an overview of surveillance studies. The irony of 'overview' is deliberate, because it reminds us that we are all in a sense implicated in surveillance, both as watchers and as the watched. Surveillance is part of our human world, and here we try to bring vision more clearly into our field of vision and to make visibility more visible. Over the last few decades a number of scholars and investigative journalists have tried to draw our attention to how surveillance is growing, and in this book I discuss some of their work. So it is an introduction not only to surveillance but also to studies of surveillance.

For some time now I have been variously intrigued, entertained and enraged by new forms of surveillance and I have made several attempts to throw light on this. It all started as I was trying to make sense of the so-called 'information society', as it emerged in the 1980s, when I concluded that some of the most politically and socially significant aspects of digital technologies would be their capacity to process personal data (Lyon 1988). In *The Electronic Eye: The Rise of Surveillance Society* (1994) I trace the historical development of surveillance in different spheres of the modern world, and in *Surveillance Society: Monitoring Everyday Life* (2001) I suggest that contemporary surveillance has novel implications for how we think about the body, the city and global relationships. I had hoped to follow this up with a third surveillance title, focusing on the subjects of surveillance and how their different responses affect how those processes work, but events intervened. Sensing the shifts that would continue to make an impact long after the attacks on the USA in 2001, I turned my attention to these, stressing the role of suspicion and fear and of challenges to human rights, in *Surveillance after September 11* (2003a).

As I worked on research towards these titles I frequently met new colleagues and students who were working on parallel tracks, and such contacts have been immensely stimulating and satisfying. I have learned much from these scholars, not only in sociology but also in criminology, political studies, human geography, ethics, computing and information studies, cultural studies, psychology, law and, of course, history, which is where my own work began. Their work may be found in a mushrooming array of books and articles and in an online journal dedicated to surveillance studies, *Surveillance and Society*. It has been a privilege to meet many of these colleagues, who come not only from Europe and North America, but also from countries including Australia, Hong Kong, India, Japan, Korea, Mexico, Singapore and South Africa. In this book I have included references to some of the best work in this exciting field, much of which is being done by researchers who are still in the early stages of their careers.

The perspective that holds these studies together has of course developed over time. While I hold to most of what I wrote fifteen or twenty years ago, I also acknowledge that I made mistakes. So in what I now write I try to correct misapprehensions, to explain things more clearly, and to indicate what seem to me to be better modes of expression or analysis. It will be evident from chapter 3, on surveillance theory, that I draw selectively and critically on several theoretical traditions, on two main criteria. One is empirical constraint. If the discoverable facts do not fit the theory, there must be better theoretical tools. As all so-called 'facts' are theory-laden, however, I admit that empirical constraint can only ever be partial. The other criterion is the values that inform and indeed give life to the theory. No theory emerges unmediated from accumulated 'facts'.

The values involved have to do with what I take to be non-negotiable starting points, such as the embodied subjectivity and sociality of human persons (ontology), and the primary imperative of all governmental systems to care for, protect, support and empower their most vulnerable members (ethics). From the critique of violence and the hints of an ontology of peace (Milbank 1990) or the exposure of exclusionary strategies and the alternative of embrace (Volf 1996) to the assertion of personhood against some unrealities of technology (Borgmann 1999; Franklin 1999) or an emphasis on trust, forgiveness and care – these are the commitments I cherish and from which I try to learn. These inform my theoretical choices in ways that connect scholarship and life (Fay 1976; Wolterstorff 1976). Other values are important (and are discussed in other publications of mine), but these two both underlie my work on surveillance and are informed by traditions of Christian social thought.

All books are the product of more than one mind – even more so in the case of a book that aspires to offer an overview of a field of study; many minds worked to make this book what it is now. As the author named on the cover, I take responsibility for what use I have made of the comments and criticisms of my kind readers and ask forgiveness for where I have not understood or made best use of ideas thus shared. I'm grateful for my academic contexts within which serious research work is valued and supported – the Social Sciences and Humanities Research Council of Canada, Queen's University in Kingston, Ontario, and within that the Sociology Department and the Surveillance Project, plus the more far-flung groups that include most prominently the international Surveillance Studies Network and authors from *Surveillance and Society*.

Colleagues from half a dozen countries who generously gave me helpful feedback on drafts of this book are Kirstie Ball, Davide Calenda, Chiara Fonio, Martin French, Kevin Haggerty, Kylie Hamilton, Jan Kahlen, Steve Marmura, Gary T. Marx, Midori Ogasawara, Charles Raab, Emily Merz Smith, Gavin Smith, Andrew Stevens and Dean Wilson, as well as an anonymous reader for Polity Press. Emily Merz Smith, a very able researcher, has contributed a lot by way of background and bibliographical searches as well as helping generally to keep me on track with the project. Andrea Drugan at Polity is a cheerful and encouraging editor. My life-companion, Sue, often reminds me in the words of the ancient sage Ecclesiastes that 'much study is a weariness of the flesh and of making many books there is no end', but she has the sense to suggest alternatives such as paddling our canoe or pedalling our tandem, which paradoxically refresh the 'flesh' in sociable ways. For the grace that keeps me going and for the invaluable help of patient friends, I am thankful.

Introduction

Surveillance studies is about seeing things and, more particularly, about seeing people. But, paradoxically, people are not what most surveillance sees today. Think of 'ambient intelligence' or 'ubiquitous computing', for example. This is the world – as yet unrealized but clearly in the making – in which all of daily life is under constant surveillance: humans are surrounded, immersed, in computing and networked technologies from dawn to dusk and in every conceivable location. Not only is the employee able to access the building or the computer terminal only with a coded key, all environments are either hardwired or wirelessly able to sense where people are, what they are doing and where they are going. Even 'wilderness' hikers have global positioning system (GPS) devices to indicate where they are at any given moment. But the people themselves are not really 'seen' so much as they yield data, or, in the case of DNA or fingerprint scans, have data extracted from them. Surveillance may be direct, face-to-face, or it may be technologically mediated. In today's world, the latter is growing fast. Each is significant in surveillance studies.

The task of giving an overview of surveillance studies can be undertaken in a number of ways, and I have chosen to try to set out some of the main fields of exploration and debate and to illustrate them with some of the best work being done in this exciting cross-disciplinary area. To get a broad picture of what is happening I begin in part I with 'Viewpoints', first describing the field and defining terms and then turning in chapter 2 to 'spreading surveillance sites'. Surveillance has become ubiquitous and taken for granted in today's world. It appears in many sectors of life, not necessarily in some developmental order, but in each certain features are displayed: rationalization, the application of science and technology, classification and the knowledgeability of subjects.

The military sphere yields both the earliest modern examples of rational discipline and some of the technical advances central to surveillance today. State administration and the census take this further, checking the details of all citizens, for example for voting or public health. Workplace monitoring and supervision represent a key surveillance history in which several dimensions of modern practice, including disputed monitoring, are writ large. Policing and crime control accent the urban context, today both with highly visible video cameras and with police dataveillance. Consumption also has to be considered as a sphere of surveillance, where again the same key traits are visible, and in the consumer sphere a particular pattern of growth is evident. Place-based surveillance began with market research, was modified by online commercial activity, and now, using locations technologies, the techniques of cyber-marketing are returned to the world of mobile consumers. Today, these spheres not only co-exist but increasingly also inter-relate.

It is hardly sufficient, however, to state *where* surveillance is happening. We need some explanations of *why* surveillance is proliferating today, *what* is behind it, and *who* is affected. How does one explain the processes of surveillance? While some treatments of surveillance focus on a single theory, the view taken in chapter 3 is that various theoretical resources contribute to explanation and understanding at different levels and in different ways. The urge to rationalize and to classify, together with the individuation of populations and a corresponding culture of possessive individualism, is basic to modernity. But the classificatory drive is also bound up with competitive capitalism, the organizational imperatives of bureaucracy and conflicts at a global level, and thus these also contribute significantly to the social order that surveillance helps to produce.

While, as Weber and, in different ways, Foucault show, self-discipline linked with 'oversight' was required for modern institutions to work and flourish, one could argue that other motifs of situational control are now superimposed on (and sometimes supplant) such self-discipline. Within this, surveillance plays a central role at a macro level in 'sorting things out' (Bowker and Star 1999), now assisted and amplified by information networks. Theoretical debate at this level – especially around the notion of 'social sorting' and its relation to governance – offers strong clues about how things work at a micro and meso level, too. In the end, however, the cases of those who are marginalized, abandoned and excluded by such sorting serve as a further reminder of the axiom that the personal is political and that this too must be theorized.

A note is needed at this point on the perspective that underpins this book. While I genuinely try to present an overview of surveillance studies and to be fair to different theoretical positions in particular, I cannot pretend that I myself take no position. As I set out the various arguments about theorizing surveillance, I draw readers' attention to valuable insights in the work of many thinkers, including those who disagree with each other. Readers will not find the work of a consistent disciple of Zygmunt Bauman, Judith Butler, Émile Durkheim, Jacques Ellul, Michel Foucault, Nancy Fraser, Karl Marx, Georg Simmel or Max Weber here (even supposing such consistent discipleship were possible). Yet the analysis done by each of these, among others, contains very helpful ideas. Foucault once invited his readers to use his work as a tool-box (cited in Haggerty 2006a: 38) from which to select useful analytical equipment, and such selection is what I do. As I noted in the preface, my choice of tools is guided both by how effectively they explain what is happening and, more significantly, by how well they comport with my basic commitments. While I find substantial agreement with others in the field, analytically and ethically, I try to find consistent ways of expressing my position. However poorly I live them, my convictions are Christian.

Part II – 'Vision' – may be read as moving from the micro to the macro level, although each has to be understood in terms of the other as well. These chapters deal with the formation and growth of what might be called surveillance systems. To understand surveillance in organizational and informational contexts both 'watcher' and 'watched' and the relations between them have to be analysed (chapter 4). Surveillance practices are probably basic to human society and start with any elementary watching of some by another in order to create an effect of looking *after* or looking *over* the latter. The fact that there are two parties, watcher and watched, is important but often overlooked. In local face-to-face contexts the gaze is mediated only by customs and mores, so mutual expectations are invoked. Such watching may also involve checking or recording, perhaps using some simple device. Some purpose is present, which may appear somewhere on a continuum between *care* and *control* (and may involve both in combination, for example with some addicts or suicide-prone persons who might seek or comply with control for their own good), although how this is perceived by the surveillance subject may make a difference.

In modern times, surveillance appeared as part of the political economy of capitalism (Marx), as a product of bureaucratic organization (Weber) and as a shift from punishment and spectacle to self-discipline (Foucault). In each case a specific kind of system and a specific concept of self are in view. With the advent of computer-based surveillance in the later twentieth century, fresh forms of mediation emerged, in which *personal data* (and thus the 'data-double' or 'software self') were central. Surveillance today is found in the flows of data within networked databases, but these still relate to organizational practices, power and, of course, the persons to whom those data refer. How the powers of surveillance are realized in local and remote organizational contexts must be considered by looking at both the *system* and the *self* and at the interaction between the two.

Moving to the meso level in chapter 5, twenty-first-century cities rely on the order-creating capacities of digital technologies to classify, sort and manage social outcomes across a range of sectors. Using personal data, techniques derived from military, administrative, employment, policing and consumer practices combine to create a complex matrix of power; a surveillance assemblage. The word 'assemblage' originates in archaeology, where it refers to artefacts that are found together – say, tools and vessels – and apparently related to each other. In Gilles Deleuze and Félix Guattari's work it takes on the idea of a dynamic interconnection between otherwise discrete items that somehow come together, an idea that is made more concrete in relation to surveillance by Kevin Haggerty and Richard Ericson. The latter note some strong contemporary desires, or urges, to bring surveillance systems together, whether for control, governance, security, profit or entertainment (Haggerty and Ericson 2000: 609). Police departments constantly try to draw different databases together, just as, on an international scale, the US Department of Homeland Security does. But marketers also evidence this urge, along with insurance companies, health systems, and the like.

In this way, in today's cities, cyberspaces may in some ways be mapped onto physical geographies, helping to create new configurations of the social as well as to erode some older ones. And personal data relating to one area, say, health records, may be sought by recruiters who pre-screen applicants for jobs. Thus the assemblages grow together, constantly putting out new shoots like ground-creepers to form new networks. Community life-chances and personal choices are increasingly affected by these assemblages, which too often serve to reinforce already existing divisions. A humorous treatment of this may be seen in an American Civil Liberties Union (ACLU) animation of a pizza-ordering system that checks the customer's identity against the national registry, warns him about the health risks to someone with his cholesterol count of his 'double meat' order, is aware of his clothing size from other consumer records, and shows his ability to pay for the more expensive product from a recent travel agent flight record.[1]

Though I mention Homeland Security, above, what I am describing is not simply the result of the 9/11 aftermath, although the 'war on terror' has contributed tremendously to the further digitizing and globalizing of surveillance. Nor can it be understood as a simple extension of, for example, class or bureaucratic power, even though these are still significant. Questions of risk and trust, of privacy and anonymity, of security and opportunity are central. Today's surveillance is a peculiarly ambiguous process in which digital technologies and personal data are fundamentally implicated and meet in software coding that classifies yet more groups in different ways. Some outcomes are relatively innocuous while others carry both deep dangers for democracy – especially as biometric, location and genomic techniques proliferate – and potential for democratic involvement, ethical critique and alternative practices.

Apparently insignificant aspects of ordinary life – banking, travelling, using the phone – are routinely recorded, stored, processed and retrieved. Those data, originating in or from our bodies, travel great distances not only within organizations or countries but also across borders. This is the theme of chapter 6. Global mobility, much prized in the late modern capitalist world system, generates large-scale surveillance as people physically cross borders through airports and other transit points, or as their data travel for trade, employment, law enforcement or other reasons. Now travel documents such as passports (for external movement) or ID cards (for internal) carry more data extracted from the body to permit global flows. Data-doubles have far greater rates of mobility than their real-life counterparts; indeed, the travels of the one affect the travels of the other (especially if one is locally defined as an 'other'). Some see in this the emergence of a global surveillance assemblage, and in some instances this is an appropriate – not to mention democratically dangerous – characterization. But significant differences also occur between different countries; surveillance experiences are far from uniform, for a number of reasons. Different cultures, different social values; these are accentuated by globalization in local contexts and serve to shape surveillance and responses to it in various ways.

This emphasis on the contexts of surveillance may be read in other ways too. If part II is mainly about surveillance systems, then part III – 'Visibility' – is mainly about surveillance subjects. In chapter 7 I explore some ways in which contemporary surveillance occurs in contexts that are already media-saturated. Electronic means of entertainment, leisure and even education operate alongside the media of surveillance and indeed are sometimes part of a two-way exchange. In film, novels and television, surveillance situations and processes are portrayed and analysed, and beyond those the internet provides games and spaces where surveillance may be explored as well as experienced. How they do this is worth examining carefully; some aid critique, some foster complacency. In the worlds of theme parks and shopping malls, too, surveillance is not merely an external process but something participatory.

The overlapping and cross-cutting cultures of surveillance may be reinforced and normalized by their interactions with entertainment media; think, for example, of the domestication of the dreaded Big Brother in 'reality TV'. As Thomas Mathiesen argues, the TV 'synopticon' where the many watch the few parallels and reproduces the 'panopticon' where the few watch the many (Mathiesen 1997). The spectacle that Foucault thought had been superseded is actually crucial to the effectiveness of some of its supposed disciplinary replacements. And as Mark Andrejevic shows, not only do many 'expressive' TV shows encourage display and visibility, but also all kinds of 'interactivity' (such as voting on reality TV) help to expand the consumption of goods and services as well as of TV itself (Andrejevic 2004a).

Chapter 8 examines the struggles over surveillance. Surveillance serves various purposes, from entitlement to control (and sometimes both those at once), and is inherently ambiguous. Moreover, in order to work, many surveillance processes depend on the involvement, witting or not, of those who are surveilled. Such persons are not merely subject *to* surveillance, but subjects *of* surveillance. In those contexts where surveillance is perceived as or has the effects of control, the fact that its subjects interact and react with surveillance means that its effects are mitigated or magnified in part in relation to their involvement. Surveillance may be questioned or attacked as well as accepted meekly. The struggles make a difference to surveillance outcomes.

For Giddens, a 'dialectic of control' is set up whereby the growing power of modern institutions calls forth countervailing responses, and this may be seen in the case of surveillance, in workplace, political and other contexts (Giddens 1985). For much of the time, and for a variety of reasons, people comply with surveillance but they may also variously negotiate and resist, and these circumstances and processes deserve exploration. For Giddens, the main thrust of counter-surveillance activities may be thought of as 'free speech', which, while an interesting and potentially fruitful thought, seems rather limited for the varieties of surveillance experienced today. At certain junctures, opposition to surveillance produces regulatory and legislative change, for instance, around the concept of privacy.

Conventionally, in the West, privacy has often been seen as the concept around which resistance to intensive or extreme surveillance may be mobilized. As we find in chapter 9, privacy helpfully alerts us to dimensions of human existence that should rightly be treated with caution and respect and, in tandem with principles such as 'fair information practices',[2] offers some vital guidance as to how surveillance should be regulated. But privacy is also hard to define and varies tremendously from culture to culture and from era to era. It is also associated with possessive individualism, with property and with a dubious notion of persons as autonomous agents (Lyon 1994: chap. 10). But privacy is not the only mobilizing idea on offer today. Many of today's surveillance issues are better thought of in social justice terms, to do with the distribution of risks and with civil liberties, where 'social sorting' and governance are guiding motifs (Lyon 2003b).

Because of the widespread, systematic and routine ways in which personal data are processed in the twenty-first century, it is appropriate to talk of the 'surveillance society'. This is not a sinister conspiracy, or a comment about everyday prison-like conditions, just a feature of social life today. Equally, because the focus of the nation-state is shifting subtly from welfare to safety, seen especially but not exclusively in a huge post-9/11 emphasis on national security, it is appropriate to talk of a 'safety state' (Raab 2005a). The safety state, needless to say, depends extensively on surveillance data, much of which originates not in official statistics but in commercial, health-care, employment and other kinds of sources.

The fact that the way in which our lives are shaped (this is 'governance') depends heavily on the kinds of data available about us means that the politics of information is an increasingly important arena for debate. As the ultimate beneficiaries – and victims – of data regimes and surveillant assemblages are not abstract categories but people, then disclosure of the ways in which coded categories affect people's lives is of paramount importance. This can be illustrated by reference to no-fly lists, genetic screening and customer relationship management, each of which is a feature of the surveillance society and the safety state and each of which shows how automated social categorization affects ordinary people's choices and chances.

Surveillance of many kinds now touches all our lives in many different ways, all the time. Our encounters with surveillance are almost constant, 24/7. To understand surveillance, however, we must first define what we mean and acknowledge its ambiguities and its benefits as well as what we may consider as its dangers. Surveillance works by capturing personal data within certain coordinates (see Agre 1994), which means that bodies, behaviours and communications, seen in the cross-hairs of space and time, are significant in ways that we might not previously have imagined. This is what surveillance studies explores and tries to explain. This relatively new field draws gratefully on insights, concepts, theories and methods from a number of different disciplines, starting with sociology. Each has a contribution to make if we are to stand a chance of getting the picture properly in focus.

PART I

Viewpoints

The first three chapters set things out from different viewpoints. The first tries to show how surveillance is an ordinary part of everyday life even though it may sometimes take extraordinary turns. Surveillance is defined here, and I also explain the ways in which it relies on having some coordinates – the cross-hairs of space and time – to capture personal data. But why do we need a field of studies to focus on surveillance? I offer some reasons for this that have mainly to do with the rapidly increasing influence of surveillance in our daily lives and in the operation of very large-scale organizations, from businesses like Wal-Mart to government departments like Homeland Security.

Chapter 2 looks at some 'sites of surveillance'. The five areas are not exhaustive but they are symptomatic. Military surveillance gives us some historical background and reminds of an important contemporary emphasis that we ignore at our peril. Government administration is again a site of ancient forms of surveillance, but there are some significant shifts today, especially where computer networks are layered over conventional bureaucracies. Workers, too, have always been watched but today they find themselves under surveillance in new ways as well as finding new modes of resisting and negotiating them. Policing and crime control appear as a 'natural' site for surveillance, but, once again, some of the implications of this are far from obvious at first sight. Finally, until a few years ago, consumer activity might have seemed as unlikely a site of surveillance as policing seems likely, but in fact marketers have been trying to find out about their customers for almost a century. Today, they sometimes employ technologies superior to those of policing or government to do so.

Chapter 3 discusses the field from the perspective of theory. How do we explain what is going on in the world of surveillance? A big mistake, easily made, is to try to 'read off' surveillance outcomes from claims made about their products by technology companies or from what we think we know about what machines can do. Just because a network of searchable databases appears to be able to track down minute details of personal life does not mean that it will do so, or that if it does that these will necessarily have a negative impact on the individual. This book does not discuss 'technology' as a separate theme; rather, an exploration of the origins and consequences of technical innovations in surveillance is integrated into the overall analysis. Thus chapter 3 focuses on the roots of surveillance theory, including concepts lifted from literature; on supposed shifts from modern to postmodern forms of surveillance, in which the socio-technical features quite strongly; on discipline and control; and finally on governance, social sorting and exclusion. The intent is to find good theoretical ways of understanding and interpreting surveillance, but the discusssion does not neglect the theme of theory and counter-surveillance.

1 The Watched World Today

> My anxiety is that we don't sleepwalk into a surveillance society where much more information is collected about people, accessible to far more people shared across many more boundaries than British society would feel comfortable with.
>
> Richard Thomas, UK Information Commissioner (cited in Ford 2004)

Encounters with surveillance

If I have to take a trip, and especially if my route from Canada passes through the USA, I check my documents carefully and calculate the extra time that may be needed for border crossings or airport security stations. Once at the airport, surveillance is evident everywhere, especially at the check-in counter and the security zone. As a matter of fact, surveillance actually starts long before I reach the terminal buildings or customs and immigration checkpoints. Reservation data already reveal important facts about me – food preferences, health status – that under certain circumstances may be made available to several agencies. As a traveller, I try to ensure a smooth and efficient passage, so I do what I can to avoid delays. As a citizen, though, I have qualms about where my personal information may end up, not because I have something to hide, but because I know that once my name is on a list it could affect my choices and even my freedom of movement.

Since September 11, 2001, many more people than previously have become at least vaguely aware of the surveillance capacities of their governments and law enforcement agencies. The deliberate demolition of the twin towers of the World Trade Center on a busy working morning has become emblematic not only of a lurking 'terrorist' threat but also of determined attempts to prevent future attacks by upgrading security and surveillance systems. The Department of Homeland Security was established in the USA as a first response, setting off a ripple effect around the world, one result of which is that 'security industries' are now seen as an economic sector in their own right. Agencies of risk assessment and management, along with their associated technical partners, seized the opportunity to develop further what had already been expanding steadily; a culture of control that has surveillance as a central activity.

A 'culture of control', as David Garland calls it (Garland 2001), increasingly characterizes many countries around the world, especially the USA and the UK. Perennial and universal desires for security, orderliness, risk management and the taming of chance have been magnified and reinforced since the 1980s, so that regulation of every area of life has become a watchword (except, in some respects, the 'free market' economy). And, as Garland says, 'in the process our civic culture becomes increasingly less tolerant and inclusive, increasingly less capable of trust' (Garland 2001: 195). If you had suggested in the 1970s that someone dropping litter in the street would be observed by a surveillance camera and ordered through a loudspeaker to pick it up, the idea would have been dismissed as the product of a paranoid Orwellian imagination. Today, it already happens on the streets of Middlesbrough, England (Cross 2006). Surveillance practices, which, as we shall see, have always been an aspect of human societies, but which emerged as a central component of modern life, are now vital to the emerging cultures of control.

Today, the cultures of control are not merely something that government agencies or large organizations are involved in. Ordinary people in everyday life seem to be adopting similar outlooks concerning risk and its antidotes. Parents of small children buy sophisticated systems such as 'nannycams' in order to watch how their paid caregivers treat their children. In 2003, an American *Parenting* magazine survey revealed that 82 per cent of mothers would secretly videotape their nanny even if they had no grounds for suspecting that their children were not receiving proper care and attention (Burson 2005). Beyond this, parents increasingly use surveillance technologies in order to watch their own children, and cell-phones seem to be the tool of choice for this. Since many mobile phones have become equipped with GPS, parents have an easy means of checking where their teenagers are, or how fast they are driving on the highway.

Parents have always been concerned about what their children might be up to, of course, but ours is the first generation that has deliberately sought techniques used by the military or the police in order to monitor their activities. Surveillance is not merely something exercised on us as workers, citizens or travellers, it is a set of processes in which we are all involved, both as watched and as watchers. Indeed, one of the most striking areas of growth for systematically keeping an eye on ordinary people is that of consumption. Throughout the twentieth century, techniques originating in market research were honed to try to second-guess what customers would want, but by the end of that century database marketing and its offshoots had become a billion dollar business.

Loyalty cards in the supermarket, for example, are a key means of tracking purchases in a way that connects back to the individual, but numerous other means are also used to profile and classify consumers. This can produce targeted marketing, once the budget, preferences and shopping times of the customer are known. Shoppers may appreciate knowing about special offers that are actually specific to them, but they may also find that they are simply not informed about other available merchandise. Conversely, some even fear that government health regulations may oblige supermarkets to prevent certain customers purchasing a product – say, people with tendencies to obesity buying doughnuts – when profiles are accessed that combine medical with purchasing data (cited in Lace 2005b: 208). Once we are identified as particular kinds of customers, it can sometimes be difficult for us to make purchases outside our box.

Defining surveillance

Before going any further, I should make clear what is meant by surveillance. Although the word 'surveillance' often has connotations of surreptitious cloak-and-dagger or undercover investigations into individual activities, it also has some fairly straightforward meanings that refer to routine and everyday activity. Rooted in the French verb *surveiller*, literally to 'watch over', surveillance refers to processes in which special note is taken of certain human behaviours that go well beyond idle curiosity. You can 'watch over' (or, more clumsily, 'surveill') others because you are concerned for their safety; lifeguards at the edge of the swimming pool might be an example. Or you can watch over those whose activities are in some way dubious or suspect; police officers watching someone loitering in a parking lot would be an example of this kind of surveillance.

Surveillance always has some ambiguity, and that is one of the things that make it both intriguing and highly sensitive. For example, parental concern and care for children may lead to the adoption of some surveillance technologies in order to express this. But at what point does this become an unacceptable form of control? Does the answer depend on whether or not the offspring in question are aware that they are being tracked, or is the practice itself unethical by some standards? At the same time, putting the question this way assumes that people in general are wary, if not positively spooked, when they learn that others may be noting their movements, listening to their conversations or profiling their purchase patterns. But this assumption is not always sound. Many seem content to be surveilled, for example by street cameras, and some appear so to relish being watched that they will put on a display for the overhead lenses, or disclose the most intimate details about themselves in blogs or on webcams.

So what is surveillance? For the sake of argument, we may start by saying that it is the focused, systematic and routine attention to personal details for purposes of influence, management, protection or direction. Surveillance directs its attention in the end to individuals (even though aggregate data, such as those available in the public domain, may be used to build up a background picture). It is focused. By systematic, I mean that this attention to personal details is not random, occasional or spontaneous; it is deliberate and depends on certain protocols and techniques. Beyond this, surveillance is routine; it occurs as a 'normal' part of everyday life in all societies that depend on bureaucratic administration and some kinds of information technology. Everyday surveillance is endemic to modern societies. It is one of those major social processes that actually constitute modernity as such (Giddens 1985).

Having said that, there are exceptions. Anyone who tries to present an 'overview' has to admit that particular circumstances make a difference. The big picture may seem over-simplified but, equally, the tiny details can easily lose a sense of significance. For example, not all surveillance is necessarily focused. Some police surveillance, for instance, may be quite general – a 'dragnet' – in an attempt somehow to narrow down a search for some likely suspects. And by the same token, such surveillance may be fairly random. Again, surveillance may occur in relation to non-human phenomena that have only a secondary relevance to 'personal details'. Satellite images may be used to seek signs of mass graves where genocide is suspected or birds may be tagged to discover how avian flu is spread. Such exceptions are important, and add nuance to our understanding of the big picture. By looking at various sites of surveillance, and exploring surveillance in both 'top-down' and 'bottom-up' ways, I hope to illustrate how such variations make a difference to how surveillance is understood in different contexts.

The above definition makes reference to 'information technology', but digital devices only increase the capacities of surveillance or, sometimes, help to foster particular kinds of surveillance or help to alter its character. Surveillance also occurs in down-to-earth, face-to-face ways. Such human surveillance draws on time-honoured practices of direct supervision, or of looking out for unusual people or behaviours, which might be seen in the factory overseer or in neighbourhood watch schemes. Indeed, to accompany the most high-tech systems invented, the US Department of Homeland Security still conscripts ordinary people to be the 'eyes and ears' of government, and some non-professional citizen-observers in Durban, South Africa have been described by a security manager (without irony) as 'living cameras' (Hentschel 2006).

But to return to the definition: it is crucial to remember that surveillance is always hinged to some specific purposes. The marketer wishes to influence the consumer, the high school seeks efficient ways of managing diverse students and the security company wishes to insert certain control mechanisms – such as PIN (personal identification number) entry into buildings or sectors. So each will garner and manipulate data for those purposes. At the same time, it should not be imagined that the influence, management or control is necessarily malign or unsocial, despite the frequently negative connotations of the word 'surveillance'. It may involve incentives or reminders about legal requirements; the management may exist to ensure that certain entitlements – to benefits or services – are correctly honoured and the control may limit harmful occurrences.

On the one hand, then, surveillance is a set of practices, while, on the other, it connects with purposes. It usually involves relations of power in which watchers are privileged. But surveillance often involves participation in which the watched play a role. It is about vision, but not one-sidedly so; surveillance is also about visibility. Contexts and cultures are important, too. For instance, infra-red technologies that reveal what is otherwise shrouded in darkness help to alter power relations. But the willing self-exposure of blog-writers also helps to change the contours of visibility. To use infra-red devices to see into blog-writers' rooms at night would infringe personal rights and invade private spaces. But for blog-writers to describe their nocturnal activities online may be seen as an unexceptional right to free expression.

Caught by coordinates

At first glance, as it were, surveillance seems to be about watching. One person watches others in order to check for inappropriate or abnormal behaviour. The pole-mounted camera in the street keeps watch for potential deviance, from criminal acts to 'undesirable' activities. But surveillance may also be about listening, from eavesdropping to phone-tapping. What is heard may in certain circumstances be used as evidence, and in the context of global fears about terrorism fairly flimsy references to violent action may count for something. Already these examples include some technological mediation, whether closed-circuit television (CCTV), wiretaps or whatever. But once we consider the range of possible mediations, the surveillance picture enlarges significantly.

Coordinates are key. Anyone who can pinpoint the time and place of some event or activity already has a handle on the situation. Those data reveal a lot. As we shall discover, the quest for personal data by large organizations has grown hugely over the past two decades. It has given rise to a new word, dataveillance, to describe this kind of 'watching' using not sight, exactly, but the amassing of details to create profiles that in a sense resemble those thus 'seen'. Dataveillance, says Roger Clarke, monitors or investigates people's activities or communications using personal data systems (Clarke 1997 [2006]). Being much cheaper than direct physical or electronic surveillance it enables the watching of more people or populations, because economic constraints to surveillance are reduced. Dataveillance also automates surveillance. Classically, government bureaucracies have been most interested in gathering such data, although employers have increasingly sought to keep accurate tabs on their workers as well.

But in recent decades organizations dedicated to 'getting to know' customers have challenged the primacy of government surveillance. In the 1980s database marketers developed new means of obtaining geo-demographic data as a means of building a picture of what sorts of people live where (hence, 'geo-demographic') so that direct mail shots could be much more accurately aimed than previously. In the 1990s, as the possibilities for online marketing grew, internet surfing was monitored to produce more data. And in the first decade of the twenty-first century several systems have appeared that have the capacity to capture 'locational' data. Tracing where you are at a given moment can be achieved using cell-phones, RFID (radio frequency identification) and other wireless devices (Lyon 2006b). An employer can check just how long his or her drivers take to reach their destinations, how long their breaks are and even what speeds they reach on the highway. Alongside this, geographic and geo-demographic information systems (GIS and GDIS) are also implicated in translating captured data into the means of sorting cities in ways that favour the already privileged (Burrows and Ellison 2004; Graham 2005).

Such coordinates are of interest to others than marketers, of course. If marketers can orchestrate mobile consumers and purchasing opportunities, the same kinds of systems can help police to track suspects on the move, airports to check the progress of travellers – whether 'trusted' or not – from check-in to gates, and even schools to monitor where students are. For example, near Houston, Texas, children wear RFID tags to alert school authorities and police when they get on and off the school bus, and a school in Buffalo, New York uses RFID to automate attendance registration (Richtel 2004). Such systems are at an early stage of development and it is not clear that they will be reliable enough for routine use, but interest in (as well as opposition to) them is widespread.

After 9/11, public interest in surveillance – such as it is – shifted back to law enforcement, as public opinion was sought on whether or not measures such as national ID cards or biometric measures in airports were acceptable in the 'war on terror' (and often, because of the way the questions were worded, a large measure of approval was found in Europe and North America[1]). But within surveillance studies, all kinds of coordinates are of interest, not least because another trend is towards data collected for one purpose being used for others. Those consumer data, for example, may be of considerable interest to law enforcement, just as drug companies are interested in medical data and insurance companies in police records.

The 'coordinates', as I have been calling them, may include all kinds of data, not just the time and place of events or activities. Personal data may be drawn from the body itself, usually with, but sometimes without, the consent of the subject, in the form of DNA traces or some biometric such as fingerprints or iris scans. Or it could be an image, such as that caught by a camera in the shopping mall or in a transit system. It may be a bureaucratic or financial item such as an identification number or salary amount. Or personal data could be part of a message that is sent or spoken – by email or telephone – or transmitted as part of a transaction. So the personal data in question have to do with time and space, bodies, information and communication.

The categories sought by surveillance can be very precise, but at their most general they include groups that touch ordinary people in several different roles. Surveillance data are not gathered about everyone in the same way, or with the same intensity. Surveillance relates to roles played in different aspects of modern life. Most obviously, workers are surveilled by capitalist corporations and government organizations in order to check that they are doing what they are paid to do. Consumers are tracked and profiled by marketers in order to offer clearer targets for purchases and promotions. Citizens have tabs on them from birth, to ensure efficient administration, especially touching matters such as taxation, health, workers' insurance, and so on. Travellers must carry passports, drivers' licences and other forms of identification linked with databases, to verify their identities and to facilitate movement. Children are increasingly observed in schools and on the street, and parents as well as educational and policing bodies engage in such 'safety-oriented' surveillance (see, e.g., Lewis 2006). Offenders and suspects may also expect a high degree of monitoring and supervision, both within institutions and, especially with the advent of remote devices such as electronic tagging, in the community. Other categories exist, but the above are the most common general ones. This is explored further in the next chapter.

Why surveillance studies?

Surveillance studies is necessarily a multi-disciplinary enterprise, although sociology seems to be deeply involved at every level. This is somewhat ironic in view of the fact that sociologists have been seen both as suitable *practitioners* of surveillance and as appropriate *targets* for surveillance. Early in the twentieth century, for example, the Ford Motor Company set up a 'Sociology' Department in their Dearborn, Michigan plant, the purpose of which was to oversee the systematic monitoring of workers. In the mid-twentieth century, however, sociologists themselves were apparently prime suspects of subversion, such that American academics in the discipline were placed under observation by the FBI at the instigation of J. Edgar Hoover (Keen 2004).

It is the case, of course, that some sociological practices may be construed as surveillance (the systematic attention to personal details for specific purposes), and the work of any good sociologist who probes below the surface of society is bound to be seen as subversive by some. We return to these issues and explore them further in this book, but it is important to acknowledge the problem from the outset. The social sciences themselves are engaged in activities that may at some levels be construed as surveillant. That is part of the reason why I subtitled this book, ironically, 'an overview'. When we study surveillance practices, we cannot exclude those practices in which sociologists, anthropologists and others of their ilk also engage.

Surveillance studies involves a number of disciplines, among which sociology offers some distinctive perspectives. What sociology offers is both some cross-cutting theories of surveillance and the empirical grounding that keeps it in touch with the real world. The work of Karl Marx on surveillance in the capitalist workplace and Max Weber on how files and officials keep tabs in bureaucracies, not to mention Michels, Mosca, Pareto or Sorel on how geo-political struggles between states stimulate the growth of surveillance, does not make the theoretical background exclusively 'sociological', of course. The work of such classical theorists is drawn on throughout the social sciences. These thinkers remind us that modern forms of surveillance are distinctive just because they grow out of central processes of modernity: capitalist production, bureaucratic organization and the increasingly globalized struggles between states.

At the same time, social science disciplines also insist on grasping the significance of the small-scale, the everyday, for their sustaining of and giving ongoing life to the larger processes that inform and shape social life. While Michel Foucault's work refers to the large-scale transformations of modernity, his work on surveillance also draws attention to the myriad small components of 'disciplinary society', those everyday 'strategies of power' that above all act on the human body (Foucault 1979). Those subjected to surveillance often resist, so that a constant tension is maintained within the web of relations. As we shall also see, from a quite different vantage point, sociologists such as Erving Goffman have crucially significant insights at a micro level. Whatever the arguments made about CCTV 'coverage' in the UK, for example, it is misleading to assume that the carapace of cameras means that surveillance is somehow total. How people respond to cameras and how bored and distracted operators pass the time in the control room invite detailed studies of the kind that Goffman initiated (see, e.g., Smith 2004).

Other major disciplines and approaches besides sociology play a role in surveillance studies, but rather than listing them (which will inevitably leave gaps), some of their insights and emphases may be mentioned. Surveillance is always bound up with questions of power and its distribution, which is a key theme of political science (even though several other disciplines have an interest in this). Reg Whitaker warns, for instance, that new forms of corporate surveillance challenge conventional understandings of political power. Profiles of individuals and groups created in the commercial realm are superseding what police and security agencies used to provide, with interesting consequences for power and politics (Whitaker 1999). Geography offers insights into surveillance studies that derive from an interest in space, which is where many power struggles of surveillance are played out. As much contemporary surveillance is remote, the stretching of surveillance relations across larger terrains also has to be interrogated. And without an historical imagination, contemporary studies will blithely ignore the precedents to today's developments, many of which existed in some form – including the totalitarian regime in the Soviet Union or the oppressive rule of apartheid in South Africa – long before the arrival of searchable computer databases and networked communications.

To mention these technologies is also to remind ourselves that business and computing studies have insights to offer in studying surveillance. A striking example is the concept of 'identity management', which began life as a set of strategies for regulating online access to sites or sections of sites but is now being transposed into the offline world of physical border controls with its biometric passports and other means of identification and verification. Because today's surveillance tends to be technology-dependent there is also a need to grasp at least the technical basics of new devices and techniques. But this also implies a view both ways: today's surveillance cannot be understood without considering it as a socio-technical system. The technologies are socially shaped as the social is informed by the technical.

None of this would be much use, however, without also knowing something about the legal frameworks within which surveillance operates – at least ostensibly – or without being able to argue ethically about the pros and cons of a given surveillance practice. Gary T. Marx observed a long time ago, for instance, that the kinds of 'categorical suspicion' made possible by new surveillance methods threaten to turn on their heads conventional Western ideas on the 'presumption of innocence'. If the category in which your personal data place you renders you 'suspicious', then you are hardly 'innocent until proven guilty' (Marx 1988: 227). And how law actually works – or does not work – in practice is also a vital consideration in surveillance studies. Privacy and data protection laws, for example, which are often taken to be the appropriate antidote for excessive or repressive surveillance, are frequently hard to enforce. Obtaining compliance is a constant headache for those involved.

To speak of law also reminds us of the key contributions to surveillance from socio-legal and criminological studies. Here the interests lie variously in the supervision of offenders, the classification and trailing of suspects, and the surveillance work of policing. Notions of 'social control' and of 'governance', tightly tied in with crime control, are vital justifications for surveillance activities. And the use of new technologies such as electronic monitoring (EM), or 'tagging', of offenders again serves to highlight some crucial features of surveillance within today's cultures of control. Mike Nellis points out that EM, the use of digital anklets or bracelets that alert authorities to the whereabouts of offenders in the community rather than in prison, is an automated socio-technical system of remote control. It depends on the informational and telecommunications infrastructure and fits neatly the current 'managerial' language of corrections. Such constant surveillance, which of course can be and is subverted, could be part of a trend towards offenders being 'managed by machines' (Nellis 2006).

Such 'management by machines' has been a persistent thread in sociological and organizational studies for some time. The social sciences were obliged to confront questions of technology as the twentieth century progressed, but so important was this that separate subfields (such as technology studies) were formed as well, which also act as a challenge to conventional notions of relations between 'technology and society'. Today, there is fuller recognition of the fact that few social relations are not mediated in some ways by technology. Equally, often at more theoretical levels, cultural studies and feminism contribute fresh perspectives that are highly relevant to surveillance. How we understand the relation, for example, between the Big Brother of Orwell's oppressive fiction and the Big Brother of so-called 'reality TV' is a question for which cultural studies offers useful ideas. In addition, issues such as the disproportionate emphasis on 'maleness' in technology and in the 'gaze' suggest that gender nuances are pertinent to surveillance studies as well. Moreover, notions of 'care' developed within feminist theories offer some constructive counterpoints to the often overwhelming concerns about 'control' in surveillance.

In this book, the important element is not the disciplines themselves so much as the insights they offer into concepts, theory, empirical investigation or even policy intervention. For example, the organizational and social micro-studies level is considered in chapter 4, alongside the discussion of bureaucracy. In chapter 5, contributions from criminology and urban studies are foregrounded as the topic shifts to surveillance in the city. The lens is opened wider in the following chapter, to include international relations and global politics, although technology studies also features here in the treatment of biometrics. In chapter 7, media and cultural studies become very relevant, in the analysis of how popular culture interacts with surveillance. Throughout, however, sociology and communication studies inform the direction of the analysis.

It is no slight to any of the disciplinary areas mentioned here that surveillance studies started to emerge as a coherent cross-disciplinary field towards the end of the twentieth century. As certain trends towards the monitoring of ordinary people in everyday life became prominent, people in different disciplines came to realize that here was a phenomenon that defied conventional disciplinary boundaries and seemed to call for concerted intellectual attention. At the same time, debates over the work of Michel Foucault, in particular, threw up many different ways of thinking about surveillance. These were to provide the foils for ongoing argument about the meaning of surveillance – paradoxically – in contexts that were mainly informed by systems that Foucault never considered, namely information technology-based organizations and networks.

Lastly, at the turn of the twenty-first century, the 9/11 attacks on America and the subsequent political prominence of terrorism elsewhere offered opportunities and pretexts for the massive expansion of security-surveillance capacities around the world. Biometrics, electronic identification card systems, smart borders, these and other items rose high on national political agendas. Surveillance of many kinds was dramatically intensified (Ball and Webster 2003). As Indian social critic Arundhati Roy notes of the USA, 'The Patriot Act ushers in an era of systematic automated surveillance. It gives the government the authority to monitor phones and computers and spy on people in ways that would have seemed completely unacceptable a few years ago' (Roy 2004: 62). This expansion, which reinforced already existing surveillance and served also to raise popular awareness, demands intellectual, ethical and political attention for the foreseeable future.

Surveillance studies is about power (among other things), and, as I argue, it is about personhood as well. True, some surveillance is aggregate and some, such as medical surveillance, may be deliberately anonymous. But even these have indirect implications for persons, whether in targeted marketing ploys or in epidemiological surveys. Whatever the purpose of surveillance, to influence, manage, protect or direct, some kind of power relations are involved. Those who establish surveillance systems generally have access to the means of including the surveilled in their line of vision, whether that vision is literal or metaphorical. It is they who keep the records, hold the tapes, maintain the databases, have the software to do the mining and the capacity to classify and categorize subjects. Whether it is the massive Department of Homeland Security in the USA or some rural school board with cameras in buses, power is generated and expressed by surveillance. Surveillance power may also be wielded by the disempowered, of course. A case in point is the female subway vigilantes in New York who take cell-phone shots of harassing or lewd males and post them to the internet to shame them (Smith 2006).

At the same time, travellers going through the security lines of airports and children on the school buses also affect the ways in which surveillance occurs and thus the outcomes of the surveillance practices and processes. Persons, by which I mean social, embodied subjects, are often aware of surveillance and they interact with it in an imaginatively complex range of ways. At the end of the day, it is also flesh-and-blood humans who are affected by surveillance, for better or for worse, and thus whose life-chances and whose choices are at stake when any surveillance system is in place that touches their lives. Several important debates about both power and personhood must be explored, but it is fair to say that both inhabit surveillance studies in significant ways.

2 Spreading Surveillance Sites

Concepts such as 'surveillance society' draw our attention to the ways in which our whole way of life in the contemporary world is suffused with surveillance. In this perspective, the gaze is ubiquitous, constant, inescapable. What once was experienced only in specific contexts such as voter registration, tax files or medical records, in each of which personal records are held by an impersonal organization, has spilled over into every dimension of daily life. Whether travelling, eating, shopping, telephoning, working, walking in the street or working out at the gym, some check occurs, some record is made or some image is captured. As Robert O'Harrow's book title says, there's 'no place to hide' (O'Harrow 2005). But such terms as 'surveillance society', while useful (Surveillance Studies Network 2006), are also potentially misleading because they suggest merely a total, homogeneous situation of 'being under surveillance' when the reality is much more nuanced, varying in intensity and often quite subtle.

Rather than thinking only of 'surveillance societies', it is helpful to think of specific surveillance sites, as they have developed historically in the modern world. Theoretically, this is a more institutional approach that separates surveillance strands out into different domains of social life such as work and leisure. This gives us a sense of the variety of surveillance situations that we might encounter, a sense of how one system gave rise to or facilitated another, and at the same time a sense of how one system may overlap with another or several others. Eventually, however, we are obliged to see that contemporary surveillance is very much influenced by the apparent imperative to be joined-up. The desire to create assemblages is strong, even if these are not always matched by the reality, which may be technically deficient or may encounter user resistance, or both. Separate strands do still exist but increasingly, using electronic information and communication networks, they are or can be connected.

In what follows, I indicate some parallel developments. This is not a chronological history of how one area grew after another, or how one institution built onto another (although there are significant elements of that process within and between each area). There is some genealogy here, the tracing of family trees, and in so far as that model is present, generations are significant, as is the question of parentage. Modernity multiplied systematic and routine surveillance in the quest for efficiency, productivity, speed and comprehensive reach. And this is expressed in the histories of many major agencies and institutions from banks to border controls and from shopping malls to security measures.

There are also some common threads, which help us to analyse similarities and differences between different sites of surveillance. Such threads include processes basic to modernity, such as the following:

Rationalization. This describes the process whereby standardized techniques are sought and reason (rather than tradition, emotion or common-sense knowledge) is prized as the guide to social, political and economic life. Whether or not surveillance systems (or any other ones) that owe their peculiar traits to the modern quest for rationalization actually work well, or better than what preceded them, is an open question. Because in the case of surveillance, personal information gathering is rationalized, there are bound to be tensions.

Technology. The application of science and technology to organizational practices, in order to support and reinforce rationalization and to speed up processes, is clearly visible in surveillance sites. Surveillance, which for most of human history has been a matter of face-to-face oversight augmented with some methods of recording basic information, is now also characterized by high-technology applications. As these become embedded in surveillance systems they sometimes help to alter the very character of those systems.

Sorting. The classification of groups – workers, prisoners, customers, and so on – into categories to facilitate management and control through differential treatment of those groups (Bowker and Star 1999) is also central to surveillance. Those who have the capacity to influence how people are classified and categorized tend to be in positions of greater power than those who do not. This process is now somewhat occluded, especially in the present context, by the use of computer software to accomplish the sorting processes. This simply pushes the question back, however, to ask how the highly consequential coding is done that distinguishes between one group and another.

Knowledgeability. The different levels of knowledgeability and willing participation on the part of those whose life-details are under scrutiny make a difference to how well surveillance works. Surveillance works best with the cooperation of those who are subject to it. Of course, the Iraqi soldier caught in a remote satellite image or the supermarket shopper whose preferences are sold to a third-party marketing company can hardly be thought to be involved in their surveillance. But what they do know and what they do with what they know makes a difference. As we shall see later, at a micro-level all sorts of strategies and subterfuges on the part of knowing subjects make a difference to how surveillance works.

Urgency. A fifth thread that has become increasingly prominent within the safety-and-security-oriented world of the present, especially since 9/11, is what might be called obsessive risk aversion and media-amplified public panic. This tends to prompt the adoption of surveillance measures of many kinds, even if already-existing measures do the same job. Some national ID card proposals fall within this category.

Each of these threads is woven in different ways into the ways that surveillance operates in the sites mentioned below.

Military discipline and intelligence

Early military discipline involved the careful scrutiny of the practices of warfare, and breaking them down into component parts to simplify them and speed them up. This was the application of reason to the routines of warfare. Although Roman armies were highly disciplined, it was not until the sixteenth century that the quest for efficiency and for the reduction of unit costs led to meticulous concern with details of drill. Soldiers were closely watched so that their activities could be more carefully controlled, and their coordination made more machine-like. Those activities that one sees choreographed on army drill squares or in elaborate ritual performances involving colourfully uniformed soldiers originated in early modern Europe and form an important part of the story of surveillance today.

Such drill squares did not exist on their own but as part of an emerging process of rationalization that also signalled the birth of the modern nation-state. An officer class was also created at this time, within a hierarchy of responsibility that prefigured those of other bureaucratic organizations. As Christopher Dandeker argues, the consolidation of the armed forces was a crucial moment in the birth of nation-states (Dandeker 1990). These forces were organizationally complex, required the greatest expenditure and involved the largest number of people. Bureaucratic administration grew from such military origins, yielding hierarchy and command structures for decision-making. Like the army, bureaucratic structures require knowledge of practices and of behaviours, that these be codified and controlled, and that higher officials (or officers in the army) take responsibility for what is done by those below them in the pyramid. The contribution to surveillance practices is evident.

The arrangement of persons within a supervisory hierarchy was not merely abstract, either. In the military camp the tents or huts were set out in ways that replicated the authority and supervisory structure. Officers' tents overlooked the main gate and arms depot, the captains' tents overlooked rows of company tents, and so on down to the lowest ranks. That is, they were carefully sorted for surveillance. In this way information was available where needed within the disciplinary structure. The layout of the place – which would become important in the factory system and eventually even in the shopping mall – was disciplinary in the ways in which it facilitated surveillance.

In later centuries, military initiatives would also make other contributions to the development of surveillance, in at least two major ways. First, the mobilization of whole populations for war, seen above all in the twentieth century, had numerous spin-offs for surveillance in general. The 'warfare state' would have been hard to justify within societies that were democratizing, without accompanying promises about what would become known as the 'welfare state'. Although they were curtailed during war efforts themselves, citizenship rights were not only reinstated but they were also extended as an after-effect of wartime measures. So while conscription meant that men (the involvement of women in the armed forces came only later) were obliged to undergo both personal health checks (for medical fitness) and security checks (for allegiance to the cause, which led to dilemmas regarding conscientious objection, for example), such surveillance measures were also carried over into peacetime. National systems of health-care, for example in the UK, came to be seen as both desirable and feasible under these circumstances, as did more universal recording of citizenship details in documents such as ID cards and passports.

Second, as whole societies, rather than just standing armies, mobilized for war, so it became important to distinguish clearly between friend and foe. Military personnel needed not only to know about internal control of army units through discipline. They also needed information for external control obtained through knowledge of the enemy – both the enemy outside and the 'enemy within'. Military intelligence, starting with simple spying, is another tributary feeding into contemporary surveillance. Externally, military intelligence developed a range of techniques, especially in the twentieth century, that have been highly influential well beyond the military. Radar and signal interception are obvious cases in point because they stimulated both new communications media and the industrial shift towards miniaturization of components (Campbell and Connor 1986). This in turn produced other possibilities for non-military communications including surveillance capacities. Microelectronics has both surveillance origins and consequences.

Even in peacetime military imperatives have continued to play a role in public policy and planning. As Jennifer Light shows, for example, in the USA urban problems were addressed in the Cold War era by drawing explicitly on military strategy – and technologies (Light 2003). The fact that such 'military' strategies may not have worked (Pressman and Wildavsky 1984) does not mean that the 'war-model' ceases to be significant. From satellite reconnaissance to the idea of 'wired cities', each of which has strong surveillance implications, military ideas migrated to quite a few other spheres. As we shall see, it is thus no accident that, particularly from the 1970s onwards, social, political and diplomatic problems were addressed as 'war' situations – on poverty, drugs and, today, terrorism. These latter situations extend considerably definitions of war, however. It is hard to see when a 'war on terror' might end, for example. By the same token, these newer ways of construing 'war' also extend the possibilities for increased surveillance. War means crisis and crisis means special measures.

Internally, as we shall see in the next section, the attempt to distinguish clearly between national populations and alien 'others' led to the

vs. the proles

Lives of Others, enemies, sword/shield, culture war

use of various devices that effectively sequestered the latter. The case of the treatment of Japanese populations in Canada and the USA is particularly egregious in this regard. In the USA, for instance, the census was used illegally to obtain data on Japanese Americans (Seltzer and Anderson 2000), but in both countries, treatment of Japanese people in internment camps was brutal and shameful. The use of national or ethnic categories to distinguish between groups considered 'safe' and 'dangerous' led to what can only be considered as profound injustice.

The role of the military in catalysing developments in surveillance continues today with the so-called 'Revolution in Military Affairs' (RMA). This is a way of not merely rationalizing but also applying computerized forms of control to the whole enterprise of military engagement. A key ingredient of contemporary warfare, as other areas, is information. And information is sought to reduce risks to those making offensive strikes, as information is sought for reducing risk more generally (Haggerty 2006b). For a number of years it seemed that the focus of RMA on remote and virtual warfare would fulfil the dreams of those who imagined that armed struggles could be 'clinical' or 'surgical' and carried out in deserts and wildernesses. However, the shift in recent years, prompted by urban guerrilla action, has been decisively if reluctantly towards attempts to bring high-technology warfare into cities. This amounts to a 'counter-revolution in military affairs' (Downey and Murdoch 2003) that now tries to combine precise surveillance with the messy and bloody realities of urban conflict (Graham 2004b). At the same time, sparked above all by the 'war on terror', this further catalyses the growth of globally networked surveillance.

State administration and the census
"to know everything"

From earliest times agencies of the state have tried to keep tabs on citizens using various techniques, starting with the census. Recorded counts of population for conscription or for taxation occurred in ancient societies such as the Roman Empire. Indeed, this may also be considered the other way round, as it were: the making of a census produces citizens as such. The kind of surveillance that records names and family details, domiciles and other property for the sake of listing bona fide citizens is actually the medium of their production. By the same token, it also distinguishes between 'genuine' citizens and other

(handwritten margin notes: "to know everything"; "a department of records in L.O.O. 3.2 shoes etc. all that files at the end")

categories such as permanent resident, illegal alien or temporary visitor. One could say that, as in some respects the timetable is to a train, producing passengers that can take advantage of the timed transport facilities, so the census is key to keeping track of and regulating a range of activities of citizens.

In modern times, the techniques and practices of state recording and regulation became formalized and rationalized in new ways. Indeed, modernity itself is in part constituted by rationalization and, by extension, surveillance helps to constitute modernity. However, one also needs to specify the ways in which this occurred, and at this point major debates appear. Put briefly, different kinds of arguments about how state practices produced intensified surveillance situations vie for attention. Marxian claims about class control suggest that surveillance may be traced back to economic power within capitalist societies. Weberian notions regarding internal rationalization counter such claims, insisting that the Marxian view, though instructive, cannot explain all. What Dandeker calls the 'Machiavellian' position (Dandeker 1990) adds nuance by stressing the struggle between external geo-political forces and the need to maintain internal power. These are examined more fully in the next chapter.

If one looks at the details of the English case, however, several important features emerge that should be noted particularly by those who are tempted by a more paranoid view of surveillance. For one thing, as Edward Higgs observes, the idea of state surveillance, especially for recording population details, often began as a means of reassuring leaders of the 'vitality of the nation' rather than necessarily of tying them with a documentary leash (Higgs 2001, 2004). Furthermore, as forms of state surveillance were elaborated in the nineteenth and twentieth centuries they often had the at least ostensible purpose of creating records of entitlement to limited rights and obligations – to vote or to have access to defence in a law court, for instance – rather than appearing as technologies of direct domination (Abercrombie et al. 1986). The fact that entitlement surveillance may also have consequences, whether intended or unintended, for social control does not mitigate the fact that entitlement surveillance also secures basic rights. Much of what we must think of as state surveillance, then, began with the collection, collation and codification of mundane details of names and addresses, next-of-kin, property values and, in the twentieth century, items like motor vehicle registrations and tax files.

At the same time, we cannot ignore the fact that state administration also gave us some of the strongest metaphors for the surveillance state, the best known of which is Big Brother from George Orwell's novel *Nineteen Eighty-Four*. In this fictional case, intended as a post-World War II warning about the totalitarian potentiality of Western democracies, the state has become pathologically absorbed with its own power and is intimately involved in everyday control of its citizens' lives. But equally powerful is Franz Kafka's nightmare novel *The Trial*, which focuses on the role of uncertainty. In this case the central character, Joseph K – note the incomplete name – is apprehended for reasons he is not told by persons of dubious authority. Bureaucracy here becomes a malignant maze of bewildering twists and turns that leave the citizen naked and confused before the anonymous gaze. Other novels, such as Margaret Atwood's *The Handmaid's Tale*, probe further dimensions of state surveillance, in this case, the gendering of power. This is explored further in chapter 7.

Modes of classification have been central to state power in modern times. While this has often been for democratic purposes, such as ensuring a universal franchise and that each eligible person has the right and the opportunity to vote, notorious cases of violently undemocratic surveillance also exist. The Nazi regime in Germany from the 1930s to 1945 offers one egregious example of state surveillance and classification in order to privilege 'Aryans' and to eliminate minorities such as 'Jews' and 'Gypsies'. Interestingly, and alarmingly, IBM Hollerith punch-card machines were used to facilitate this sorting process (Black 2001). South Africa under the apartheid regime from 1948 to 1993 offers another example. In the latter case, many are aware of the notorious centralized information-based police state that depended on the much-hated 'passbooks', which were meant to contain the personal history and movements of every African worker. They were linked to fingerprint-based ID cards. While the power of the South African state did indeed depend in part on the apartheid system of classification, however, the administrative surveillance machine was in considerable disarray long before the regime itself was dismantled (Breckenridge 2005).

Today, state administrations around the world continue to rationalize, but now in peculiarly late modern ways, using, first, office computerization and, now, more fully, 'e-government' as the way in. The 'informatizing' of the nation-state has been largely undertaken in the

name of administrative efficiency and as part of the broad restructuring and economic cost-cutting that has affected all major countries of
the global north since the 1980s. In Canada, as in many other countries, there is a vocal 'e-government' movement, fostering citizen
access to government information through electronic environments,
as well as online voting and other features. These, too, require further
surveillance, however, especially through the entry process, which
requires some kind of reliable – and, many argue, universal – identifier for gaining access to government sites and services.

At the same time, since the attacks on New York and Washington
in 2001 and subsequent terrorist bombings in Bali (2002), Madrid
(2004) and London (2005), many countries have increased the intensity of their surveillance and intelligence-gathering operations both
within and between their jurisdictions. This is examined further
under the heading of 'policing and crime control', although it should
be noted that these developments now also connect the routine collation of personal data in relation to property and employment, on the
one hand, with international relations and foreign policy, on the other.

The modern state is involved in other kinds of personal data collection and analysis as well, including, prominently, data relating to public
health. In 1878, for example, the US Marine Hospital Service (forerun-
ner of the Public Health Service) was authorized to collect morbidity
reports regarding cholera, smallpox, plague and yellow fever from US
consuls overseas in order to institute quarantines to stop the diseases
spreading in the USA. By the early twentieth century, the Surgeon
General had begun to collect data on notifiable diseases. In the UK,
however, public health activities developed especially in relation to the
attempts to discover how many adult males were fit for fighting in the
Boer War, and that initiative developed into the kinds of public health
institutions that are known today. The development of genetic science
has raised further surveillance questions about public health data collection because of the focus on future predictions (Nelkin and Andrews
2003), and the World Health Organization's International Health
Regulations ensure that questions such as these have a global scope.

Work monitoring and supervision

Alongside the nation-state and military activities, working life offers
some self-evident starting points for surveillance studies. Many terms

that refer to work superiors actually contain the idea of surveillance within them: 'supervisor', 'overlooker', 'monitor'. Almost anyone employed by someone else would expect that their activities will be watched or recorded. The workplace also provides some paradigmatic models of surveillance. For example, although Jeremy Bentham's Panopticon plan was for a prison, he obtained the idea from his brother Samuel's plan for worker control in a factory. (The Panopticon, as we shall see, was intended as an automated form of surveillance where the architecture enabled a single unseen observer to watch over many people at once.) Industrialization, in its infancy when Bentham wrote at the end of the eighteenth century, brought fresh problems for employers to solve. How to ensure workers do what is required is an ancient dilemma; the factory system gave it added urgency as wage labour became central to the new industrial economy.

A fine example is furnished by Josiah Wedgwood's Staffordshire (England) pottery business, called 'Etruria', founded in 1759 (Roethlisberger et al. 1939, cited in Macintosh 2003: 42). Wedgwood saw profit opportunities in royal patronage, rising living standards and colonial demand for 'homeland' products, and devised a means of upgrading his former small-scale guild shop to an enterprise capable of vastly increased production, modelled on a metal-manufacture oper-ation owned by John Bolton. However, the available workers were land-less peasants and serfs who were used to relaxed routines that included numerous 'holy days' and less than sober pastimes. Wedgwood wrote a book of 'potter's instructions', which, like military drill, broke tasks down into their component parts. Drinking, gambling and swearing were also outlawed in his outfit. At first, Wedgwood oversaw the oper-ation himself, but when the business grew too large to permit this he installed overseers and clerks and initiated a system whereby workers had to place a named ticket in a box on arrival at work. He also arranged the various sheds of his shop into a continuous production sequence that served not only to expedite production but also to enable worker discipline, as each had specific tasks within the overall process.

By the nineteenth century, Karl Marx and Friedrich Engels observed and analysed new means of exploitation using the cash-nexus as the sole line of responsibility and connection between employer and employee. They were very aware of enterprises like Wedgwood's, which by now had multiplied in the British Isles. Within the new factories workers were typically brought together under one roof and new modes of discipline had been tried to ensure that they performed the tasks expected of them. As E.P. Thompson stresses, their work was increasingly timed as well as being carried out in enclosed spaces (Thompson 1963). Those coordinates, crucial to surveillance and control, were central to nineteenth- and twentieth-century production sites.

During the twentieth century the embryonic practices of worker discipline that had begun piecemeal in earlier centuries sedimented into accepted routines in all industrializing countries. So-called 'time-and-motion studies' developed within F.W. Taylor's schemes of 'scientific management' in the USA as the rationalization of labour control developed apace. As with Wedgwood's early experiments, 'Taylorism' required intimate knowledge of each task and thus careful supervision to ensure that the tasks were accomplished appropriately.

Today's employee supervision and monitoring may be more sophisticated but it builds on the rationalizing trends of the past few centuries. From entry keys in the form of bar-coded cards to video-surveillance, keystroke-counting, active badges and location technologies that enable employers remotely to check on mobile workers, the idea of worker supervision has changed little except in intensity. I recently visited a call centre in Bangalore, South India, for example, and several features already alluded to here were present. The young workers, nearly all new university graduates, had to go through security checks at the main door of the building and in their own suite, before entering the centre itself. At the entry to the main terminal room all articles – bags, pens, paper, and the like – had to be left behind. In the high-security area containing the terminals and phone headsets the workers were watched from above by ceiling-mounted cameras, were monitored automatically by the machines themselves, which timed their calls and counted their keystrokes, and also could expect constant oversight from supervisors who walked between the desks. Of course, how this is received, and sometimes resisted, tells a further story, which is explored more in chapter 8.

Whereas for Bentham or Marx the work*place* was the physical site of work, today the issues of worker surveillance have expanded in both time and space. Workers are often in places physically distant from their employers, but this now prompts practices of remote 'oversight' using devices that workers use on the move, such as cell-phones, laptops or GPS-enabled vehicles. Workers may also find that they are pre-screened for police records or disease before they even start their

Some workplace surv. in LOO - lunchroom scene ?
hierarchi

employment, or that their monitoring extends into non-work time as, for instance, they check emails from home. These surveillance expansions are related in turn to what is often referred to as the 'new managerialism', which is engaged, as Gary T. Marx puts it, in 'measuring everything that moves' (Marx 1999). Because in this sphere, as some others, measurement has come to be equated with validity and effectiveness, a constant quest for more observations, reports, records, checks and analyses is engendered (see, e.g., Ball and Carter 2002).

Policing and crime control

The word 'surveillance' has a natural affinity, it would seem, with policing and what today is often called crime control. Police routinely place certain persons 'under surveillance', meaning that they are specifically and carefully watched when they are suspected of committing an offence. Early policing units in the modern world were often connected with the military, but as police developed their own styles of operation as distinct units, they became a 'civil police force', paid for from the public purse. Their purpose, rather than to fight abroad, was to 'keep the peace' at home. For this, they needed to know, and often to *see*, the areas over which they had authority.

As this section shows, the 'natural affinity' between policing and surveillance has some contradictory and ironic aspects to it. Policing is closely associated with the growing urbanization of modern societies; it is a feature of cities above all. Increasingly, in contemporary cities, surveillance by police is general rather than specific and relates as much to offences that have yet to happen as to ones that already have. This is especially true of remote and partially automated surveillance using CCTV systems or 'video-surveillance'. Moreover, the processes of collecting intelligence about an urban area are still very dependent on military techniques. Indeed, this has become more marked in an 'age of information' (Haggerty and Ericson 2001).

Not only this, but the idea of 'public' policing, which has seldom been a complete process in any country, is today challenged by the rapidly growing presence of private policing or what George Rigakos calls 'parapolicing' (Rigakos 2002). Such private policing is often coordinated with its public counterpart, and is geared to creating 'safe spaces' in cities where particular kinds of 'disorder' receive attention in the effort to 'restructure' the city above all for commerce. Shopping malls and 'tourist' areas of cities receive close attention in this regard. These broader contexts help to make sense of the huge growth of urban CCTV and other kinds of high-tech surveillance over the past decade or so (see Coleman 2004).

The idea of creating the ideal city is an ancient one. Ever since the fabled Tower of Babel and the related urban space of Babylon, the city has been the site of numerous experiments in political-economic aggrandizement and social engineering. The geometry of space in Roman cities, according to Richard Sennett, was intended to discipline bodily movement such that, as citizens looked up towards Hadrian's Pantheon, for example, they would be induced to comply with the desired order (Sennett 1996: 116). As public lighting became technically feasible in early modern cities, so the idea of being visible in urban space was more connected with social control. Paris was perhaps the first 'city of light' when police chief Nicolas de la Reynie installed thousands of lanterns at the end of the seventeenth century. By the end of the twentieth century, however, many cities had helped to bring about the reversal of the Roman ideal. No longer did citizens merely see and comply with the architectural demands of urban space; the urban spaces were themselves enabled to see the citizens, as it were, courtesy of CCTV.

Several studies in surveillance focus on policing and crime control and together they yield some very important insights. In the 1980s, many public questions were raised in the USA about the use of 'undercover' tactics by police. Gary T. Marx showed that such tactics were part of some broader trends, especially those involving the use of new technologies (Marx 1988). The historical drift from relatively unpoliced rural to more policed industrial-urban settings in the context of an increasingly bureaucratic state led to the quest for more admissible evidence and hence to covert practices. Criminal investigations drew on new surveillance technologies – mainly video and audio at first – that permitted those practices, but this in turn put a new spin on the practices themselves. As Marx notes, 'The intelligence role can be defined in a way that creates an insatiable appetite for information while limiting action taken on the basis of information collected' (Marx 1988: 88).

In the 1980s Marx explored a number of unintended as well as intended consequences of the move towards undercover policing using both informers and new technologies, and reserved his most strenuous critique for the latter. He warned about the development of 'maximum security societies' in which he saw dossiers, including computer records, playing a greater role; actuarial approaches becoming dominant, in which decisions are made on the basis of predictions about future behaviour; engineering strategies appearing that environmentally limit choices; transparency increasing such that traditional boundaries are weakened that once protected privacy; and more self-monitoring that supplements police work. All these trends have become more prominent, as Marx suggested they would, and so, too, has time borne out his prediction that they would become less recognizable in a consumer society. The velvet glove, as he said, hides the iron fist.

Another study, set this time in Canada but with ramifications for many other countries, looks at the role of policing in relation to risk. That sense, noted by Marx, of information-based policing creating an insatiable appetite for more data, and of systems that seem to be self-augmenting, is also highlighted by Richard Ericson and Kevin Haggerty. Not only this, they say, but local control is also lost and trust becomes a feature primarily of the abstract system. Indeed, they go further, arguing that the very discourses of sociology, which once centred on 'deviance, control and order', are giving way to ones that favour 'risk, surveillance and security' (Ericson and Haggerty 1997: 448). Relevant signs of this include police cruisers in Toronto that resemble mobile offices, complete with wireless laptop systems on which the central police computer system can readily be accessed. Vehicle licence details can be retrieved instantly, for example, and linked with other data, in order to create a collage of salient fragments on which decisions about potential prosecution may be based.

Risk communication systems need surveillance because they focus not on the moral discourse of deviance but on calculating probabilities, and at the same time deviance becomes a technical problem requiring an administrative solution. 'Contingent categorization' takes the place of 'coercive control', which means that all are suspect until the system clears the way to entry, inclusion or a ban. Thus what is probable or possible for individuals is determined by surveillance-generated biographical profiles. Policing is thus transformed into systems of 'remote control' as distant actions have local effects, and as once-delayed actions are instantaneous. Here again the new surveillance technologies are prominent, but now they are seen as part of broader social-cultural trends of information-dependence and a framework of risk.

Such trends may also be seen in the rapid and far-reaching rise of CCTV. In this case the world capital both of CCTV itself, and of careful, critical analysis of CCTV, is the UK. One fifth of CCTV cameras world-wide are in the UK, which is also the largest market for CCTV in Europe. The chances of being 'seen' by a camera while going about one's daily business are extremely high in the UK; indeed it is likely that your image will be captured around 300 times (Coleman 2004: 4). In Britain, CCTV is central to the attempted creation of 'order' in streets and public spaces and may be read directly from the policies and targeted spending first of the Conservative government of the early 1990s and of 'New Labour' since then. There is both an apparently 'self-augmenting' trend visible here and a very 'visible hand' of policies that guide the particular trajectories of CCTV deployment.

The expansion of CCTV in British cities is also surrounded by some interesting anomalies and contradictions. The UK population, though wary of some forms of surveillance such as national identification cards, seems in general to be content with the massive colonization of the streets by CCTV. People seem to believe that somehow they – and their children – are safer with cameras installed above them. The much publicized case of James Bulger, a toddler murdered by two young boys in Bootle, Merseyside, in 1993 seemed to have been a symbolic moment of reassurance about the utility of CCTV because grainy images of Bulger being led away were caught and helped with the apprehension and identification of his killers. Britons got used to CCTV as it was used in campaigns against Irish Republican Army terror attacks and later as similar equipment was again installed after the 9/11 attacks on New York and Washington.

Yet as Clive Norris and Gary Armstrong say, 'the use of CCTV cameras offers no simple panacea to the problem of crime and raises serious issues about justice, equality and fairness' (Norris and Armstrong 1999: 205). So why are they so popular as a 'solution' to crime? Norris and Armstrong propose several important reasons, in addition to the underlying social, economic and political pressures that point to CCTV as an attractive option. Negative findings about CCTV tend to be dismissed by the industry and the media. The well-known displacement effect of cameras on crime encourages each successive town council or police force to claim the 'need' for local CCTV cameras once they are installed nearby, and, at the same time, the presence of CCTV is seen as an incentive to bring business to an area. Rare but serious crimes such as terrorism, murder or rape may be caught on tape to aid an investigation. Again, from a police perspective, CCTV helps 'manage the problem of informational uncertainty', making it clearer what sorts of disturbance are unfolding, and whether or not to intervene, and how.

Policing is today associated with crime control and an emerging 'new penology', which depends on information, on gauging probabilities, on a risk calculus and on algorithmic methods. It tends to work towards a model of pre-emptive activities – as in the film *Minority Report*, preventing the crime *before* it occurs – for which intensive surveillance is required. Crime control and policing are particularly connected with a 'culture of control' (Garland 2001). Regulation, inspection and control have been promoted to a central theme of social life as control in general is reinstated as a political theme. Among several means, information technology and new management are popular with police forces, both public and private ones. Controls are sought especially against 'undeserving' claimants and 'dangerous' offenders – and, even more, 'terrorists' – with the result that it is the poor and the marginal who are most deeply affected. At the same time, pleas from police for the public to be pro-active in passing on information about suspicious persons or incidents have never been more frequent. Not only in neighbourhood watch schemes, but through police TV shows and other means, ordinary citizens are also expected to contribute to the processes of police surveillance.

Consumption and making up consumers

While law enforcement and military intelligence seem to be obvious sites for surveillance, the world of consumption seems at first sight to be less so. After all, it is in the realm of consumption that the powerful ideologies of the 'unregulated market' and of 'freedom of choice' flower and flourish. Yet during the twentieth century the processes of marketing goods and services became increasingly 'managed' and the names and personal data of consumers became highly valuable items to corporations. By the start of the twenty-first century, not only was the processing of consumer data valued for its primary purpose, to streamline and to make more specific the targeting of customers, but those data had also found very significant secondary purposes in law enforcement and even in the post-9/11 'war on terror'. Indeed, consumer data are now implicated in the regimes of governance of all societies in the global North.

The story starts with the efforts of Alfred Sloan and the development of market research in the 1920s. What began in the workplace as 'scientific management' with the work of F.W. Taylor and others was slowly transposed into the sphere of consumption in practices of 'social Taylorism' (see Webster and Robins 1986). Here, the focus was less on the worker, more on the household. Sloan worked for General Motors, and pioneered the attempt to use scientific management principles for commodity markets and consumer behaviour. Data on buying habits were collated to build profiles on consumers, and by the 1930s the help of International Business Machines Inc. (IBM) was enlisted to provide data services. Demographic and socio-economic data on consumers were collected in order to manage better their activities. As Vincent Mosco suggested at an early point in research on consumer management, this increased surveillance capacities considerably, and raised questions far beyond ones of the 'privacy' of the personal data collected (Mosco 1989: 37–8). As he put it, such 'social management' is a subtle form of social control.

Although IBM was involved from the 1930s in handling personal data for market researchers and 'social Taylorism', the advent of modern computing was to enable large-scale changes to occur in the marketing industries. By the 1980s so-called 'database marketing' had taken its place as a means of sifting through massive amounts of personal data that simply could not have been processed without the use of computer power. Geo-demographic marketing research and targeting began using zipcodes and postcodes to cluster populations according to shared spending and lifestyle characteristics. General features of a given population could be read fairly accurately from demographic data in specific neighbourhoods, helpfully coded by postal services, and these could be concatenated with more personal identifiable data in order to fuel the direct mail advertising industry. *We Know Where You Live* was the title of a NOVA film that brought to life a world of targeted advertising and credit bureau data-sharing seldom guessed at by most consumers (see also Larsen 1992).

A number of important studies have been made of the growing economic significance of personal data, and the way was led by Oscar

Gandy's classic *The Panoptic Sort* (Gandy 1993). He combines analysis of the sorting and classifying aspects of the Panopticon with the process of profiling consumers. His is an empirical study of the 'political economy of personal information' that concludes by outlining the discriminatory technology at work. Marketers promote the ongoing rationalization of the market by identifying individuals who share certain attributes that make them particularly attractive as potential consumers. The discrimination occurs as certain potential consumers are discarded while others are 'skimmed off' as 'high-quality targets of opportunity' (Gandy 1996: 152). Gandy's work stresses the ways in which information today plays a crucial role in the development and reproduction of systems of power.

Even as Gandy was writing about the panoptic sort, another development was occurring that would vastly increase the power of database marketing, namely the commercialization of the internet (and younger readers may have to be persuaded that there was once a time when no advertising appeared on the internet!). Surfing activities could readily be added to geo-demographic data to create a marketers' cornucopia of information that would enable far more precise details of customer preferences, choices and histories. The debate that was resolved in favour of commercialization led directly, says Manuel Castells, to the 'transformation of liberty and privacy on the internet' (Castells 2001: 170). Not only do individual consumers have their surfing activities followed from site to site, but companies use the internet as a marketplace for exchanging data, frequently selling customer email addresses, phone numbers and home numbers to others. At the same time, of course, customers participate in this system by using the internet for online purchasing and leaving a trail of data as they do so.

The internet quickly became a platform for many kinds of surveillance, not only directly commercial, but also, for example, as an adjunct to workplace surveillance. Employers could check directly on internet clickstreams and by remotely monitoring keystrokes, but they could also more easily perform background checks on potential employees. Especially after 9/11, the internet came into its own as a means of running security screens on job applicants. 'Backgrounds Online' for example, saw a 33 per cent rise in requests in November 2001 (Lyon 2002b: 350). Not only this, but the FBI's 'Carnivore' system uses 'sniffers' to check millions of email messages, and the international

'Echelon' intelligence-gathering system uses even more powerful online tools to check on diplomatic negotiations, organized crime, terrorism and groups believed to pose a political threat. One of the fascinating features of this is that it is often commercially based personal data that is first sought, even in the execution of workplace or law enforcement surveillance.

If database marketing (and the 'panoptic sort') was the first phase of computer-assisted consumer surveillance, and online monitoring of surfing activities the second, the third phase is one that brings these two together, the use of so-called 'location technologies'. Although these techniques are as yet nowhere near fully developed, it is important to note that they represent the attempt to do in the real world what already happens virtually – to trace and track actual movements of consumers and to use the data for marketing and other purposes. The term in vogue is 'm-commerce' (where the *m* is for 'mobile'), and as Mark Andrejevic points out, this is where mobile surveillance is becoming dominant, and where the most mobile are the most surveilled (Andrejevic 2004b). In terms of the panoptic sort, however, this is only to be expected. The most attractive consumer prospects will be 'creamed off' even as others are simply cut off. Mobile surveillance using location technologies is in its infancy right now, but this is an area with important potential (Lyon et al. 2005).

Throughout the development of these phases of consumer surveillance, the practices known as 'customer relationship management' (CRM) have expanded steadily. Once a reference to specific information technology 'tools', CRM now draws attention to an overall business strategy. Although it continues to use techniques such as data mining, it is also seen as a vital way for businesses to remain competitive. Corporations manage the flow of data between service representatives and marketing departments in order to offer differential treatment to different kinds of customer, those whose history demonstrates greater or lesser profitability for the company.

This is a reminder of the broader context of this and other aspects of surveillance studies. The emerging industry of personal information management contributes to the processes whereby social divisions are variously created, mitigated or exacerbated. As Susanne Lace comments, in relation to research in the UK, 'We have found that those with limited incomes pay more, or get less, for a range of goods and services', and this in turn relates, *inter alia*, to 'how personal information is used'

(Lace 2005b: 221). The questions raised by surveillance are not merely about 'privacy' or even 'social control'. They are about governance, openness and fairness.

Conclusion

The chapter began by observing that otherwise useful notions such as the 'surveillance society' can give the impression of homogeneous and negative power. In fact, surveillance crops up in many domains, some of the most important of which have been discussed in this chapter. Surveillance not only appears in different ways in these different sites, but it also meets different kinds of responses, depending on the circumstances. People may more readily part with their personal data, for example, when they believe that there is some clear benefit or reward for them. Thus the use of loyalty cards in a supermarket or of frequent flyer clubs from airlines may be perceived entirely in a positive light. Special discounts and member privileges are the dominant feature from the consumer viewpoint, so less attention will be paid to the potential for harm through the sale of personal data to others or through profiling that could be used to exclude some from participation.

The common threads mentioned at the beginning help us to see features that reappear in different contexts and yet with varying connotations and consequences. These threads are rationalization, technology, sorting, knowledgeability and urgency. Rationalization refers to the desire for calculability, seen for instance in the 'new managerialism' in the business goal of 'measuring everything that moves'. For Weber, the classical theorist of rationalization, this spelled bad news for human freedom, and many in surveillance studies tend to agree with him. The thread of technology is seen in the commitment to finding better and better technical means of achieving surveillance, which today means networked databases, increased automation and the use of new sources of personal data such as biometrics and DNA.

Each of the first two threads facilitates the third, which is sorting, or classification. Again, this may be seen as a goal, a policy, or a desire. The 'phenetic fix', as I dubbed it elsewhere (Lyon 2002a), is a classificatory urge sold as a solution. Sorting occurs between different groups of consumers, offenders and suspects, employees and citizens, but also in areas we have not yet explored, such as patients, children or travellers. Persons in each group may to some extent be aware of the process by which they are categorized for particular attention, and may well respond in ways that could subvert or at least mitigate whatever negative effects are believed to be present. This is 'knowledge-ability'. Perhaps Weber underestimated the degree to which the recipients or rationalized systems would respond to modify outcomes?

Lastly, I suggested that a certain urgency is today attached to surveillance processes. This relates in part to the post-9/11 contexts of 'crisis' (see, e.g., Brodeur and Leman-Langlois 2006) but more generally to a world in which risk and risk management have risen up the ranks of priority. It may just be a desire for greater efficiency and speed in production or marketing that generates a sense of urgency, but it is reinforced by the widespread sense of 'exceptional circumstances' prompted by the 'war on terror' rhetoric of the early twenty-first century. This constant thrust to find new and better modes of surveillance also challenges those concerned about such developments to seek fresh ways of raising awareness and minimizing potential harms. But that is to anticipate. We cannot examine that question until we have thought more carefully about how to explain how surveillance works and how it contributes to the production and reproduction of social life today.

3   Explaining Surveillance

Surveillance has rapidly become a central topic of public debate and political concern. Post-9/11, wiretaps became controversial in the USA. CCTV coverage is questioned in the UK. Australians worry that an unwanted ID card system may be foisted on them. Simultaneously, surveillance appears as a popular theme in the mass media, and high-technology companies are making large profits with constantly evolving new devices. These, and other, developments are clear about contemporary surveillance. But beyond these observations, explanation is needed. Why are these things happening, what are the underlying trends, and why does surveillance occur differently or why is it experienced differently in different organizational and national contexts? The field of surveillance studies will not be worth much if no such explanations, or only weak explanations, are on offer.

While each area in which surveillance occurs has to be considered in its own right, and subjected to theoretical interrogation suited to its specific characteristics, there are some ways in which surveillance theory has to be discussed in a broader terrain; that is the main purpose of what follows. Because surveillance is occurring across national boundaries, is often mediated by similar types of computer software and hardware, and because its growth is frequently related to overarching goals such as 'national security' or 'safety', it must be theorized in ways that transcend its local and specific manifestations. In other words, the global, technological and policy aspects of surveillance demand some wide-ranging theories to make sense of the big picture.

At the same time, however, the quest for an abstract grand theory of surveillance is a wild-goose chase, particularly if it is yoked with particular concepts and is supposed to have universal relevance. The theoretical task is better seen as an ongoing conversation in which concepts or theorems that prove helpful should be explored and used, but even if they loom large they should not be permitted to dominate the debate. Concepts such as the Panopticon have been unhelpfully overused, for example. The task of theory in this context is to show the connections between the real lives of ordinary people and the modes of surveillance that serve to watch, record, detail, track and classify them. That is, to make good surveillance theory, which actually explains what is important without becoming overly abstract or paranoid or technologically deterministic, the practices and processes of everyday life must always be kept in focus.

The elements of any theory include being historical and open to empirical constraint and moral critique. The sorts of elements that may be helpful in providing an orientation would include the following. Although it often has protecting, entitling or caring components, surveillance expands primarily as a means of power in modern societies, due to military, geo-political and economic dynamics expressed through bureaucratic organizations. From the late twentieth century, however, applications of digital technology stimulated by the same dynamics have helped to produce cross-system similarities, system networking and integration and the further extension of surveillance into everyday life, which overlay and interact with previous surveillance formations. In earlier and later forms, sovereign power and active subjectivity together shape how well surveillance power works in any given setting. Vision and visibility have been central to surveillance since early modern times, but this ocular emphasis also affects our understanding of non-visual analogues – such as 'dataveillance' –that feed off direct visual imagery.

Throughout the chapter, I try to keep in focus what it is that theory attempts to explain. To obtain the best kind of leverage, we have to be aware of theory that explains, firstly, the origins of surveillance in modern societies and thus, in a sense, what drives surveillance; secondly, the main ways in which surveillance operates in any given period, with the accent on the present; and, thirdly, the effects of surveillance on individuals, groups and the overall structuring of social relationships. In short, we can distinguish between theory that helps to interpret the causes, the courses and the consequences of surveillance, even though it is also helpful to see these together in their interconnectedness.

In what follows, I survey various aspects of surveillance theory, starting with its roots in several disciplines, moving through a discussion of 'modern' and 'postmodern' theories to more specific debates over 'discipline' and 'control', and concluding with a look at 'governance' and at the 'ban' as potential key concepts in surveillance theory. Each of these constitutes a general theoretical issue in surveillance studies, and must always be linked back to specific situations, processes and practices for the theory to be worth anything. But they are also issues that relate necessarily and strongly to critical and normative positions that must also be articulated and open for inspection and questioning.

The roots of surveillance theories

Among the many problems encountered by students of surveillance is that the field is large and sprawling and concepts and theories are drawn from a wide range of sources. Where to begin? And does the theory that originated in one domain such as the workplace really apply in another, such as the domestic or the consumer realm? How helpful are the popular concepts that are drawn from the work of George Orwell (Big Brother) or Michel Foucault (the Panopticon)? A good place to start is with those areas in which surveillance has been theorized for a long time, such as workplace management, military power or criminal justice.

As Elia Zureik points out, 'worker monitoring, fragmentation of tasks, the separation between mental and manual tasks, and regimentation of work' were noted by scholars such as Karl Marx, who saw them as a means of subordinating labour to capital (Zureik 2003: 31). But as he goes on to say, these themes are linked with workplace surveillance, especially through the application of new technologies that affect power relations. There is a sense in which such surveillance expresses an ongoing theme, that those who establish some means of watching over others are demonstrating that they do not trust those being watched, in this case workers. Workplace studies of surveillance often follow Foucault's focus on the micro-techniques of discipline that target and treat the body as something to be observed and tested (see Staples 1997: ix), and Zureik also shows that subtle, discursive approaches indicate how different uses of technology may produce different outcomes. But he reminds us as well that the larger questions of political economy – some of which derive from Marx – still must be borne in mind.

Turning to the second area, military power, Christopher Dandeker shows how important warfare and military development were – and still are – to the growth of Western liberal democracies (Dandeker 1990, 2006). As such, he argues, they have helped to expand surveillance into a central position in the constitution of nation-states. This argument is derived especially from Max Weber's theories but also from the 'Machiavellian' approaches of Italian theorists such as Pareto and Mosca. The early modern state had to supervise its citizens as well as to distinguish its domain of power separately from them. As war was a major feature of the life of those states, military organizations were often the first to bureaucratize and surveillance was an outcome. The state's supervisory powers over society extended in order to facilitate military objectives, something that became even more clear as 'welfare states' were created after World War II. Moreover, as long as the existence of bureaucratized and technologized military power is seen as a means of maintaining peace, the military–surveillance connection will persist.

Thirdly, as far as criminal justice is concerned, surveillance has also been a key feature of numerous developments, from making Victorian streets visible for policing (Cohen 1985) to equipping officers with high-tech devices for undercover tasks (Marx 1988). Indeed, to hear that someone is 'under surveillance' is almost automatically to assume that they are being monitored and tracked by police agents of some kind. But why might increased general surveillance, including the use of new technologies, occur at some times more than at others? Durkheim's theory of crime illuminates this issue well. When the gap between the relatively well-off and the relatively disadvantaged is growing, he argues, each group will come to see the other, increasingly, as a threat to their security. There may be both real and perceived increases in crime rates, because of the widening inequalities gap, and the better-off will respond by supporting more draconian counter-measures and broadening the definition of 'crime'. This includes obtaining technologies of self-protection, thus further excluding the more marginalized and targeting offender and innocent alike. As Perri 6 suggests, Durkheim's ideas may be extrapolated to suggest that more surveillance would follow, especially to maintain vigilance over public spaces, which would affect some 'suspect' categories disproportionately, thus adding to their stigma (Perri 6 2003).

As may be seen from these three examples, without intending to establish 'surveillance studies', some early social scientists spoke at least indirectly of surveillance issues, mapped the field in a preliminary way, and drew attention to modern disciplines of capitalist supervision (Marx) or military-bureaucratic record-keeping (Weber), or to the likelihood that surveillance would increase at times of growing social and economic inequality (Durkheim). One could add other examples as well, such as the accenting of the eye in the urban metropolis, which was central to the work of Georg Simmel (1950). For the latter, modernity entailed the creation of a 'society of strangers', the ideal breeding ground of surveillance surrogates for the sorts of trusting relationships that one might expect in contexts where longer-term and personal relations predominate.

More specifically, one could consider the ways in which classical social and political theories focused – so to speak – on the eye. Without even invoking Jeremy Bentham's Panopticon, such ideas may be viewed more broadly within the 'scopic regimes of modernity' (Jay 1989), dating from Descartes. The eye was privileged to the extent that much later twentieth-century theory reacted with anti-ocularcentric critique. Narrowing this down to how some may 'watch over' others, it is already clear that the 'watching' may be metaphorical (the work-timing machines in the factory, the office files and the city plan) as well as literal. It is important to consider the implications of Enlightenment 'ocularcentrism' and its twentieth-century critique because 'watching' metaphors and considerations of the 'gaze' lie behind much surveillance theory, even when actual eyes and images are not in view.

The question of vision and its critique is highly significant in surveillance studies, not least because the very concept of surveillance presupposes it. More broadly, as we shall see, knowledge is sought on the subjects of surveillance, and new techniques may be deployed to provide this. In his piece on 'digital rule', for instance, Richard Jones shows how the Foucauldian 'gaze' has given way in many cases to fresh forms of surveillance that rely on digital technologies (Jones 2000). Nonetheless, while a variety of restrictions on time and space are evident – though no longer typically in enclosed spaces – forms of control, exclusion and punishment persist. Watching over, monitoring or overseeing may in some cases be transposed into an electronic key, with consequences that cannot safely be overlooked (as it were).

Modern and postmodern surveillance theories

Modern surveillance theory relates to those classical treatments that understand surveillance as an outgrowth of capitalist enterprises, bureaucratic organization, the nation-state, a machine-like techno-logic and the development of new kinds of solidarity, involving less 'trust' or at least different kinds of trust (see Lyon 2001: 109ff.). Postmodern surveillance theory, on the other hand, deals with what William Staples thinks of as new forms of 'vigilance and visibility' – technology-based, body-objectifying, everyday, universal kinds of surveillance (Staples 2000: 11).

One does not have to accept the validity of other debates around the terms 'modern' and 'postmodern' to use them as helpful markers. Moreover, they may best be thought of as changing attempts to deal with major shifts in the social, economic, political and cultural land-scape rather than as internally 'theoretical' movements. It seems to me that new kinds of theory are required to deal with some profound alterations in the organization of everyday life and in global relations that were accented from the 1980s onward. Although no one concept can be expected to undertake the task of encapsulating unprecedented transformations of social experience, 'globalization' is very relevant here, and 'postmodernity' also speaks well to the issues (see Lyon 1999 for fuller justification).

One particularly useful dimension of the concept of 'postmodernity' is precisely that it still refers to and assumes 'modernity'. Without debating whether we have ever been modern (it is a good question – see Latour 1993), it is important to remember that even if the concept of postmodernity – or 'postmodern theory' – is accepted, it does not ne-cessarily supersede what obtained previously. With regard to the ele-ments of postmodern surveillance mentioned above, it is clear that certain kinds of techniques and technologies for surveillance were common long before recent times, that targeting the body is not a new idea, and nor is local surveillance or even large-scale capture of popula-tion details (think of censuses, in use since ancient times). Rather, these elements have come to the fore, and now dominate the surveillance landscape in ways that they did not previously. These are general char-acterizations intended merely to provide a contextualizing big picture.

The main contours of modern theories of surveillance derive from analyses such as those mentioned above, including Marx, Weber and

Durkheim, but with two interesting additions. One is the (largely but certainly not explicitly) Weberian work of the French sociologist and legal scholar Jacques Ellul, and the other is the theoretical influence of the work of novelist and social critic George Orwell. The one bequeathed a strong interest in the technological dynamics of surveillance, and the other a model (or 'ideal type', if one is to see Weberian influence here as well) of a total surveillance society by which the degree of surveillance power in a given setting may be gauged. Both these figures also lent a moral seriousness and political urgency to the development of surveillance theory in the mid- to late twentieth century.

Ellul painted with a broad brush, the dominant stroke of which is '*la technique*'. This is a cultural orientation towards 'means' rather than 'ends', which also yields part of the commonality with Weber's work. This orientation makes the insertion into social life of many artefacts and technical processes seem desirable, plausible. *La technique* constructs the social world that the machine needs, feeding on itself and expanding in an all-embracing and usually irreversible fashion. Thus, for instance, Ellul was among the first to note the effects of technologized policing; it requires that more and more be supervised in the hope of apprehending more effectively those who violate rules and laws. *La technique* in police work steadily puts all under subtle surveillance (Ellul 1964).

Ellul's work, concerned as it is with the critique of totalitarianism, was recognized as a significant contribution by many early surveillance studies researchers and writers. Gary T. Marx's work on undercover policing and Oscar Gandy's on the personal information economy are cases in point of theorists who take some significant cues from Ellul. And the idea of 'surveillance creep', now widely used in the field, also originates in Ellul's work, via Langdon Winner's concept of 'function creep' (Winner 1977), although it was also used by Marx (1989) in relation to DNA fingerprints. In Winner's hands, this term, or, rather, the tendency to which it points, is used, for instance, of the establishment of digitized identification card systems, which tend to be expanded to include other functions not originally envisioned by their promoters (this is discussed further in Lyon 2001: 111–13).

Orwell's work, on the other hand, has provided some of the most enduring, best-known and publicly accessible concepts in surveillance studies, above all the figure of Big Brother. Theoretically, the notion that nation-state surveillance arises from certain political imperatives, relating to military and geo-political struggles, and may embrace a whole society in negative and repressive ways, is connected with the work of Mosca, Pareto, Sorel and Michels. But in much academic as well as popular imagination, these theoretical ideas are brought to life in Orwell's fiction. The centralization of state power, the use of technologies such as the ubiquitous telescreen to bring the face of Big Brother into every corner and through which citizens could also be monitored, the twisting of language to create 'doublespeak' – all these are familiar dimensions of Orwell's sinister state-centred surveillance society.

One other aspect of Orwell's work is worth mentioning, however, and that is his ambiguity regarding the actual location of the *Nineteen Eighty-Four* society. While many considered his work as a critique of state socialism (and the old 'communist' countries behind the 'iron curtain' or Eastern Europe), Orwell did not let Western liberal democracies off the hook so easily. It is clear that his work, along with that of theorists as diverse as Hannah Arendt or Anthony Giddens, sees totalitarian tendencies – among which state surveillance would figure prominently – as immanent within any bureaucratically organized nation-state. This has become an abiding theme of surveillance studies, that it is precisely within liberal democratic nation-states where record-keeping, monitoring and observation become routine and technologically augmented that restrictions on liberty – and, especially post-9/11, mobility – may be anticipated.

One prominent theorist who does argue for the central role of surveillance in modern life is Anthony Giddens. Lamenting the dominance in late twentieth-century sociology of Marx-influenced theories, on the one hand, and what he calls 'industrial society' theories, on the other, Giddens insists that surveillance (and militarism, the other neglected factor) must be seen in its own right and not merely as a product of capitalism or bureaucracy (Giddens 1985). For Giddens, surveillance refers to both the accumulation of coded information and the direct supervision of social life (Giddens 1985: 13), and it may become a significant means of domination. While he sees the dangers of totalitarian tendencies in bureaucratic administration, Giddens also wants to distance himself from the more cynical reason of Nietzsche or Foucault's 'ubiquitous power' and leave history open to democratizing possibilities.

While Giddens' work makes a welcome break with the relative neglect of surveillance in social theory, two observations must be made about his contribution. One, the distinction between 'supervision' and 'coded information' becomes more and more difficult to maintain in a digital world where coded information becomes a *means* of supervision. Computerized surveillance contributes to the collapse of that distinction. Two, Giddens' assumption that surveillance is primarily a feature of nation-states is hard to sustain when personal data, used for regulation purposes, are promiscuously processed in many non-government realms, but with undoubtedly governmental consequences.

Towards postmodern surveillance

All these examples in the previous section add up to what I am calling, for want of a better term, 'modern' contributions to surveillance theory. By the later twentieth century, however, it became increasingly clear that surveillance was undergoing some serious alterations, as the political-economic context moved towards 'consumer capitalism' and as new digital technologies were adopted in organizations. This meant, for example, that those thinking in primarily 'Orwellian' terms had to consider surveillance practices well beyond the nation-state – in advertising and marketing, for instance – and involving technologies that have greater speed and capacity and are much more subtly interactive than anything previous. The new technologies make automation and permanent record-keeping possible, the body may be watched, assessed and manipulated in new ways, everyday surveillance is local and immediate, and yet the data of large populations are captured for sorting and sifting.

This last point is especially significant, but must also be handled with great care. Any social and political theory that attempts to incorporate the technological is vulnerable to charges of 'determinism'. That is, the impact of new artefacts and systems may easily colonize the argument, such that already existing situations and processes are downplayed and 'indigenous' factors may be obscured by an exaggerated view of technical capacities. At the same time, to ignore or downplay the role of digital technologies in helping to create today's surveillance landscape would seem to be blindness of a perniciously perilous kind. Without the enablement of new technologies, the extension of 'vision' would be restricted (Marx 1988: 217–19), cross-system usability and networked integration would be impossible, and 'social sorting' – the pervasive digital discrimination that makes possible different treatment of different categories of population (Graham and Wood 2003; Lyon 2003b) – could not occur on the scale that it does today.

The more 'postmodern' versions of surveillance theory, as Staples says, underscore technology-based, body-objectifying, everyday, universal kinds of surveillance. To review these: the technologies make surveillance amenable to automation and place increasing reliance upon the data-double or the virtual self. Mark Poster makes some important observations on this, suggesting how post-structural theory helps us to see databases as 'discourses' and data-doubles as simultaneously independent and dependent entities (Poster 1996). For Poster, this means we live in the era of the 'superpanopticon'. So, far from producing Foucault's 'interiorized' subjects, aware of their self-determination, database discourse produces objectified individuals with dispersed data 'identities' of which some may not even be aware. The body is no longer a bastion to be protected as 'private space'. It is already part of the superpanopticon.

The body-objectifying aspects of postmodern surveillance may be seen in the very visibility of bodies to surveillance agencies, which is now almost constant in some contexts, and in the rising attention paid to the body itself as a source of surveillance data. This aspect is not limited to external agencies, either. As new sorts of surveillance seep into all life-spheres, some engage in self-surveillance of quite precise and systematic kinds. Think of keep-fit 'fanatics', for instance, who constantly check times, pressures, weights and rates, or of the ways in which some women use scales, body-fat indicators and calorie charts in forms of low-level self-surveillance (Bordo 1993). As far as the external agency use of body data is concerned, the use of biometrics and DNA is further discussed in chapter 6.

The everyday character of postmodern surveillance refers to the ways in which the regulation of daily life now goes far beyond criminal or workplace deviance. Surveillance categories now include geo-demographic lifestyle groups, psychological classifications, educational differences and health distinctions. Some of these reach back to birth or even before birth in an attempt to gauge future life-chances. In the UK, for example, a child registry database established in the Children's Act (2004) may even be used to check on children's daily fruit intake (Roberts 2006). As Deleuze would say, surveillance comes out of specific enclosures to permeate all of life. Surveillance is universal in the sense that no one is immune from the gaze. Surveillance is also universal in the sense that wherever new systems are adopted, they tend to have a similar technological character.

William Bogard uses Jean Baudrillard's work as a springboard for showing how surveillance is simulated (Bogard 1996). The speed with which computer systems operate makes it possible for them to overtake themselves, as it were, and to try to second-guess or predict events. This is an instance in which technological capacities contribute directly to the changing character of surveillance, enabling it to have a decidedly future orientation. The idea is to see first, to anticipate. Of course, early sociologists such as Auguste Comte believed that they could foresee and thus change the course of events, and in film-fiction the classic recent treatment is Steven Spielberg's adaptation of Philip K. Dick's short story 'Minority Report', where murders are 'seen' in advance by clairvoyant 'pre-cogs'. But surveillance as simulation brings this out of philosophy and fiction into practical police work or marketing. Pattern recognition software used in parking-lot CCTV, for instance, is intended to alert operators to 'suspicious behaviour' *before the event*.

What actually happens on the ground and in daily life, however, is likely to display a mixture of 'modern' and 'postmodern' features of surveillance. While risk management and new modes of governance may well be seen in pre-emptive data-mining or 'predictive' CCTV, watching for behaviour patterns rather than actual offences, in most countries the power of the state is still strong. Public space CCTV systems, for example, though they may be run on a commercial basis, or be outsourced to operating companies, are still operated in conjunction with police departments, and images from them may still be demanded by state intelligence authorities (Norris and McCahill 2006). However 'postmodern' the situation, the 'modern' is still present in the word and in the social reality.

Inside and outside the Panopticon

Some surveillance theories that may be considered to straddle the 'modern' and the 'postmodern' rubric originate in the work of Michel Foucault or Gilles Deleuze, neither of whom, paradoxically, had much time for ideas of 'modernity' or 'postmodernity'. It took Michel Foucault, writing in the mid- to late twentieth century, to pinpoint a precise shift to modern scopic regimes, above all in the Panopticon, with its powerful explanatory proposals (Foucault 1979). The semi-circular architecture of Jeremy Bentham's envisaged prison height-ened inmate visibility through individual back-lit cells and reduced or eliminated 'inspector' visibility through the use of blinds in the central inspection tower. Power lay primarily with the inspector, who could see without being seen, the uncertainty thus generated being the very means whereby his power was guaranteed.

For Foucault, the disciplinary gaze of the Panopticon is the arche-typical power of modernity, the model of discipline that would suffuse all social institutions. Interestingly, however, archaeological work has recently uncovered some ancient observation sites that appear to be 'panoptic' *avant la lettre*, thus potentially relativizing Foucault's claims about the uniquely modern character of such surveillance (Yekutiel 2006). Nevertheless, his work certainly gave a new lease of life to some quaint ideas of Bentham's, ideas that were influential during the nine-teenth century but which in their details might otherwise have remained in some dusty history of failed plans for prisons. Instead they have become paradigmatic for thinking about some aspects of surveil-lance (see Lyon 2006a).

Despite what seem to have been Foucault's intentions, the idea of unilateral power vested in the inspector is what animates a number of studies carried out following the logic of the Panopticon. This has yielded a rather one-sided account of surveillance that focuses heavily on the subtly coercive experience of living with the uncertainty of being seen, which for better or worse also lends itself to updating for an era of almost invisible electronic surveillance. In this account, as Foucault himself said, 'visibility is a trap' (Foucault 1979: 200). But not only does this kind of account distract attention from the subtle inter-play between surveillance power and the attitudes and activities of those subject to surveillance, it also places all the emphasis on forms of rational control. The impression is given that surveillance is unam-biguously imbued with the controlling interests of sovereign power.

Bentham was a driven secular social reformer, a major contributor to the British utilitarian school of thought. Late eighteenth-century Britain was buzzing with ideas for urgently needed penal reform, and other contributors to this came from the evangelical wing of Christianity. But

Bentham's vision differed from these in that, while he shared the idea that moral reform and not retributive punishment alone should be central to the prison experience, he insisted that the 'fabrication of virtue' (Evans 1982) should occur without any religious underpinnings. So although he prefaced his Panopticon plan with words chosen from the biblical Psalm 139 – 'Thou . . . spiest out all my ways. If I say, per-adventure the darkness shall cover me, then shall my night be turned to day' – he turned his back on any notion that the surveillance should be about *caring* for the individual (the parallel theme of Psalm 139) and focused exclusively on the mechanisms of *control*.

Nikolas Rose summarizes nicely what the Panopticon was all about, for Foucault: 'the diagram of a political technology, one that was indi-vidualizing, normalizing, based on perpetual surveillance, classifica-tion, a kind of uninterrupted and continuous judgment enabling the government of multiplicities, reducing the resistant powers of human bodies at the same time as it maximized their economic and social utility' (Rose 1999: 187). But several processes are in play in Foucault's model. One is concerned with discipline, as seen sharply in the Panopticon plan, but the other focuses on bio-power. Where the first helps to normalize individuals, the second, through devices such as the census, socializes people by group or by category. In this second case, individuals are affected by virtue of their group membership or association. Even in the Panopticon, however, classification of pris-oner types occurs, so that bio-power is also present there.

Although Foucault claimed that his was a history of the *present*, he studiously omitted any mention of the role of mass media or comput-ers in contributing to the kinds of discipline and bio-power into which he had otherwise demonstrated such insight. Others, however, have taken his ideas into the realm of digital surveillance, showing how the Panopticon might go electronic (e.g. Poster 1996; Zuboff 1988). One could be forgiven for scepticism as we trace the path from a prison that was never built but whose principles supposedly permeated modern societies to electronic forms of surveillance that Bentham could never have dreamed of and Foucault curiously ignored.

It is important to recall that Foucault saw his work on surveillance in several other contexts that are explored, for example, in the *History of Sexuality* (Foucault 1976) and other writings, and centred on other concepts, such as the 'confession' (see, e.g., Cole 2006) And, impor-tantly, it is not always possible to generalize about the Panopticon. For one thing, the primary referent of the diagram is a prison, and thus although some of its operations may work in other contexts such as the workplace, the degree to which surveillance subjects can walk out of the surveillance site does make a difference. For another, a key element of the panoptic is its contribution to what Foucault called 'soul-training', so although visibility may be centrally significant to, say, CCTV systems, without the soul-training element there are limits on how far CCTV may be said to be panoptic (Haggerty 2006).

In *Discipline and Punish* (Foucault 1979) Foucault saw surveillance taking place in enclosed spaces – prisons, workplaces, schools – where people are confined. Each context has its panoptic principles at work; containing, shaping and including subjects within a system of automatic power. Foucault's arguments suggest how self-discipline is promoted through panoptic and related methods. The uncertainty about whether or not one is being watched creates the desire to comply with whatever is the norm for the institution in question. Through the process is developed an inner compulsion to 'do the right thing' as prescribed by the organization, which produces the desired 'docile bodies'. This brief account accents the power/knowledge dimension as it is tied to the visual and highlights what many have thought Foucault intended to achieve, an exposure of and a critique of 'vision' for its role in modern forms of domination.

Without doubting that the panoptic paradigm throws light on some very interesting aspects of the development of surveillance, it must also be said that it is also subject to a number of important criticisms. For one thing, it pays little attention to the growth of the mass media and thus the persistence of the 'spectacle', a theme that was initially suggested by Thomas Mathiesen in his work on the 'synopticon' (Mathiesen 1997) and is discussed in chapter 6. For another, despite some imaginative efforts, it is hard to bring together all the diverse aspects of digitally enhanced surveillance with the power/knowledge dynamics of the vision-directed Panopticon. Moreover, Foucault had additional observations on subjectivity that remain relevant after these critiques have been considered (see discussion in chapter 4).

The present discussion turns, then, to questions of how surveillance theory might go 'outside' the Panopticon, first in relation to digital technologies and the 'control society' thesis, and secondly in relation to another Foucauldian theme, that of governmentality (or, less clumsily, governance). Implicit in Deleuze's idea of the control society is a critique of panopticism, that such surveillance has been superseded by other forms of power than discipline, mediated by electronic technologies. And in the 'governmentality' argument, surveillance is seen as one strand, or one strategy, in broader conceptions of power.

This debate about surveillance after the Panopticon is conceived in a variety of ways, among which is Roy Boyne's proposal that 'post-panopticism' be considered a successor to the panoptic paradigm (by definition, however, this position docs not have the coherence of the panoptic perspective) (Boyne 2000). First, from Zygmunt Bauman, Boyne brings the idea that forms of consumer seduction are replacing the panoptic regime. Second, he suggests that self-surveillance may be carried out so effectively in Western capitalist societies that it makes the original panoptic impulse redundant. Third, he refers to William Bogard's claim that simulation, prediction and action before the fact may reduce the need for older forms of surveillance. Fourth, Boyne brings in Mathiesen's contention that the mass media synopticon, where the many watch the few, acts alongside the Panopticon, where the few watch the many, thus relativizing its effects. Finally, the arguable failure of the Panopticon to produce docile subjects is seen as a final challenge to panoptic theory.

In a terse but trenchant piece called 'Postscript on the Societies of Control' Deleuze sketches the shift from 'discipline' to 'control' (Deleuze 1992). Whereas Foucault had theorized surveillance in the context of confined fixed spaces like the Panopticon, Deleuze proposed that such old sites of confinement were no longer the only or the primary sites of surveillance. The erstwhile 'analogical' sites are now paralleled by new digital means, an idea similar to that of Paul Virilio, who writes of the rapid free-floating control of the 'vision machine' (Virilio 1994). The new surveillance is individualized and competitive, appropriate to the new businesses that emerged from later twentieth-century restructuring, where constant monitoring checks worker activities and individual inducements provide incentives for compliance.

According to Deleuze, individuals in the disciplinary society could be individuated and amassed using signatures and numbers. Now all that is required is just the code for 'dividuals' so that they can pass through the system of universal modulation: swipe the card; place the thumbprint on the screen. Work can be contracted out; consumers can service themselves; patients are passed through the delivery system as fast as possible; offenders may be tagged. In fact, the Deleuze 'control society' thesis bears a striking similarity to a theory proposed around the same time in the English-speaking world, the idea of a 'new penology' (Feeley and Simon 1992, 1994). Proponents of this theory argued that rather than ascribing guilt and blame to individuals and imposing punishment and treatment, the new penology is concerned with 'techniques for identifying, classifying and managing groups assorted by levels of dangerousness' (Feeley and Simon 1994: 180). New risk management approaches to crime invite surveillance in order to make assessments rather than individualized forms of suspicion-based surveillance.

Others who have taken up this theme in a general way include Michael Hardt and Antonio Negri, who argue in *Empire* that the 'crisis of government' that followed the 1960s consumer boom involved a general turning against established authority that led to an apparently 'post-disciplinary' situation (Hardt and Negri 2000). No longer could authorities rely on the old inner compulsions, fostered in part by panoptic regimes, and in their place two kinds of strategies appear, the 'repressive' and the 'democratic'. The former, based in the workplace, disaggregate privileged and marginalized workers, using new technologies to watch over the marginalized especially. The latter have to do with democratic, dispersed and distributed methods, based around processes of consumption and producing new forms of inclusion and exclusion.

The *Empire* argument is in turn very reminiscent of Zygmunt Bauman's analysis of 'acceptable' and 'flawed' consumers, in which the latter are discarded from the system for their failure to comply (Bauman 1998: 38). What Bauman omits, however, is the ways in which flawed consumers (by which he means mainly the poor) may be actively excluded through social sorting processes. Today, the 'commercialization of suspicion' means that surveillance technologies appear even in everyday life in domestic, family and, of course, work settings. These are discussed in chapter 5.

The panoptic idea still has some merits for surveillance theory in that some surveillance does still occur in enclosed spaces, above all in prisons, with which the diagram was associated in the first place. Again, the uncertainty of being watched may still act as a deterrent to deviance, which is why some CCTV systems may be said to 'work' even if the cameras are not actually switched on or recording. But for explaining much other surveillance today, theory has to leave the Panopticon behind. In its least helpful versions, it acts as a metaphor for total power over hapless victims. There are much better ways of considering surveillance theoretically that explore the actual workings of power in electronic grids, the experiences of those subjected to and interacting with surveillance systems, and how the complex politics of systems and subjects are worked out in practice.

Governance, sorting and the 'ban'

Another way in which Foucault's work has been used in relation to surveillance is to consider 'governmentality' or governance. As David Garland says in relation to the culture of control, the 'criminal justice state is, in this area at least, shedding its "sovereign" style of governing by top-down command and developing a form of rule close to . . . "governmentality" – a modality that involves the enlistment of others, the shaping of incentives, and the creation of new forms of cooperative action' (Garland 2001: 125). This does not mean, necessarily, that forms of regulation are always present in governmentality or that this shift is negative in other ways. Indeed, Garland himself believes that the complex world of late modernity demands that the governmental capacities of civil society be harnessed to work alongside the nation-state.

Theoretically, Foucault saw governance not as a site of control but as one of freedom, albeit a bounded freedom. This is the thought behind Nikolas Rose's volume *Powers of Freedom* (1999). Rose argues that current regimes of government relate to the ways in which 'freedom' – as the enlargement of human capacities to act – has become a key motif. If surveillance has to do with strategies of control, then these have to be thought of, says Rose, as the price paid for the regimes of government through freedom (1999: 273). Rose stresses that Foucault was not arguing for an epochal 'disciplinary society' except in the sense that such societies are ones where strategies and tactics of discipline are active (1999: 234). And Deleuze's work should be understood in the same way, exploring the new possibilities and complexities of 'control', only now, rather than disciplining the subject from scratch within set locales, we find surveillance 'designed in' and dispersed throughout the flows of everyday existence.

Rose emphasizes that his is empirical but not realist work, in the ethos of inquiry of, but not hidebound by, Foucault. Governance in all its ambiguity and complexity has some strong resonance with surveillance studies, as Kevin Haggerty argues pointedly, above all in the knowledge-dependency of governance (Haggerty 2006). Visibility is vital for governance. Knowledge of all kinds is used to manage population groups through identification, categorization and monitoring. And because studies such as Rose's are not committed to grand theory constructs such as 'postmodernity' or even 'control society', the focus is always maintained on specific surveillance projects, each of which has its own rationale and which is regarded by its subjects in different ways. But Haggerty also rightly regards the governmentality approach as self-limiting when it refuses to look at the actual systems of rules and relations among political actors. He pleads that however much may be learned from governmentality perspectives, surveillance studies keep a place for realist investigations of the experiences of subjects of surveillance and of specific analyses that show which groups are able to use surveillance power to their ends.

It is to such ends that a number of surveillance studies have concentrated on the processes of 'social sorting' as a means of understanding how actual surveillance practices have particular outcomes (Lyon 2003b). Such studies learn from but go beyond governmentality, to indicate how patterns of power, inequality and injustice form in concrete situations and what their wider social and political consequences may be. In terms of some classic lines of cleavage, one may explore how, for instance, gendered, racialized and class-based divisions may be mitigated or reinforced by contemporary regimes of governance and associated routines of surveillance (see, e.g., Amoore and De Goede 2005).

Thus, for instance, Ann Bartow suggests that women are targeted in specific ways through online marketing techniques, where the 'highly valued demographic' of females between 25 and 49 are prized customers. She argues – though more work should be done in this area – that women are especially vulnerable to online consumer profilers (Bartow 2005). Equally, surveillance studies may investigate ways in which 'racial' groups are specifically targeted, not only through obvious post-9/11 developments such as intensified profiling at airports (Lyon 2003b), but also through genetic testing. Oscar Gandy argues that race and gender markers within predictive models such as those of health-care result in 'unequal distribution of harms'. Moreover, as past decisions are often linked with future options, such hardships tend to cluster within what are called patterns of 'cumulative disadvantage' (Gandy 2006b).

Another important surveillance-based challenge appears in the work of Roger Burrows and Nicholas Gane, who show how social class theory is confronted by current marketing practices. They argue that the use of geo-demographic data to sort groups of persons according to where they live is now so significant that it challenges some conventional ways of conceiving social class (Burrows and Gane 2006). Geo-demographic classifications are widely used in the marketing industry, but as Burrows and Gane note, the connections between these and sociologies of class have hardly been made.

Rating different urban zones was first a task of policy-makers trying to determine priorities for housing grants and only later, ironically, to discriminate between categories of rich neighbourhoods. Consumption patterns are explored by collapsing several sociological variables such as class, housing, life-course, income, health and education into neighbourhoods. This produces crude designations such as 'young influentials' or 'pools and patios' or, perhaps slightly less desirably for marketers, 'ethnic underclass'. Within informational capitalism, however, Burrows and Gane argue that such classifications are becoming sociologically significant in new ways. Digital media are helping to restructure the geographical-social spaces of everyday life, even as they are sorted for preferential and routine service in areas such as road or internet use.

However, consumers also become aware of how they are sorted as details of the classification systems become available on the internet and as they are connected with postal codes associated with one consuming group or another. This means, for Burrows and Gane, that Weber's conventional distinction between class (as life-chances) and status (as lifestyle) may be harder to maintain. Life-chances, for example in the housing market, may be linked with cultural attachments in ways that help determine chances and choices. And the power to classify, the governance, is in the commercial, corporate realm, not that of the state. Identity – or, rather, identification – comes to be articulated once again with place. So while self-sorting occurs as people seek association with neighbourhoods and postcodes they think are commensurate with their social standing, the processes of geo-demographic sorting are still arcane, technologically opaque to many ordinary people and capable of making substantial differences to the capacities of consumers to make those self-sorting choices in the first place.

Another way of learning from but also building upon the work of Foucault is to consider the relation between structured power and ordinary everyday life. Giorgio Agamben's work, in particular, offers fresh insights on what he calls 'sovereign power' and 'bare life', ideas that relate closely to new surveillance regimes of categorizing and exclusion (Agamben 1998, 2005). In this work, however, surveillance studies come full circle, once again to focus on the activities of the state and on citizens or non-citizens. Starkly, Agamben sees the world from the point of view of concentration camps, where death was adjudicated and life directed (for a current application see French 2007).

Agamben argues that Foucault and others have never succeeded in bringing together ideas about the sovereign state and institutions such as the prison (as in *Discipline and Punish*) with notions of everyday bio-power (as in *The History of Sexuality*). In a new sense, says Agamben, totalitarianism and democracy have certain things in common. In *State of Exception*, Agamben argues a contemporary case that the declaration by President George W. Bush that he is 'commander-in-chief' in a 'war on terror' has a longer history, in which, as it were, the exception has become the rule (Agamben 2005). In the 'state of emergency' after 9/11 the Bush administration authorized the indefinite detention of non-citizens suspected of terrorist activities and their subsequent trials by a military commission. Agamben claims that the state of exception, which was meant to be a provisional measure, became in the course of the twentieth century a normal mode of government, and was accented after 9/11.

For Didier Bigo, Agamben's analysis of the 'ban' that systematically excludes some groups (Agamben 1997) invites consideration of a further post-Foucault neologism, the 'ban-opticon' (Bigo 2005). While the majority of citizens of the global North are normalized through their involvement in consumer capitalism in the kinds of ways mentioned earlier, a focused surveillance is reserved for the *sans-papiers*, the potential terrorist, the refugee – those 'trapped in the imperative of mobility'. Police, military and other professionals combine their efforts to become the new 'in-security professionals'. The 'opticon' has a specific purpose, to 'ban' some, to exclude. Mixing files from different sources leads to new classifications.

Thus for Agamben a genealogical line may be drawn from Nazi camps of the Second World War, through camps for Japanese detainees in the USA and Canada in the same period, to off-shore facilities such as Guantánamo Bay in Cuba (used for post-9/11 'terrorism suspects') or Australian detention centres for unprocessed refugees. It could be argued, of course, that these are just the obvious, sharply defined 'camps' for excluded persons, and that many indeterminate statuses are maintained through the use of *Gastarbeiter* permits, permanent resident cards, and the like. But to explore these would be to go beyond the point of this excursus, which is to show that while surveillance studies may benefit from the insights of governmentality scholars, there is also a place for detailing the actual conditions produced by specific regimes of governance, for examining the politics of surveillance, and for understanding the ways in which those who are subjects of those regimes respond and react to their circumstances.

Theory and counter-surveillance

If surveillance studies needs a theoretical companion, I have suggested, better choose a general approach such as governance than specific all-embracing concepts such as the Panopticon. Even with such a companion, surveillance studies should try to retain its own integrity by allowing for the contributions of more realist analysis that concern themselves with theorizing actual conditions, processes and subjectivities of surveillance. These will pay attention to crucial dimensions such as socio-economic class, race and gender which today must be applied in areas of literal (CCTV) as well as literary (data-mining) 'watching'. This is not to mention 'watch lists', those constructions of multiple networked databases, data-mining and cross-departmental memos that play such a role in today's 'ban-opticons'.

Recall, too, that Foucault himself saw power as productive and as calling forth countervailing power. Many studies of resistance suggest the need for theory that includes how people engage with surveillance. This can be at the level of movements, specific anti-surveillance organizations (such as the International Civil Liberties Monitoring Group or the New York Camera Players) or everyday apparently *ad hoc* negotiation and resistance (see Gilliom 2001). Theorists such as Kirstie Ball (2003), Hille Koskela (2003) or John McGrath (2004) show how in ordinary life people raise questions, refuse to cooperate ('I ain't going to pee in no jar'), limit their exposure or comply cautiously as a means of challenging surveillance powers. And of course the resistance may indicate an element of some other kind of related movement (civil liberties, feminism, anti-racism, freedom of movement and identification, etc.).

In the end, then, surveillance studies has to go beyond general (even totalizing) theories of discipline or control to look at specific ways in which this or that institution is involved in surveillance and how the surveillance is modified by the compliance or refusal of its subjects. This may itself be met by counter-measures, of course. Border resistance by 'undesirable' groups of would-be entrants into national domains has, for example, prompted professionals to move the checking upstream, as witness the advance passenger information and passenger name record system at airports. This becomes part of the narrative approach to theory that I am advocating here.

Alongside this lies a theoretical thread, indeed, one might say a commitment, that I believe is centrally important: that is, to some notion of embodied personhood. The kinds of subjectivities that have to be stressed over against the overly structural or technical approaches of some theorists are based in social realist views of materiality that are neither ex-carnate (downplaying the body) nor hyper-carnate (making it central to social explanation) (see Lyon 2006a). It is embodied persons who are affected by surveillance, positively or negatively, and embodied persons who engage with it, again, for better or for worse. Thus the contributions of Michel de Certeau (1986) become highly significant for surveillance studies, as do those of Paul Ricoeur, which stress the story told by the self – for instance, in 'self-identity' – as the complement to the 'body' (Ricoeur 1992; see also Lyon 2001: 72). This is especially relevant to ID card systems. Care for the self and for the other is also germane as a motive for engaging research on surveillance in the first place, especially in the world of the 'ban' that affects most deeply and cruelly those whose 'otherness' is negatively construed (see Lyon 2003a: 149–55).

At the same time, it must not be forgotten that capitalism, bureaucracy, government departments, corporations, police, security agencies, and so on, each play their part in creating the wider world of surveillance in which subjectivities are imbricated. Surveillance is only ever a means to other ends, of governance, which may include both care and protection. Both the classical theorists and more recent cultural theorists have important insights for understanding these varied dimensions of surveillance, but in the end the real value of such ideas is only realized in relation to two other factors: one is the constraint of real-world empirical conditions against which all theories stand, fall or at least prove their usefulness and illuminating qualities; and the other is the commitments that, no less than the empirical conditions, inform those theories. For me, such commitments are expressed in a quest for the kind of justice that takes special account of the very vulnerable, the most marginalized, and requires a dual response: one, that their voices be heard and their stories told; and, two, that the large-scale institutions, networks and processes of surveillance be held accountable for their uses of personal data. This is how a theory of embodied personhood speaks to the contemporary realities of ubiquitous surveillance.

Conclusion

Let me try to summarize what has been said about theories of surveillance and suggest what their implications are for doing surveillance studies. By looking historically at how explanations of surveillance have developed, analytically at how surveillance processes and practices work, and critically at what the main outcomes of surveillance are, we can put together an account of the causes, courses and consequences of surveillance.

As far as the causes of contemporary surveillance are concerned, they may be traced to the growth of modern forms of capitalist and bureaucratic practice, but they also acquire some distinctive characteristics of their own. Individuation, for example, is basic to both modes, but later is highly amenable to incorporation within computer-based systems. The consolidation of administrative power in nation-states, and the drive for capitalist control of employees, raw materials and markets provides a constant catalyst for surveillance. The desire for rationality, efficiency, speed, plus, variously, for control and for the care of populations (in the welfare state, for instance) also prompts improved surveillance. At the same time, as Durkheim reminds us, modernity also brings with it rising levels of social inequality and conflict that foster the quest for better policing and the search for techniques to quell dissent. Brought up to date, and seen on a global plane, technology-assisted surveillance may be seen as a product of the accelerating growth of a North–South gap, further exacerbated by responses to violent resistance.

If those are the causes of surveillance today, then what we actually see happening is the increasingly technological basis of surveillance, which exhibits several characteristics. The shift towards risk management, from welfare state to safety state approaches, from the social bases of crime to the new penology and from an older, more paternal management style to a 'new managerialism' of actuarial accounting, bespeaks a hardwiring of the calculative mode. That which can be counted counts. That which moves must be measured. Alongside this are two other features: a drive for classification, which in surveillance terms means 'social sorting'; and another for system integration, seen in 'joined-up' government services or, more abstractly, in the augmenting of surveillance assemblages. None of these 'shifts' are in any sense complete, however. These are trends and tendencies. Old practices and new mix in varying configurations. Across several domains, this is the *course* of significant surveillance developments.

Last but not least, the *consequences* of these processes are as follows. A constant quest for integration means demands for 'interoperability' – such as for standard machine-readable travel documents (MRTDs) in regions such as North America or Europe. This also produces constant pressure for data collected for one purpose to be used for another. How useful, not to mention cost-effective, if consumer data from telephone or credit card companies can be used for police investigations or crime prevention, one argument goes. Networked forms of surveillance also create a world in which more and more mundane everyday activities are subject to checks and controls. Swiping cards, recalling PINs, producing photo ID, all these and more are now taken-for-granted protocols for daily living. And they produce a surveillance world which is skewed increasingly towards the future.

The aim of the risk-based, managerial approaches discussed here is to pre-empt events (such as crime or violent attacks) rather than merely check on past events or be aware of what is happening now. Such a focus on probabilities, simulations and extrapolations from data turns some surveillance to an apparently abstract mode of reasoning and, it seems, deflects attention from the real-life embodied persons affected by it. Could this be why, in current 'emergency' situations that produce 'states of exception', the rule of law – which, for instance, in a phrase like *habeas corpus* has an obvious reference to actual bodies – may be thought dispensable? It is abstract 'categories of suspicion' rather than observable acts that render people guilty until proven innocent.

At the same time, these surveillance systems do not always work in the ways expected, for at least two reasons. On the one hand, the technologies simply may not live up to the manufacturers' or, more likely, their political proponents' claims. On the other hand, the systems may be resisted or at least negotiated by those who are affected by them. Examples of the former appear here and there throughout this book, while examples of the latter are discussed specifically in chapter 8 as well as elsewhere. Such factors must be built into any satisfactory theory, however. Whatever drives surveillance, and whatever its overt or covert logic, the fact that surveillance systems may be unworkable or subject to subversion should not be overlooked.

PART II

Vision

The next three chapters say a lot about surveillance systems. That is to say, vision or the 'gaze' is accented. Although I make the case that both watcher and watched must be borne in mind if we are to understand surveillance aright, in this part of the book the main stress is on how surveillance systems work. In the final part of the book, to fill out the story, 'visibility' rather than 'vision' becomes central as the emphasis tilts towards the self, the subject, rather than the system of surveillance.

Chapter 4 is about the organization of surveillance, from face-to-face situations through bureaucratic files to digital interfaces. Surveillance is an ancient feature of human society, but has been intensified and broadened to become a defining element of contemporary life. The interaction between surveillance systems and subjects is stressed in this chapter, although there are hints, too, that there is more to these two concepts than at first meets the eye. The systems are 'relations of ruling', as Dorothy Smith suggests (Smith 1990), but they also involve what Foucault calls bio-politics, in relation to population statistics, and anatomo-politics of the body itself, for managing people through iden-tification, categorization and monitoring. Accompanying this are the regulatory rules that often govern these processes, and which repre-sent a meeting place of systems and subjects.

Chapter 5 opens out more broadly to consider some spatial dimen-sions of surveillance, with special reference to urban life. Here the quest for security and safety is important, hence the concern with policing and regulation in the city. But cities are also sites of con-sumption, from the suburbs to the central business district, and in each surveillance is at work, sorting between different neighbourhoods to match marketing ploys with lifestyles and checking that the down-town core is safe for shopping and tourism. Since 9/11, many routine urban concerns have been overlaid with extra security and surveillance concerns, particularly those relating to the movements of populations by rail, road and air. In this context, it becomes difficult to disappear; anonymity is almost unavailable in the city.

Chapter 6 takes us beyond the city limits, and, indeed, beyond the nation-state as such. Surveillance today may focus its attention on bodies as never before, but, paradoxically, it has gone global at the same time. Personal data travel as much as if not more than those persons to whom the data refer, and this becomes very clear at airports and other national borders. Identity is secured in plastic ID cards and documents such as passports, but these in turn refer to databases that may be limited to frequent traveller information but may also hold national registries. They are intended to facilitate the mobility of those who travel for business or tourism while at the same time creating friction that slows the movement of migrant workers and immigrants. They seem to develop faster than policy analysts and social critics can describe or question them. Yet as with other systems, these are ambiguous and not closed to critique.

At all three levels, surveillance may be stretched across time and space, sometimes in new ways. Organizations may adopt similar routines – such as entry cards – in all their departments, but urban areas, too, may start to resemble each other, say, with their installing of CCTV or road-toll systems. On an even larger canvas, the gaze may reappear across 'national' boundaries – for instance in biometric border rituals – thus inaugurating new 'transnational' regimes along with their cognate local practices. But that is to anticipate.

4 Information, Identification, Inventory

> Many of the facts presented by the bureaucracies did not even exist ahead of time. Categories had to be invented into which people could conveniently fall in order to be counted. The systematic collection of data about people has affected not only the ways in which we conceive of a society but also of the ways in which we describe our neighbour.
>
> Ian Hacking (1990: 3)

As we noted in chapter 1, to understand surveillance in organizational and informational contexts, both 'watcher' and 'watched' and the relations between them have to be analysed. In this chapter, the organization of surveillance is explored. Some kind of information relating to the person becomes important to another person or agency and so the information is attached to an identifiable individual. The Department of Employment needs to know how long a certain group of people has been out of work but they also need to know to whom benefits must be paid at this time. In order to organize the information, classification must occur, which categorizes the information to create meaningful content. What results is a list of things found, an inventory,[1] attached to the name or identifier of the persons who are the subject of the inquiry. How each person or his or her activities are classified is likely to make a difference to his or her life, however. The act of classification is a moral one because each standard or category valorizes one viewpoint and silences another; it can create advantage or suffering (Bowker and Star 1999: 5).

The inventory, or list, plays a leading role in the history of modernity and especially of doing science. But even at a mundane domestic level, shopping lists help to coordinate our activities in time and space. They represent prioritized schemes for what is really needed, and will often be subdivided according to which store is visited first or the order of the aisles in the supermarket. On a much larger scale, bureau-cracies also use lists as a means of organizing reality according to organizational priorities, and the file itself is central to this (see, e.g., Yates 1989). Identification, categorizing and monitoring permit coor-dination in time and space across a government department, across a national border, indeed, with imperial governments or transnational corporations, across the globe. In the latter case, particularly, we also see the role of information and communication technologies. Elec-tronic coding 'freezes' policy in ways that are more consequential even as they are less evident.

This chapter starts by looking at face-to-face forms of surveillance and moves on to consider the changes wrought by 'file-based' or bureaucratic surveillance. It then examines some features of surveil-lance involving an electronic interface, which also differs in certain respects from earlier forms of surveillance. Increasingly, in an histor-ical frame, surveillance is interested in gathering information about individuals and listing them in categories, a form of inventory. But it does not achieve this in an abstract, objective way. As surveillance cat-egories make people up to fit them, so those thus identified may also assert what they claim are their identities, those ways of thinking about themselves that make sense to them.

Face-to-face, file and interface

Surveillance is as old as human history and has always been ambigu-ous. It starts with anyone 'watching over' others for some purpose, whether caring for children or supervising workers or registering cit-izens. In what follows we trace some important surveillance themes, from face-to-face watching to the impersonal gaze of the computer system. The main focus is on the kinds of information sought and revealed by surveillance practices. We explore how this alters, over time, from the informal and unsystematic supervision of 'pre-modern' times, through the formal, classificatory schemes of 'moder-nity', and into the complex and fluctuating world of digital networks that some dub 'postmodern' (Staples 2000).

As long as no one imagines that artificially designated historical periods are enclosed temporal spaces with no overlaps or flows between them, one can locate surveillance techniques in pre-modern, modern and postmodern times. However, because of the risk of falsely assuming that one period gives way to or is succeeded by the other, it is best to think mainly of the distinction between types of surveillance relation. First, the ones we might call pre-modern are direct or *'face-to-face'* – the 'foreman' observes the labourer at work, for example. The present is foregrounded; space coordinates are local. Second, modern surveillance methods are rationalized using accounting methods and *file-based* coordination, involving more complex mediation, present- and past-oriented, local and national, and tend to be inclusionary, encouraging sameness, uniformity, homogeneity. Third, so-called 'postmodern' methods are digitally mediated, based on behavioural and biometric traits, future-oriented, micro- (body) and macro- (globe)oriented, and tend to be exclusionary. An electronic *interface* (or interfaces) comes between the subject and the surveillance system, helping to re-shape surveillance once more in distinct ways.

It should be stressed that these – face-to-face, file-based and interface (or pre-modern, modern, postmodern) – are merely heuristic devices; helpful means of finding out more. They are artificial and analytical distinctions in the sense that they may overlap and they may all be found in the same context at the same time. In the Indian call centre I visited in 2004, for instance, face-to-face supervision of call centre 'agents' was undertaken by management supervisors snaking between terminal stations, worker records were constructed and maintained by the organization, and fluctuating flows of data were obtained through CCTV images, keystroke monitoring and auto- mated call-timing systems. Face-to-face, file-based and interface sur- veillance techniques co-exist in the call centre.

We explore these surveillance developments by considering the interactions between what might be thought of as the 'surveillance system' and the 'surveilled subject'. The distinction is analytical, however. Subtle interplay and even co-construction are at work between these two. The emphasis is less on the mere development of surveil- lance systems as technical or political apparatuses, and more on the interactive development of such systems, as products of both surveil- lors and surveilled. Information is crucial to this process. How infor- mation is used to identify the subjects of surveillance and to 'sort things out' (Bowker and Star 1999) must also be related to how those 'subjects' are formed, see themselves and what they consider to be their 'identi- ties'. Equally, the rules that regulate surveillance situations also must be borne in mind as the meeting place for systems and subjects.

Geoffrey Bowker and Susan Star make a further important observation about classifying or 'sorting things out': 'The sheer density of the collisions of classification schemes in our lives calls for a new kind of science, a new set of metaphors, linking traditional social science and computer and information science' (Bowker and Star 1999: 31). In an updating of Karl Marx's notion of technology as 'frozen labour', they suggest that today's information technologies 'embed and inscribe work' in ways that are hard to see but that freeze values, opinions and rhetoric in technology. Software may now be viewed as 'frozen organizational and policy discourse' (Bowker and Star 1999: 135). That is to say, to understand today's classification schemes we have to bear in mind their carriers, digital technologies. They make a difference to how surveillance is organized, as we show below.

Face-to-face surveillance

If surveillance is the routine and focused attention to personal details for the purposes of influence, protection, management or control (as defined in chapter 1), then how is this surveillance achieved? How do those who wish to obtain details relating to personal activities, records, conversations or transactions actually do their surveillance? Ancient manuals on governing, such as the *Arthashasra* by the fourth-century BC Indian writer Kautilya, made much of the importance of having adequate information on subject peoples (this was *realpolitik*, as opposed to Plato's idealism). And even two centuries earlier the Chinese military strategist Sun Tzu also stressed having knowledge of the enemy as a means of obtaining advantage on the battlefield.

Not only was clandestine watching important in ancient times, so was listening in, eavesdropping and confessing. Hearing as well as seeing was and is a means of surveillance. Beware, warns the enigmatic Ecclesiastes of the Hebrew scriptures (600 BC), a 'little bird' may permit unauthorized access to affairs or secrets of state. What might be heard from behind a curtain in a Shakespeare play such as Hamlet has startling and tragic effects. And while practices of confession to a priest have often been explored, many Christian churches in Europe, North America and elsewhere also practised more deliberate forms of surveillance, intentionally checking up on congregation members. These 'church courts' existed until relatively recent times.

In pre-modern contexts face-to-face watching, spying and peeping are each important, but so too is the census and other means of recording personal details. In an intriguing historical reconstruction of the thirteenth-/fourteenth-century village of Montaillou in the Pyrenees (and now in modern France), Emmanuel Le Roy Ladurie describes a complex system of eavesdropping (Le Roy Ladurie 1979). The village was the last bastion of a Cathar (or Albigensian) heresy which the church authorities wanted to stamp out. An Inquisition Register was made by Jacques Fournier, Bishop of Pamiers and later Pope of Avignon, which was Le Roy Ladurie's primary source. It shows how a very complete surveillance apparatus existed such that ordinary peasants had to watch what they said, and to whom, lest a priest or even a neighbour-turned-stool-pigeon report them. 'One piece of tittle-tattle might mean prison, or having to wear stitched to one's clothes the yellow cross, symbol of ignominy imposed by the Inquisition on heretics' (Le Roy Ladurie 1979: 14). Of course, it is ironic that one of the best sources for understanding the daily life of a fourteenth-century community, and how they knew so much about each other's lives, comes from an inquisitorial report. But in any case *Montaillou* does suggest that, Inquisition or not, there is evidence that small-scale communities know fairly intimately about each other's lives and that such knowledge may be turned to regulatory purpose.

Listening-in may also use very modern methods, of course. An obvious example is the massive international Echelon system for monitoring international telephone, telex, fax and email communication. It has its headquarters in the USA but a striking physical presence elsewhere, such as the receiver-transmitters resembling gigantic 'golf balls' of the tracking station on Menwith Hill in Yorkshire, England. More prosaically, listening, perhaps using disguise, is still a common mode of surveillance. During the Cold War in the 1960s, at my own university, Queen's, RCMP (Royal Canadian Mounted Police) agents sought subversives on campus. They reported to their superiors that Arthur Lower, in the History Department, was a 'man of extreme thought, *if not definitely Communist*' (Hewitt 2002: 60). From immediately after the Second World War the RCMP had a systematic check on the 'Red Menace' at Canadian universities. The RCMP sometimes had officers in plain clothes taking courses, such as Constable M.J. Spooner. In 1969 science student Charles Edwards was investigated by the RCMP, which led to an official complaint to the police from Queen's Principal John Deutsch.

Near the start of the modern era, however, a shift started to occur that can most clearly be seen in the workplace. Indeed, the very idea that there would be a 'workplace' as distinct from the home is a relatively modern one. In the pre-modern world much labour was of the 'subsistence' kind. People worked in order to provide the basic necessities of life. But as the growth of waged labour occurred, organized by early capitalist industrialism, so control problems arose, often referred to as the 'indeterminacy of labour'. Labour tended to retain responsibility for the conception and execution of work tasks, while the capitalist owners tried to control the content of the work.

The workers kept control over their capacity to labour to an extent, by selling only labour *time* to the capitalist, rather than an agreed amount of labour. Thus the capitalists hired overseers to try to ensure that workers at least approached the limits of their potential labour power. For early British writers on the matter of the new production – such as Charles Babbage, Andrew Ure and Robert Owen – this was a key problem. And, clearly, there were costs associated with direct visual surveillance and managers could never be sure that workers really were working as hard as they could. In the twentieth century, Frederick Winslow Taylor believed he had found the solution: separate the conception of work tasks from their execution and make 'scientific' managers responsible for the former and workers responsible for the latter. Thus, as Graham Sewell says, workplace surveillance was 're-inscribed as "performance monitoring"' (Sewell 1999: 3). The question then became: are the workers achieving the management-set performance targets?

This discussion of face-to-face surveillance could begin elsewhere than the workplace, of course. The gradual advent of modernity was eventually to produce a world of rationalization, science and technology and a profound cultural commitment to progress. It would stress the benefits of democracy, invent the nation-state and create a whole new world of 'professionals' (see, e.g., Kumar 1985; Lyon 1999). Each of these elements has some interplay with surveillance. Watching others was progressively placed on a more rational footing within the burgeoning bureaucracies of modernity and would eventually be augmented by technological as well as scientific means. The nation-state and democratic processes would come to depend on an

increasingly elaborate administrative structure that entailed surveillance, first to ensure that all participated and then that all were
checked for their ongoing capacity to pay taxes, fight wars or contribute economically.

File-based surveillance

Bureaucratic organization, one of the hallmarks of modernity, is a key
generator of surveillance. Indeed, surveillance is one of the features
that constitute bureaucracy as such. Naming, identification, counting,
classifying, record-keeping, and so on, are all important in bureaucracies. Bureaucracies may be found in workplaces, government
departments, hospitals, schools, prisons, churches and other religious
institutions, among others. Bureaucracy, for Max Weber, was part of
the modern means of ensuring legitimate power and of democracy, as
well being an outgrowth of rationalization. It relies on a hierarchy of
offices through which communication channels flow, the use of files
and of secrecy about some matters, spheres of authority defined by
rules and regulations, and the separation of administrative duties
from private affairs. Weber thought bureaucracies were technically
superior forms of social organization because of the calculability of
their procedures, which minimize uncertainty in risk-taking, and the
ways that all would be treated equally, by minimizing arbitrary decisions. Once the decision has been taken on which persons to track or
what information to gather, bureaucracy is the machine that does the
basic processing.

However, Weber also feared a world in which bureaucracies would
rule because those working within them would secure power for
themselves, avoid the scrutiny of their political bosses, or become
obsessively attached to their rules for their own sake rather than for
the ends they were meant to serve. He noted especially the tendency
for bureaucracies to accumulate more personnel or more files than
was strictly needed for the task in hand, and that notion of the 'infor-
mation-hungry' institution has a strong resonance in surveillance
studies. As we shall see, it is amplified in the digital era.

Bureaucracy is a basic mode of surveillance because of its supervisory and information-gathering capacities. This rests especially on
knowledge of the files – a mastery of information stored centrally in
the organization – and on rational discipline, which gives bureaucratic

surveillance its unemotional, calculating, machine-like quality (Dandeker 1990: 9). Dandeker's work places surveillance even more centrally within the basic structures of modernity than Anthony Giddens' does (Giddens 1985), especially by drawing attention to what James Rule calls 'surveillance capacity'. This concept comprises four components: the size of files, the degree of their centralization, the speed of information flow from one point to another, and, crucially, the number of points of contact between surveillance systems and subject populations, or how far the lives of the latter are transparent to bureaucratic scrutiny (Rule 1973: 37–40).

Rule's was the first sociological study to deal with everyday surveillance by corporations as well as the administrative departments of the nation-state, and Dandeker's was the first to take seriously the role of warfare and the military in promoting and perpetuating bureaucratic approaches in government and corporate contexts. Each of them incorporates into his account some sense of the likely implications of computerization on bureaucratic structures. For Dandeker, this was already (in the 1980s) affecting the ways in which knowledge and discipline are combined, and could not be reduced to class relations, the so-called 'logic of industrialism' or the rationalization of power. At the same time, he warns that, given the potential to increase rationalization, rosy views of decentralized power and democratized work should be treated with some scepticism.

One important aspect of bureaucratic or file-based surveillance, which is perpetuated and reinforced by digital or 'interface' surveillance, is classification. This is where the inventory comes in. Classifications became singularly important within bureaucratic organizations during the twentieth century and especially in those that had to do with policing, law-enforcement, welfare and social control. As Stanley Cohen points out, within the 'professionalization of deviancy control', classification of different groups became a central tool (Cohen 1985: 191). From its 'unorderly and inefficient' eighteenth-century beginnings, crime control gave way to a 'regulated, ordered universe' in the nineteenth century. Criminals had to be separated from the poor, the poor were split into deserving and undeserving, and the criminals divided between the mad and the bad (Cohen 1985: 192). What started in the asylum was extended to the prison, and Jeremy Bentham's contribution here was considerable. Whatever the 'failures' of classification, as Cohen points out, difficult ideological questions can be evaded and professional interests are unthreatened. What is needed, officials will tend to claim, is more and better classification.

Whatever the specifics of classification, then, the urge to classify continues. The categories may shift from 'dangerous' to 'treatable' to 'high-risk', but all the time the classifications are expanding or altering to accommodate new groups. Asylum seekers, immigrants, ethnic minorities, religious adherents, come to mind today. As Foucault says, '[T]he exercise of power itself creates and causes to emerge new objects of knowledge and accumulates new bodies of information' (Foucault 1980a: 51). The professionals, be they social workers, probation officers or welfare administrators, are in positions of power because they can make claims about the boundary of the category and who fits in it. And, of course, different categories are treated differently. As Cohen observes, 'The power to classify is the purest of all deposits of professionalism' (Cohen 1985: 196).

Again, while this is true, and considerable power does indeed reside in professional classifications, how people respond to them is another matter. And it may mitigate the apparently overwhelming sense of being trapped in a category. On the one hand, theoretically, Ian Hacking discusses a 'looping' effect that occurs with categorization, such that when a group of people are classified, this is associated with certain laws or regularities concerning others in that group. Knowing this, people may change their behaviour. Equally, the knowledge or criteria may have to be changed because people no longer fit the old classification. This in turn may further affect the people classified, such that more looping occurs (Hacking 2004: 297).[2] Of course, as Hacking also remarks, some classifications are 'inaccessible' to those classified, but the classifications may generate institutional practices with which the classified may well interact, thus once more creating looping effects.

However, there is little in Rule or Dandeker to suggest exactly how outcomes other than a sort of computer-assisted iron cage would develop. While their studies are marvellously suggestive for understanding the roots of contemporary surveillance, little attention is paid to those who are its subjects, the surveilled. Hacking's comments about looping remind us about the interaction between surveillance and the surveilled. Before turning to 'interface surveillance', then, we should consider for a moment the view from below.

The view from below

The work of Weber, Rule and Dandeker illuminates the workings of bureaucracy, but by definition they tend to be top-down analyses. Modern organizations have also been studied from the perspective of those directly affected by them, and this is vitally important for understanding surveillance. Erving Goffman's work is still the best example of this, especially in his description of 'total institutions' such as asylums, convents or prisons. As he says,

> In total institutions there is a basic split between a large managed group, conveniently called inmates, and a small supervisory staff. Inmates typically live in the institution and have restricted contact with the world outside the walls. The staff often operates on an eight-hour day and is socially integrated into the outside world. Each grouping tends to conceive of the other in terms of narrow hostile stereotypes. (Goffman 1961: 18)

Goffman said that 'whole blocks of people' are handled in these institutions, where almost every aspect of their lives is ordained.

Goffman's interest, however, was in the ways in which 'inmates' (the term he used ironically for staff as well as patients) found ways of not fulfilling the intentions of the institutions. While patients were watched over with the intention of changing them in specific ways – depending on the institution – they did not necessarily become model cured patients, knowledgeable students, pious novices or reformed criminals. As Ian Hacking says, 'The changes are not deliberately brought about by the system of control, but instead take place in the presence of another person, and by virtue of this presence. . . . Each person learns to behave whether by concealing one's feelings, by affirming one's central role or by a tactical effacement' (Hacking 2004: 294).

The point is this. Seen from below, the surveillance aspect of the 'total institution' creates circumstances that have effects on those whom the institution deals with, but those effects are not necessarily those intended by the institution. This insight is crucially important in surveillance studies, because there is a frequent assumption that surveillance systems are all-powerful, after an Orwellian fashion, rather than contingent, fluid and unpredictable. Such effects of surveillance sometimes occur through categorization (which, as we shall see, also implies identification). While Goffman had little time for so-called 'labelling theory' within the 'sociology of deviance', he did think that institutional categories were consequential. They may be directly so, such that people might alter their behaviour on their basis, but more likely indirectly, when categories are incorporated into the rules of the institution.[3]

Some recent empirical studies of bureaucratic classification do indicate ways in which resistance may be generated (and this case will also be discussed later). John Gilliom, in particular, in his *Overseers of the Poor* (2001), has shown how very poor 'welfare mothers' in rural Appalachia in the USA, aware of their classification by the so-called 'CRIS-E' computerized 'benefit' system, adopt forms of subterfuge and dissembling in order not so much to 'beat the system' as to simply provide subsistence for their children. Some, for instance, like Marie, give the impression to the caseworker that her partner, Bill, is merely the father of their child from a 'drunken, one-night stand' (Gilliom 2001: 113) rather than her faithful live-in spouse. She has violated the 'spouse in the house' rule. To beat the truth-making claims of the welfare system, she is reduced to lying.

Power/knowledge

Analyses of bureaucratic surveillance, based on the 'file', show how important knowledge is for power within organizations. But the idea of a supervisory gaze, counterposed to a 'view from below' is not always the best way to conceive those relations of power. It suggests, as Foucault would say, that power is a commodity, that it is 'owned', or that it resides in one place rather than in another, where perhaps 'powerlessness' is the order of the day. For Foucault, however, knowledge and power are inextricably bound up with each other. The power mechanism in a bureaucracy, for example, is encapsulated in the file, which is simultaneously the means of acquiring and accumulating knowledge *and* the means of controlling those processes and persons to which the file refers.

For Foucault, a number of 'disciplines' or practices create knowledge and power, and these are techniques for observing, monitoring, shaping and controlling behaviour. This is why surveillance is so central to Foucault's work. The disciplines may be seen, say, in a prison, but they are not reducible to such institutions. They work across a range of institutions. All involve obtaining knowledge of those working or living within that social context, and that knowledge becomes the means of supervision and administration. By organizing knowledge of a particular group within the relevant files, these practices render the groups amenable to intervention or direction. To 'see' people, either literally in direct supervision, or metaphorically through knowledge contained in the file, is to create a power relation. Classification is crucial as well, as a technique of power, because it makes several entities known in particular ways, so that they can be acted on accordingly.

All this means that, for Foucault, power is both creative, in that it produces situations or particular kinds of people, and repressive, in that it places them in negative relations to others. At the same time, such power is always contestable; never absolute or invincible. At the end of the day, insists Foucault, people are made up through these practices. Individuals are constructed; identities are produced through these practices of power. All of which throws a different kind of light on surveillance and power relations in any context, drawing in ordinary everyday practices to the ongoing development of the institution in question and underscoring what feminists have argued for a long time, that the personal is political (Fraser 1989).[4]

How, then, might Foucault's ideas be applied in an area of practical management, such as human resources? Barbara Townley shows how a Foucaudian perspective illuminates the relational exchange between the promise of work and how its execution is organized (Townley 1994). The personnel manager needs knowledge of the workforce, of the activity or labour undertaken, as well as of the individual worker (Townley 1994: 13). Human resource management (HRM) may be seen, then as a 'discourse' and a set of practices aimed at narrowing the gap between the capacity to work and its exercise. It produces knowledge that makes the work arena visible for governance purposes. In short, it is surveillance. Through its techniques, and, in digital times, its devices, HRM provides the means of making activities and individuals knowable and governable.

As Townley suggests, this perspective also allows for more nuanced treatments of class, race and gender issues in the organization. In the realm of HRM, for instance, the very terms used to describe these managers has gendered dimensions, starting in the mid-twentieth century with 'welfare workers' (they were predominantly women at the time) in situations where male agendas ruled. The micropolitics of power also allows for contestation as the precise and everyday practices that constitute governmentality – all of which relate to knowledge, how people are seen – may be exposed and challenged (Townley 1994: 16). Townley argues that this approach to HRM practically permits opportunities for participation, and for the development of a politics – allied to feminism – which through careful critique and challenge may produce positive change.

Interface surveillance

Just as face-to-face forms of supervision did not vanish with the advent of file-based bureaucratic forms, so such disciplinary types do not disappear as contemporary electronic controls proliferate across the social landscape. Yet, just as some features of watching over others alter as officials rationalize what was previously done informally and sporadically, so interaction with new technologies (especially within new political economies) makes a difference to how power relations between systems and subjects develop in the present.

Several different kinds of approaches may be taken to this. Back in 1988 Gary T. Marx noted the rise of what he called the 'new surveillance', listing a number of ways in which new technologies transcend distance, darkness and physical barriers, transcend time through data storage, retrieval, analysis, combination and communication, are less visible, often involuntary, capital- rather than labour-intensive, involve decentralized self-policing, have shifted from targeting individual suspects to categorical suspicion, and are both more intensive and more extensive (Marx 1988: 217–19). Given his other analyses of ways in which subjects interact with the means of their surveillance, this is clearly not a species of technological determinism. Marx is simply stating programmatically what some new technological capacities mean for surveillance and that these ought to be taken seriously by anyone trying to understand surveillance today.

Another approach to interface surveillance derives from Foucault's work on the Panopticon. In the hands of Shoshana Zuboff, for instance, the Panopticon appears clearly enough, despite its electronic guise, in American pulp mills where she undertook ethnographic studies in the 1980s (Zuboff 1988). For her, the use of computers has a transforming effect in the workplace. The 'Overview System', for example, gives management a full bird's-eye view of the minutiae of the plant, indicating where blame may lie for accidents and mishaps: with the equipment, a sleepy operator or poor management decisions.

Zuboff sees the allure of panopticism for management: it yields the 'heightened visibility' that promises better control. Management 'gaze' can also capture the 'objective facts' of worker performance, and the 'omniscient observer' can thus 'induce compliance without the messy conflict-prone exertions of reciprocal relations' (Zuboff 1988: 323). Even Zuboff's comments on 'anticipatory conformity' suggest that the panoptic 'works' as 'normalizing discipline' in these contexts. Other research on workplace surveillance raises questions about this.

What of the Panopticon in other contexts, perhaps those where 'vision' seems even more in evidence? Majid Yar's exploration of CCTV as 'panoptic' makes some very telling points. While some see only an Orwellian spectre of 'Big Brother' gazing down from the pole-mounted cameras in every large city, and others, sensitized by Foucault, fear the fatal force of discipline in the same devices, Yar suggests that things are much more complex. He complains that Foucault 'pathologizes' vision by seeing everywhere the panoptic 'machine which . . . produces homogeneous effects of power' (cited in Yar 2003: 5). In contrast, he says, our experience of vision is generally much more 'polyvalent and complex'.

For Yar, Foucault's subjects are dominated by the gaze; it constitutes and positions them. But, Yar counters, limiting things to an epistemic level (power/knowledge) marginalizes emotional and other responses to the gaze; the norms are thought of as disciplinary imposition rather than positions voluntarily held by subjects; and the apparent passivity of Foucault's subjects, in which they seem to internalize behavioural repertoires, neglects any possible active role of subjects. With regard to CCTV, Yar shows that one can indeed find evidence of subtle emotional responses to cameras, that norms are not merely imposed, and that subjects find many ways of subverting as well as evading the gaze of CCTV. He notes that those, from teens in the mall to the Camera Players of New York, who use the presence of cameras as invitations for display are precisely subverting that which a Foucauldian analysis would seem to suggest are homogeneous effects of power.

A further approach derives from the work of Gilles Deleuze in his very brief essay enigmatically entitled 'Postscript on the Societies of Control' (Deleuze 1992). The four-page *mélange* of thoughts starts by observing that Foucault noted the shift from 'societies of sovereignty' to the 'disciplinary society' – in places of enclosure like prisons, factories or schools – but that this was never meant to be seen as a permanent condition. Deleuze claims that its successor is now with us in the 'society of control'. 'Control systems' now permeate our lives like 'sieves that transmute from point to point' (Deleuze 1992: 4) – a simile that captures nicely one aspect of contemporary surveillance. Taking this further, Deleuze suggests that they initiate an endless process that is never complete, and where the final judgement is always postponed (as Franz Kafka pictures bureaucracy in his novels).

In the disciplinary society, surveillance lies between the poles of the *individual* signature and the *mass* number, but in the control society the code – as password – subsumes both. Now 'dividuals' take their place, seen in data or samples within the dominant regime of computers (which have replaced energy machines or earlier 'simple machines'). The corporation has moved to centre-stage, socially, but it, too, has this fluid, undulating character, as marketing has become its *raision d'être*. Individuals are not so much 'enclosed' any more as 'in debt' (by which Deleuze seems to mean tied to the corporation). Deleuze credits his colleague Félix Guattari with the notion that a 'universal modulation' is set in train, in which computers track each person's position at all times, and concludes with the subtle thought that 'the coils of the serpent are even more complex than the burrows of the molehill' (Deleuze 1992: 7).

Serpents on one side, this approach is very suggestive, and many have taken up Deleuze's hints and allusions to construct fuller theories of control. Alexander Galloway, for example, takes further the idea of passwords and coding to propose that 'the protocol is to control societies as the panopticon is to disciplinary societies' (Galloway 2004: 13). He argues that the distributed network, the computer and the protocol make up the new apparatus of control today. We shall explore later various versions of this thesis, and comment only that they tend to see the subject only in roles such as that of the hacker. Protocol and code seem to require some kind of 'immanent critique' in this view, which begs the question of how technically unqualified people are to be engaged in the politics of surveillance today.

One may, then, find in Foucault a hermeneutic key for disciplinary society in the Panopticon, or, in Deleuze, one for 'societies of control' in the code. But to specify further what this code might be in relation to personal data one could do worse than revisit a series of terms that is often associated with the 'new surveillance', namely the 'data image' (Lyon 1994: 19), 'data-double' (Haggerty and Ericson 2000) or 'digital persona' (Clarke 1994). Computer scientist Roger Clarke refers to the latter term as one that is useful for understanding how networked computing establishes a 'model of the individual' through collection, storage and analysis of personal data. At the same time, he argues, the digital persona may also be potentially threatening, demeaning or socially dangerous because of its uses in monitoring (and thus possibly controlling) people through their data (Clarke 1996).

For Haggerty and Ericson (2000), the data-double emerges consequent on the interest of surveillance not in complete bodies to be controlled, but in fragments of data emanating from the body. The body is 'broken down into a series of discrete signifying flows' (Haggerty and Ericson 2000: 612) from photos, chemicals and other entities so that it can be observed. Eventually, says Mark Poster, this data-double means the 'multiplication of the individual, the constitution of an additional self' (Poster 1990: 97). But its purpose is to differentiate between this and other data-doubles so that discrimination can occur. The data-double created by banks enables different kinds of accounts to be held by different categories of people; that of loan companies to determine who gets credit, and so on.

The data-double – frozen in the electronic codes, as Bowker and Star (1999) might say – is not a representation of the person, but the double nevertheless has effects in the daily, embodied life of that person. Indeed, in some circumstances evidence from the data-double may take precedence over the word of the embodied person. In cases of identity theft, for instance, people whose credit card accounts have been fraudulently used by others may find that it takes many years to persuade banks, credit bureaux and other agencies that they are trustworthy customers. The virtual life of the data-double is perceived as more real, for practical purposes, than the physical life of the victim, exhausted with trying to tell their side of the story.

A third example of interface surveillance is found in William Staples' work, in which he refers rather to postmodern surveillance (Staples 2000). This goes beyond modern, bureaucratic surveillance in a number of significant ways. It is systematic, methodical and automatic (like the video camera system in the bookstore as opposed to the visual watching in a corner store); it relates to bodies, by making us visible to others through credit cards, location technologies and DNA or biometric systems; it is localized in everyday life wherever people are (and as Gary T. Marx [1988] – and before him Jacques Ellul [1964] – says, surveillance keeps an eye on all, not just suspects); and it involves risk-assessment that produces, among other things, threat-lists that place whole populations under suspicion, or at least under scrutiny.

For Staples, the postmodern is fragmented, uncertain, time-space-compressed and consumerist (all of which could be read, more obscurely, in Deleuze). This surveillance has two further key features. One is that it is based on an algorithmic assemblage (and a culture of control) in everyday life. This is intended to keep us in line, check details, assess deviations and exact penalties in what Staples calls 'meticulous rituals of power' (Staples 2000: 3). It also involves new criminological approaches such as a shift to high-technology social defence methods like CCTV, but also increased use of tagging and other electronic curfew techniques. This kind of surveillance, one might add, has been growing post-9/11, especially with new border controls including biometrics, new national ID cards and a range of techniques such as hotlines (like neighbourhood watch for terrorism) and corporate 'security' checks on prospective employees within the security-industrial complex.

The second aspect of postmodern surveillance is that it is pre-emptive, and this relates to Deleuze's point about computers tracking people in transit rather than enclosing them in physical spaces. As we shall see, others have leaned on Jean Baudrillard's analysis of simulation to suggest how surveillance is often before the event and intended to predict or to prevent rather than merely to record or to find out about something or someone after the fact. But the 'tracking in transit' point is also worth pursuing. The shift of surveillance from fixed locations and 'enclosures' to mobile contexts is clearly a feature of the present. Theoretically, Agamben notes that 'zones of indistinction' rather than specific sites are where power now operates, and, empirically, these can most clearly be seen in relation to what might be called 'mobile surveillance' (Agamben 1998; see also Murakami Wood and Graham 2006). This point relates to a shift in both space (out of enclosures) and time (from past to future) in surveillance. The coordinates of data capture are changing.

Identification and identity

Let us return to an issue raised at the start of the chapter, that surveillance depends on identification, for classification, and that the identification may well be doubted, questioned or resisted by those who feel that the 'data-double' does not accurately represent them. We have seen in this chapter that a number of dominant varieties of surveillance studies tend to underplay the role of the active subject in surveillance processes. The impression is often given that surveillance systems are more powerful and controlling than is the case, because the emphasis is placed on the technological capacities (and their supposed smooth and efficient functioning) of the system concerned, or because a model of how surveillance works neglects important factors in the equation. Those important factors may have to do with the failure rate or the errors of the system, or they may inhere in the inadequate view of the persons who are under the gaze. Such persons may be variously construed as over-cognitive, incapable of choosing their own normative stances, or unable to respond imaginatively or critically to the surveillance systems that collect, store and analyse their data.

It is worth exploring in a little more depth the question of identification, as this is a theme that recurs throughout this book. Most kinds of surveillance require some kind of identification process, so that data may be sorted accurately and only those entitled to certain benefits receive them, or only those who by some criterion have become uncreditworthy are refused credit. Indeed, identification codes provide a fine example of the 'freezing' process discussed earlier, where policy is coded into software. These codes in particular are becoming more central to getting by in everyday life (Dodge and Kitchen 2005). Some kinds of surveillance actually arise from the desire to provide identification in the form of 'identity cards' that will act as proof of citizenship or as a ticket to certain kinds of entitlement. But the notion of 'identity' here is misleading because the cards are really a means of 'identification' and may or may not be connected with a sense of 'identity' (which might inspire loyalty, for instance) on the part of the individual (see, e.g., Raab 2005b).

Within the social sciences much attention has been paid to 'identity', especially in the wake of globalization trends of the past thirty or forty years. 'Identity politics', 'social identities' and other such concepts have become very important, as are the issues to which they refer. Manuel Castells devoted a whole volume of his 'information age' trilogy to *The Power of Identity* (Castells 1997), in which he explored how the 'self' is in his view ranged against the 'net' within this world of information infrastructures. The emphasis tends to be upon the issues of the 'expressive' self and the recognition of identities in a world of global flux, fusion and confusion.

In contexts such as this, it is vital to stress that questions of identity must be balanced with the consideration of other, less voluntaristic, action-oriented perspectives. As Richard Jenkins points out, people's life-chances and prospects are affected at least as much by the ways that they are *identified* as by their *identities*, if not more so (Jenkins 2000). Over against Anthony Giddens' stress on 'reflexive self-identity' as a key feature of modernity, Jenkins suggests that categorization is far more important. Giddens' concept, he says, privileges the preoccupations of affluent intellectual elites, but social categorization has far greater warrant as a key to modernity. Anyone engaging in surveillance studies understands how important categorization is.

For Foucault, as noted above, the individual is constructed, in an ongoing process, as a particular identity. So rather than identity being something essential, basic or taken for granted, Foucault sees identity as malleable. The HRM manager, discussed above, may wish to form particular kinds of identities in his or her employees, by which they would come to define and situate themselves. But the means of doing so is through classification and tabulation, to maximize the usefulness of each employer to the organization by creating particular kinds of order in the categories, where clarity and calculation are central. The employer may improve productivity by these means; equally, the hospital administrator may seek more healthy patients, or the school principal, more educated children. Although some valuable work is done from a Foucauldian perspective on 'becoming a subject' or a self, the stress tends to be on how people are 'made up'.

Yet there exists a curious dialectic, suggests Jenkins, between self-identification and identification by others. That dialectic is essential to categorization, but surveillance studies has often leaned towards the pole of stressing the role of the 'system' rather than the 'self'. Those consequential processes of categorization that, as Jenkins rightly notes, should be central to any sociology of modernity – and in our case, specifically to surveillance – always occur in conjunction with the ongoing processes of self-identification involving the active, conscious subject. This subject, along with others, makes a difference to the effectiveness of the intended processes of social categorization, often through the looping process identified by Hacking. In this way the efficacy of surveillance, identification and categorization can never

merely be 'read off' the technologies, the systems or even the intentions of the surveillors.

Conclusion

To understand surveillance in organizational and informational contexts, both 'watcher' and 'watched' and the relations between them
have to be analysed. This may seem to be a departure from the spirit
of many works in the 'surveillance studies' genre, which stress the
strength of panoptic power, constituting and positioning the subject
in its thrall. Paradoxically, it is often just because surveillance studies
is prompted by genuine concerns for human freedom, dignity or
rights that the case for carceral control or Orwellian oppression is
made in these kinds of terms. But unfortunately such over-
determined portrayals not only do a disservice to social science, by
fostering the erroneous view that we all lie under the 'homogeneous
effects of power' or some such humbug, but they also fail to respect
the active subjects for whose lives they claim to speak. How this is perceived by the surveillance subject may make a difference.

I have argued in this chapter that both surveillance 'system' and
'subject' have to be seen together and in relation to each other in order
to produce adequate accounts of surveillance. I have also suggested
that (sometimes for apparently good reasons) surveillance studies has
often tilted towards a focus on the surveillance system, its technologies and its powerful institutions, to the neglect of analysing the activities of those who are its subjects. The Panopticon provides one
potentially misleading case in point. For all the insightful guidance of
Foucault on how people are made up, the tendency within a number
of studies influenced by Foucault is to neglect or downplay the active
role of the subject. But as Michel de Certeau says, '[B]ehind the
"monotheism" of the dominant panoptical procedures, we might
expect the existence and survival of a "polytheism" of concealed and
disseminated practices' (de Certeau 1984: 188).

But it is not only the Panopticon. Notions such as the assemblage
or the data-double may also give the impression that surveillance
is one-dimensional and that there is little that its hapless victims can
do to contain, thwart or even annul it. Thus I urge a more subtle analysis that takes into account both institutional classification and self-
classification, identification and identity, data-double and embodied

self, system and subject. This is a plea not for seeing connections between basically binary categories, so much as for subtlety in examining how each is constituted in relation to the other. Such an approach to organizational and informational surveillance will go a long way towards throwing light on what are currently blind spots of surveillance studies. It will also help the effort to understand the dynamics of surveillance in broader urban and global contexts, which are examined in the next two chapters.

5 Security, Suspicion, Social Sorting

> The politics of the right to the city amount to the hidden politics of code as the agency of software structures urban access and exclusion in subtle but powerful ways.
>
> Stephen Graham (2004a: 329–30)

The organization of information, discussed in chapter 4, expands to the level of urban life in this chapter. Picking up on themes from that chapter, it is important to remember that classification does not merely 'sort things out' in an objective or neutral way. It is based on practices of meaning-making and judgment calls and is the medium through which those practices continue to occur. In the spaces of the city, surveillance helps to classify areas as, for instance, 'hot spots' – whether these are defined by police, marketers or sports fans – and to determine who should be present when and where, who is 'out of place', and who is likely to be visible to whom while they are there. In the UK if you are young, black and male, for instance, it is more likely that your image will come up on CCTV screens than images of other group members also on the street. But this is not the product of 'objective' surveillance. Previous attitudes and experiences guided the camera operators' choices of focus, and the resulting sorting has consequences for those singled out for attention.

So if face-to-face situations yield the first significant surveillance clues, the next ones appear in the community, on the street and in the city. In these settings, surveillance has become increasingly general and even taken for granted. Few look up to check the position of the traffic light or wall-mounted cameras, even fewer stop to ask why the supermarket clerk always asks so politely for the loyalty card at the check-out. Yet urban policing depends more and more on devices that check compliance with traffic rules; the safety of the shopping mall is thought to be dependent on cameras that can 'see' potential trouble-makers and wrongdoers; and without swiping the loyalty card it is impossible for the supermarket to keep track of the customer's purchases so that savings and different levels of service can be offered depending on the shopper's practices.

The basic coordinates captured by surveillance, as ever, are time and space. In this chapter, more than the others, the spatial dimension comes to the fore. In going about daily life in urban spaces, surveillance is experienced constantly. Why it is growing in these ways and why the consequences are not fully understood has much to do with the factors examined in this chapter: the subtlety of electronic surveillance, the steady but scarcely perceptible ways in which systems feed off each other and – in more than one way – grow like weeds, and the cultural contexts of post-9/11 panic and fear, on the one hand, and the simultaneous desire for business as usual, on the other, that justifies specific developments and deflects attention from their effects.

Sorting the cyber-city

Twenty-first-century cities rely on the order-creating capacities of digital technologies to classify, to sort and to manage social outcomes across a range of sectors. The urban water utility may depend on the automated sorting of customers by postal or zip code to determine how they are treated depending on their neighbourhood and their past record with the company. Road-use may be decided by automated tolling systems that permit access only to drivers who can pay. Internet access and speed may vary depending on what kinds of commercial transactions are made by surfers. The supermarket may offer deals to certain groups of shoppers and not others, depending on their knowledge of transactions contained in loyalty cards (some of these examples occur in Graham 2004a).

Using personal data, techniques derived from military, administrative, employment, policing and marketing practices combine to create a complex matrix of powers: a surveillance assemblage. This 'assemblage' is, as the word hints, a coming together of disparate elements to create a loosely associated surveillance entity. While it grows out of identifiable desires, above all the political-technological quest for 'integration', it constantly undulates, pulsates and mutates (sometimes in response to failure or friction). Through its operation, cyberspaces may in some ways be mapped onto physical geographies, helping to create new configurations of the social as well as to erode some older ones.

Between the local organizational level of surveillance and the global flows of personal data in surveillance networks lie the urban spaces where surveillance is perhaps most evidently present. Surveillance, as understood here, is among other things an outcome of establishing information infrastructures as the basis for administration, production, marketing, entertainment and law enforcement. It involves garnering personal data for a variety of purposes in a quest for greater efficiency, convenience or safety. Its ethics and politics are inherently ambiguous, but at the same time surveillance is never neutral.

What happens in information-oriented cities is that everyday life – residing, working, travelling, being entertained, communicating – is articulated with electronic networks, databases and devices. This transcends the obvious sense in which numerous gadgets and systems in everyday use are coded with software. From the kitchen fridge and microwave to the living-room entertainment centre to the car, highway, transit system, elevator, office and beyond, software is now part of the material fabric of life (see Amin and Thrift 2002: 125). The articulation I have in mind here is with surveillance technologies that are increasingly 'designed in' to the flows of everyday life (Rose 1999: 234).

The outcomes of this interaction with automated and remote checking, recording and classification systems may in some circumstances have profound effects on the shaping and ordering of city life. These are often not those outcomes that are anticipated by the pundits, such as the reduction in travel enabled by the use of new communications media or the switch away from paper-based documents made possible by electronic text processing. Such changes represent the mistaken attempt to read social changes off technological developments. In the cases mentioned here, city travel has increased along with communication density and paper-use proliferates even as electronic information storage and transfer expands.

As Manuel Castells points out, paradoxically, advanced telecommunications helped to slow corporate relocation away from New York, and not vice versa, and in France, the first mass-diffused system of computer-mediated communication, Minitel, did nothing to reduce urban density (Castells 1996: 377). Indeed, Minitel was also used by students to arrange street demonstrations against the government, just as, in 2005, rioters in Paris used blogs and cell-phones for guer-rilla-type tactics of protest against police discrimination involving North African minorities. At the same time, since the rise of so-called 'anti-globalization movements', police and security monitoring of the internet, cell-phones and similar devices is increasingly attempted as a means of pre-empting protest and demonstration. Castells spends less time on such matters, holding that 'most surveillance will have no directly damaging consequences for us – or, for that matter, no con-sequences at all' (Castells 2001: 180).

However, it is just these unanticipated consequences of reliance on electronic infrastructures that are in focus here, and especially those that affect relative degrees of access and power in the city. It is a truism that cities have always been divided and zoned in ways that reflect the interests of groups distinguished by their wealth, income, class, status, ethnic background or gender. The term 'ghetto' speaks to ethnic sequestering, 'the wrong side of the tracks' to enclaves of poverty, and 'central business district' to the well-heeled commercial core. The emergence of urban electronic infrastructures does not necessarily produce quite different divisions so much as overlay existing ones with additional, sometimes cross-cutting distinctions. Nonetheless, they help to shape the city no less than highways and high-rises do.

If we take the case of surveillance in a Japanese city like Tokyo, however, variations on the general theme do occur. Urban space has always been intensively surveilled in Japan. In the Edo period (1600–1868) different caste groups were expected to remain in their sector of the city, with strict limits on both speed and the means of mobility (Murakami Wood et al. 2007). The *machi* or neighbourhoods had gates between them and were watched from guard-houses. However, the largest surveillance network was directed to fire-risk and was locally rather than centrally managed. With the coming of rail-ways, urban spaces were often shaped and surveilled around stations, themselves sometimes built by department stores. So when the Tokyo subway system was attacked by the Aum Shinrikyo sect with sarin gas in 1995, one of the earliest responses was to increase CCTV coverage in areas that were traditionally well surveilled, namely rail and subway routes.

Many treatments of 'global cities' focus on their role as economic powerhouses. Writers such as Castells argue that such cities are not so much 'places' as 'processes'. The emphasis is on why megacities continue to grow despite the technical possibilities for decentralization and flexibility. Beijing, for instance, is now a city bigger than Belgium. It boasts upwards of 70,000 taxis. Saskia Sassen shows that global cities have new roles, beyond the traditional centres of international trade and banking. They are concentrated command points for organizing the global economy, key locations for finance and specialized services and sites of both production and consumption (Sassen 2001). This being so, it is hardly surprising that more conventional urban inequalities are also reproduced in new ways in the global cities of both North and South. In Bangalore, for instance, hailed as India's Silicon Valley, one can see some very direct unequal relationships between the shiny electronics-based technology parks and the predominant situation of poverty and social deprivation (Madon 1998).

Beyond such direct correlations between transnational corporate wealth in high-tech software and hardware and a massive lack of adequate basic infrastructure for the majority, more subtle modes of reinforcing social and economic divisions are also visible – or, more properly, *in*visible – in some urban areas. In order to understand how surveillance affects today's cities we have to consider both the technologies involved and their uses in particular contexts. How populations are clustered in order to single out different groups for different kinds of treatment may be thought of as 'social sorting'. This is done using software algorithms, informational codes that have social consequences. Examples are drawn both from consumer contexts in which choices and life-chances are affected and from contexts in which more stringent forms of control are evident, and where some kind of law enforcement is the aim.

Interestingly enough, these apparently separate and distinct spheres of surveillance activity overlap in some ways – the domestic purchase of insurance services, for example, also relates to policing criteria in neighbourhoods – and they are also increasingly inter-related at the level of data. Different databases may contain personal information that is common to more than one, and under certain circumstances personal data acquired for one purpose are used for another. At the same time, other kinds of techniques are constantly appearing that help to refine or to elaborate what already exists. Genetic screening, location tracking, radio frequency identification (RFID) and biometric measures each add a further dimension to the social sorting potential.

Taken together, then, this combination of surveillance systems may be thought of as an 'assemblage'. And it is this phenomenon with which surveillance studies – and, of course, all urban dwellers – have to deal in the twenty-first century. Although the ways in which social power is allocated and struggled over have much to do with capitalist businesses within a kind of national *and* international system and with bureaucratically run organizations, the argument here is that information infrastructures, the digitizing of everyday life and surveillance, in particular, have to be introduced as key explanatory factors today (see also Sassen 2006 for a wide-ranging discussion of the place of digitized systems in today's world).

True, the aftermath of 9/11 is also giving rise to much technological opportunism as the state strengthens its law-and-order arm, but the surveillance assemblage, with its unique social sorting capacities, was already developing before the terror attacks on New York and Washington in 2001. The assemblage may be exploited by security and intelligence bodies, of course, one example of which is the use by the US CIA of confidential Belgium-based SWIFT bank account information in 2006 (Bilefsky 2006). This is part of a secret arrangement to try to trace money-flows among suspected terrorists. Also, as I noted earlier, the assemblage may mutate either through internal shifts, the fragmentation and failure of some of its components, or due to friction created by its users and subjects. But the idea of assemblage is a reminder that, both potentially and actually, surveillance increasingly operates in tenuously or tightly articulated ways across previously bounded domains.

Social sorting: codes and consequences

Why anyone ever dreamed that cyberspace would be primarily a realm of freedom defeats logic. The very term 'cyberspace', used first in 1982 by William Gibson in *Burning Chrome* and later, more popularly, in *Neuromancer* (1984), hints strongly at its dark side. And its etymology, in mid-twentieth-century cybernetics, does more than hint. Originating in the Greek *kubernetes*, for the one who steers a ship, cybernetics is the science of control, of regulation through feedback loops. Originally, it had to do with the processes of production. Today, since the convergence of computing with telecommunications in the 1970s and 1980s, we can say that the cyber-realm is one of *remote* control or regulation at a distance.

How this control and regulation are achieved is unique to computer-based systems of surveillance; it is control by code. The hardware and software of such systems are coded in specific ways. Lawrence Lessig, whose book *Code and Other Laws of Cyberspace* (1999) helped to establish this point, says that cyberspace is regulated by code, for good or ill. The big mistake is to imagine that cyberspace is in any sense 'unregulated'. In a moment we shall look more carefully at how codes regulate cyberspaces, but I want to take the point one stage further. It is not merely some virtual – as in 'immaterial' – realm that code operates. Control and regulation in the messy material spaces and places of the city also operate by code.

One caveat. This is not meant as a mere attack on cyberspace as a realm of 'unfreedom'. The cyberspaces of today's world are arenas, cockpits or terrains of struggle. A careful exploration of the social and material realities of cyberspace does induce cynicism about utopian visions, but this by no means paints social analysis into a dystopian corner. Coding can operate in ways more consonant with notions of participatory democracy and organizational accountability than they all too often do at present. Code's regulatory properties mean that, calibrated appropriately, they may have protective and socially supportive aspects. Some codes may also be built into systems in the forms of 'privacy-enhancing technologies' or 'PETs' (see, e.g., Burkert 1997; examples include user-friendly toolbars that enable users to see how websites may handle personal information before they decide whether or not to transmit sensitive data online).

As someone who has spent a fair amount of time talking with others about contemporary surveillance, I have noticed a constant refrain from those whose historical memories are still in good shape. They acknowledge that constant monitoring does occur today but ask whether it really is all that different from the days of small-scale local communities, where everyone knew everyone else and such mutual monitoring was taken for granted (even though it may have been resented or regretted by some). An example of ancient 'knowledgeable communities' is provided by the medieval village of Montaillou, discussed in chapter 4. My response, however, is that today's situation is very different, not only quantitatively but qualitatively as well.

The data may seem trivial (shopping preferences, for example), but when combined with others may help build a (rather partial) profile. And it is not merely a partial profile. It is a profile that, in many cases, simply suggests what *sort* of person is here. The category, not the character, is all-important. As well, in most cases the data are collected whether or not we agree to that collection process, and now so many agencies garner our data that it is simply impossible to keep track. As Lessig (1999) observes, village 'surveillance' was carried out by peers, other human beings. Today's is done by machine, and, moreover, the machine is voracious in its appetite for personal data. It notes not merely the differences between you and the next person, but many facets of behaviour. And searchable records were not in view in the village: '[N]ow the default is that all monitoring produces searchable records' (Lessig 1999: 151).

Lessig goes on to show how concerns of manipulation and equality accompany profiling. Targeted advertising, for example, may influence desires in new ways, but profiling may also shape actual behaviours of certain social groups as individuals are encouraged by feedback to fit the expected patterns. As for equality, Lessig writes from the USA, where equality in the marketplace was an assumed ideal from the start. But subtle distinctions of rank are based on profiles, such as those generated by frequent-flyer systems, which ensure that the best seats and the first meal choices go to the most frequent flyers. These kinds of status differences are increasingly exploited by surveillance-as-social-sorting, which depends on collected data to provide the grounds of discrimination.

In an urban context the use of status differences may be related to a rethinking of 'digital divides'. Stephen Graham (following Perri 6 and Jupp 2001) argues that digital divides take various forms, not only unequal access to new technologies, but the 'powerful and often invisible processes of prioritization and marginalization as software and code are used to judge people's worth, eligibility and levels of access to a whole range of essential urban spaces and services' (Graham 2004a: 324). Computer algorithms are used at database and telecommunication interfaces in order to provide different levels of service to users who have been automatically 'sorted' according to some criteria. The Canadian group RBC Financial, for instance, sorts customers according to their CLTV (customer life-time value – to the business, that is) along with KDD (knowledge data discovery, which includes data-mining techniques), in order to nurture certain segments by providing superior customer service (see Pridmore and Lyon 2005). These criteria may be opaque to the end-user and even to the operatives within the firm.

Personal information may be collected, then, in order to determine – in these cases – levels of service, access and speed of passage. Once the data are collected, the system can automatically (without human discretion), continually (24/7) and in real time (with no delay) make determinations about outcomes. The rapidity of one's internet access, for example, depends in part on the user profile gleaned from sophisticated surfer-tracking (Winseck 2003), and the speed with which one may be able to 'fast-track' through airport security depends on the use of biometric passes for what Peter Sloterdijk calls the global 'kinetic elite' (quoted in Graham 2004a: 239).

A number of issues are raised by such social sorting surveillance. Some sorting will always be practised by corporations trying to maximize their profit or their market share, and, whatever customers think, it is doubtful that it is intrinsically unethical or negatively discriminatory. There may be cases of unfairness, such as efforts to exclude financially vulnerable groups from access to banking or credit services, or the deliberate and usually illegal practice of 'redlining' certain zones in a city, now reappearing as 'weblining' through geo-demographic discrimination (Stepanek 2000). But the larger issue is probably the one that emerges when one thinks sociologically about the unintended consequences of many corporations simultaneously increasing their reliance on such methods. The reinforcing of social and economic inequalities by such means is hardly the 'fault' of some individual firm, but it is a tangible reality for those whose lives are systematically disadvantaged, as it is for those who are privileged by these practices.

Life-chances, choices, exclusion

We turn now to some further examples of the consequences of coding in primarily urban contexts. The first set are commercial, to do with the consumer sphere, whereas in the subsequent section we shall examine some security coding, relating more broadly to citizenship. The aim is to demonstrate just how decisive the codes are for people's life-chances and how they affect their everyday choices, even to the point of being excluded from certain opportunities. How, then, does 'consumer seduction' operate?

The term 'seduction' in the commercial context refers to the efforts of marketers to persuade consumers to buy goods and services.

Specifically, I have in mind the ways in which database marketers, using varieties of customer relationship management (CRM), cluster geo-demographically their potential consumers, in the hope of singling out for special treatment those with the highest likelihood of being substantial spenders. In parallel ways to the 'categorical suspicion' that attends certain groups of 'likely' offenders, such 'categorical seduction' serves not only to 'woo' consumers but, in a sense, actually to produce them for corporations.

In similar ways, broader processes of social sorting privilege certain consumers, clients and citizens over others, through differential pricing mechanisms or through shorter and longer wait-times. The corollary, of course, is that the same automated processes produce neglect or abandonment for other groups. In some cases they may be actively excluded, but in most they simply receive inferior treatment or are passed by in the marketing drive. The so-called 'freedom of choice' that supposedly characterizes market economies is, if not a chimera, at least somewhat compromised by such practices.

Some of the other cases mentioned by Graham include basic ones like the use of urban roads and the location of food stores (Graham 2004a). Electronic road pricing has become an obvious political choice in an era of great congestion, and so it is in Toronto, for example. The main east–west corridor, Highway 401, which at some points already has sixteen lanes, including both 'collector' and 'express', has been supplemented, on the north side of the city, by Highway 407, with an automated tolling facility, to avoid bottlenecks. At most times of day you can pay to cruise along at the speed limit or above, even when the 401 is in stop-start mode in all lanes (see Bennett et al. 2003). San Diego's I-15 takes things further, however, offering fluid conditions at all times. As the road gets busier, drivers are informed that the tolls are rising, causing demand to drop off accordingly as the less well-off use the exit ramps, thus ensuring continuous free flow of traffic.

Geographical information systems (GIS) are used to map cities, to reveal their shifting social and economic composition in great detail. Although GIS may be used for purposes such as crime-mapping or neighbourhood targeting for social services, Tsung Leong argues that a very important purpose is to 'understand, control and direct market behaviour' (Leong 2001: 765). Geo-demographic profiling, a practice that has existed since the 1980s, is vastly enhanced by today's algorithmic coding and searchable databases to enable the simulated

mapping processes which are then taken as the basis for actual decisions about where to locate stores, banks or sports and entertainment
facilities. Unprofitable bank branches and small local stores tend to
close as more profitable locations for new enterprises are pinpointed
by GIS mapping using geo-demographic data.

Even without direct mapping of socio-economic data onto geographical neighbourhoods, processes of CRM may still have a differential impact on zones within a city. Susanne Lace refers to the advent
of 'glass consumers' who have appeared in a world of intensive information-gathering on the daily lives of ordinary people. As she says, the
'properties and capacities of glass – fragility, transparency, the ability
to distort the gaze of the viewer – mirror' our vulnerability (Lace
2005a: 7). Banks, insurance companies, employers, welfare departments, health-care facilities and retailers all want to assess the risks
attending our dealings with them and the value that our interactions
with them represent. On the basis of this knowledge they will make
offers, deny opportunities, treat us differently from others in apparently similar circumstances. This may or may not be compared with
postal or zip code data to connect more closely with territorial realities,
but even without it, the likelihood is that certain geographical areas
will be favoured or marginalized as an indirect outcome.

These developments represent qualitative differences with earlier
(1950s, 1960s) 'redlining' practices that proscribed certain areas in the
city, rendering them difficult for (would-be) residents to obtain mort-
gages or insurance (Perri 6 2005: 28–9). The huge quantities of data that
can be processed mean that much finer-grained classifications are possible, based sometimes on hundreds of thousands of calculations with
individual algorithms for each case, to which may be added data-
mining procedures for even greater depth. Retail sector loyalty cards
permit more precise targeting of offers, often linked with postal codes.
Perri 6 observes that miniaturization and data storage mean that personal information may also be stored longer, which means that organizations 'forget' and therefore 'forgive' less in the personal information
economy (Perri 6 2005).

That these personal information regimes have consequences in
urban areas is becoming increasingly clear to sociologists and geog-
raphers. As well as the simple differences of treatment accorded to
one area favoured over another because of its profitability to corporations and relatively low risk for policing and insurance, self-fulfilling

prophecies may also set in. There are incentives to behave differently – move out – if your area is deemed risky for insurance purposes, or if you obtain a lower credit rating there. Equally, if loyalty card data discourage stores from remaining open in relatively deprived areas, they, too, may move out, creating a 'food desert' in run-down urban areas.

Risk, policing, security

If categorical seduction describes a world in which an opportunity calculus identifies certain groups as potentially profitable consumers, then categorical suspicion bespeaks one in which a risk calculus identifies certain groups as potential offenders. Of course, risk is involved in some consumer contexts, but it predominates in law enforcement and related contexts. Such risks emerged from earlier conceptions of social control in the city, among them Michel Foucault's, which saw the panoptic principle of hierarchy, surveillance and classification spreading well beyond prisons into quotidian urban life.

More particularly, argues Stanley Cohen, one finds late nineteenth- and twentieth-century attempts to map visions of the city, such as the Chicago School's 'moral mapping', those concentric zones 'on which grids of crime, delinquency, suicide and other forms of social disorganization were projected' (Cohen 1985: 220). For Cohen, writing towards the end of the twentieth century, such mapping produced both inclusionary and exclusionary policies, but tended to tilt towards the latter. The inclusionary tendency would entail the use of 'bleepers, screens and trackers', while the exclusionary would relate to 'walls, reservations and barriers' (Cohen 1985: 230). Although the use of electronic control devices was clearly coming into focus in the 1980s, later developments were to make for changed circumstances. The use of new networks of control in the city would digitize exclusion as well.

By the late 1980s, Gary T. Marx argued that 'the state's traditional monopoly over the means of violence is supplemented by new means of gathering and analyzing information that may even make the former obsolete' (Marx 1988: 220). He noted that this new surveillance is justified by positive goals: to combat crime and terrorism, to protect health or to improve productivity. Marx acknowledged the tendency to see prison-like techniques spreading into the wider community, but also noted that 'techniques and an ethos once only applied to suspects or prisoners are applied to the most benign settings' (Marx 1988: 220).

Hence his telling neologism, 'categorical suspicion', the sense that simply inhabiting a categorical niche is enough to attract suspicion. Thus Marx warned that the USA was accelerating down a road towards the 'maximum security society'.

Such warnings have done little, it seems, to help halt or slow this development. Indeed, the development of newer technologies combined with the post-9/11 media-amplified expansion of cultures of fear and their supposed solutions has increased reliance on the kinds of methods that Marx was concerned about. In addition, as we shall see, the 'soft surveillance' (Marx 2006) of the present draws in many more willing – and sometimes unwitting – subjects of surveillance. In the late 1990s Richard Ericson and Kevin Haggerty wrote about 'policing the risk society' and showed that the use of digital technologies is transforming the ways in which order is created and maintained in urban areas (Ericson and Haggerty 1997). Old barriers of time and space are eroded such that jurisdictions and hierarchies are challenged, and 'remote control' becomes increasingly feasible.

The communication systems in use create the territories and populations that are policed. 'They use the electronic infrastructures in police vehicles – computer terminals, mapping systems, video cameras, voice-radio systems, still cameras and so on – to trace their territories and those who populate them' (Ericson and Haggerty 1997: 436). Through cooperation with external institutions such as insurance companies, involving use of police risk communication rules, or through selling occurrence reports to insurance companies, police work now contributes to the processes of urban design and of creating environments that are conducive to consuming (and that discourage the presence of non-consumers). The sorts of strategy described as 'responsibilization' (Garland 2001: 124–7) stimulate the development of informal crime control – neighbourhood watch, for example – alongside more formal police activities in so-called 'public–private partnerships'. Other agencies, from the commercial to the volunteer, are thus enlisted to be 'responsible' for crime control.

Inspection devices are also used to trace people into their spaces, using contact cards, registration of certain groups such as sex-workers, special events, business and residential security reviews, and so on. What one sees in private security settings such as shopping malls is more widely diffused in the community. As Ericson and Haggerty say, 'A focus on population categories, precise movement through territories, pervasive surveillance devices and aesthetically pleasing design makes coercion embedded, cooperative and subtle, and therefore not experienced as coercion at all' (Ericson and Haggerty 1997: 436). This, again, is soft surveillance.

Contingent categorization, then, becomes a means of control in the digital city, and it is a means of control in which old lines become blurred – lines that once distinguished police work from private security, or law enforcement from consumer management. This is part of what Gilles Deleuze sees as a shift away from Foucault's disciplinary society to what he called 'societies of control' (Deleuze 1992). Richard Jones refines this to 'digital rule' (2000). As it happens, such digital rule may occur with fairly unsophisticated equipment as well as with advanced dataveillance. Video surveillance or CCTV is a case in point. As Jones observes, CCTV may be used not necessarily so much for 'hard' surveillance as for providing a 'real-time resource coordination and management system' (Jones 2000: 17). Deleuze's 'control society' may not be fully developed anywhere, and in any case it will continue to operate alongside older methods of 'discipline', but evidence of the trend helps us understand the movement towards a wider definition of governance.

As Norris and Armstrong point out in their now classic study *The Maximum Surveillance Society* (1999), CCTV has grown immensely in the UK and seems set to become a more digital system as facial recognition facilities and system integration are seen as the logical next steps. The integration of CCTV systems includes both public and private policing, as McCahill has shown (McCahill 2002), and extends the process discussed by Ericson and Haggerty where police work is characterized primarily by 'knowledge brokering'. Large-scale automated algorithmic surveillance would seem, as Norris and Armstrong argue, to follow from this, given the already existing emphasis on intelligent scene monitoring, automatic licence plate identification and facial recognition. As they say, the coupling of databases with cameras and automated recognition systems means that 'not only is it possible to create a log of the movements of individuals as they move through space, but it is also possible to automate assessment of all people's moral worthiness as they enter a locale based on information contained in the database' (Norris and Armstrong 1999: 221).

It is no accident, however, that CCTV cameras proliferate in urban areas that have become the focus of government initiatives to 'regenerate' the city. The idea is to control the streets of the city with a view to its economic revitalization. As Roy Coleman points out, this is a neo-liberal street-cleansing programme that aims to remove the signs of social inequality from public places (Coleman 2004: 221). The urban space is re-made in the name of 'safety' (which in turns plays on public fear), but simultaneously the structured degradations of some 'undesirable' areas are hidden. For Coleman, as this 'social ordering strategy unfolds the right to decide who walks through a city's streets will also impact upon the right to protest and public campaign in the city against, for example, shops dealing in sweatshop goods or those encouraging environmental destruction' (Coleman 2004: 233).

Surveillant playspaces

At another level, the city is the place to find playspaces, locations for concentrated consumption associated with leisure time. They include shopping malls, theme parks, casinos and sporting and athletic events. Most if not all have a high level of surveillance associated with them. Indeed, it is in these leisure contexts that some of the most stringent surveillance occurs, either of participants or of would-be participants and interlopers. In each case, surveillance is designed into the facility, and in several instances – casinos and the Olympic Games – the context is one in which new surveillance technologies are tested and trialled. As a case in point, in 2006 the use of powerful microphones to pick up 'suspicious' talk was proposed for the 2012 UK Olympics, an idea already tested in London's City of Westminster (Pienaar 2006; Porter 2006).

Shopping malls have become classic surveillant playspaces because, for all their emphasis on entertainment and as community meeting centres, malls are intended to be places of continuous consumption. This is built into the architecture and the ground plan, which lead consumers from location to location or oblige them to pass certain products *en route* to others, but it is also the purpose of the ubiquitous surveillance systems in the mall. While the cameras may have the intention of checking for shoplifters or monitoring the ways that staff use the till, they are also intended to keep shopper traffic moving and to minimize the risks of non-consumers – especially young people hanging out or panhandlers soliciting for loose change – contaminating the purchasing environment.

Shoppers may baulk at the ways in which surveillance now occurs in the store, with cameras, removable tags and now RFID devices, but in most contexts this is taken to be socially beneficial. The exclusion of non-shoppers may also be seen positively as contributing to 'safety', which is the pretext given for installing the equipment in the first place. Whether any such effects are real, or whether all CCTV systems can do is check identities after the fact, is a moot point. Evidence from German shopping malls in Berlin, at any rate, suggests that the effectiveness of CCTV for its stated purposes is limited. Their chief purposes are operational: keeping shoppers moving (Helten and Fischer 2004).

As with shopping malls, theme parks also use surveillance in the interests of control in order to keep the facility operating at full capacity. Alan Bryman argues that the key features of Disney theme parks – theming, hybrid consumption, merchandising and performative labour – would be less effective without control mechanisms in place (Bryman 2004: 131). The parks extract fairly high entry fees as the first deterrent to the non-well-heeled 'guests' and then ensure that they are closely watched over, often by Disney characters, to ensure that all visitors adhere to the rules.

Clifford Shearing's early account of Disney surveillance includes a vignette of his own daughter's attempt to walk barefoot in Disney World, which was quickly curtailed by a themed guard (dressed in the police uniform of the Bahamas) who informed her that for 'visitors' safety' such behaviour was not permitted (Shearing and Stenning 1985). If he were to visit Walt Disney World today he would find biometric controls in operation – fingerprint scanners are now in use in all four Orlando theme parks. Indeed, such is Disney's expertise with biometrics (it has the USA's largest commercial application) that at least one of its executives advised the Federal Aviation Administration on airport security after 9/11 (Harmel and Spadanuta 2006).

Like shopping malls, again, Disney theme park layouts are designed to channel visitors' movements in certain directions. They are supposed to take photos only at particular locations; they are kept in line, literally, in queues whose length is disguised to make them look shorter than they are (airport security has learned from Disney here); and the 'interaction' with performers is virtually scripted. Control is expressed through some exhibits (in Epcot, particularly) and through the transformation of the physical environments that gave the 'raw materials' for the parks. Like McDonald's staff, Disney's employees are themselves tightly controlled and under constant surveillance and monitoring, with rules, scripts, training and technology to keep them on track. As consumers, visitors are also closely surveilled and controlled on several levels.

Yet as Bryman also observes, the surveillance and control at Disney, though powerful, is far from complete, and plenty of opportunities occur and are taken for resistance (Bryman 2004). He brings mainly micro-social evidence of consumer and worker resistance both to theme parks themselves and to the wider processes of Disneyization. Visitors may use unofficial guides found on the internet, or break minor rules of the parks. Workers may retain their official smiles while making life difficult for visitors who annoy them – separating parties on rides at the last minute, or cutting heads from the shot when asked to take photos. Consumer resistance to Disneyization is frequently encountered in themed malls, suggests Bryman, while workers, tired in particular of the emotional labour expected of them, may quietly 'work to rule', doing only the minimum necessary. Thus the efficiencies sought through surveillance in theme park contexts may be considerably less than fully realized.

A further 'surveillant playspace' that employs a panoply of monitoring devices is the casino. These are often sites where new surveillance technologies are tested. In Las Vegas, most casinos feature state-of-the-art systems for catching the unwary cheat, from Biometrica's 'Face-in-a-crowd' facial recognition software, used in conjunction with CCTV, or a system called 'Visual Casino', a database accessible anywhere in the establishment on Compaq's iPAQ devices that are held by casino guards. Using systems like this, casinos can keep watch constantly over customers, and security officials can check on their hand-held devices for records of known offenders so that incidents can be dealt with quickly and efficiently (*Gambling Magazine* 2005). During a recent visit to a security operation in a Durban, South Africa, casino, I was informed that the biggest risk of loss actually comes from staff. They are the ones who must deliberately show what they do to overhead cameras.

Face-recognition systems used with CCTV also appear at sports and athletics events, often because the turnstile or controlled entry points give ample opportunity for clear pictures to be obtained. Soccer matches in the UK have long been key sites for surveillance of this kind, but the events that are truly marked by exceedingly high levels of surveillance are the Olympic Games. Ever since an Israeli team was attacked by Arab guerrillas in 1972 in the Munich Olympic Village security has been heavy at the Olympics. But after 9/11 the stakes were even higher such that the Athens games of 2004 turned the village into a maximum-security establishment. As Minas Samatas explains, 'The security of the Athens Olympics, based on electronic super panopticism, is not only a Greek police and security operation, but an international endeavour, including American, British, French, German, Spanish, Australian, and Israeli intelligence comprising the "Olympics Advisory Security Team"; all this is connected with the Schengen Information System, Europol and even NATO sky surveillance' (Samatas 2004: 115).

Emerging technologies and the assemblage

The main focus of what we have looked at so far is algorithmic surveillance based on personal data gleaned from consumer activities and from official, public and commercial records. Apart from alluding to some possibilities for facial recognition, in association with CCTV and related searchable databases, no mention has been made of other kinds of data that originate in the body or from some means of monitoring body behaviours and activities in space and time. However, the contemporary city is also an emerging site of such surveillance potentials, using, for example, biometric, genomic, location and tracking technologies. Moreover, the increasingly fluid inter-relation between databases containing these kinds of traces means that profiles relating to risk and others relating to opportunity may be linked. To reiterate, it makes sense to speak of a surveillance 'assemblage' in today's cities.

Once again, it is important to note that social and political futures cannot be discerned from technology vendors' brochures. But at the same time, each of these technologies is already in widespread use and already their impacts are felt in significant ways within wider contexts of socio-technical development. Some of these have made their public appearance as practical 'solutions' within the post-9/11 'war on terror', whereas others started life in retail or other contexts. They may migrate from one to the other as well. Biometric devices may be used to sort out suspects at airport security but also to filter fraudulent customers at the bank machine; RFID tags may be used to track stock on the Wal-Mart shelf or be placed in US passports to authenticate travellers as no-risk.

The various anti-terrorism measures that have been taken in many countries around the world since 9/11 and the subsequent attacks in Bali, Madrid, London and Amman involve, prominently, new surveillance technologies. Or, more correctly, they involve technologies that may have been in development for some considerable time and lacked only the opportunity or pretext for their deployment. They include devices and systems in public transit systems and at borders and airports, which are obvious from the point of view of those trying to increase the public perception of safety, plus many more subtle means of identifying persons with malign intent to do violence. These include the use of data-mining techniques to locate possible 'terrorist cells' and of CRM-type measures, for example to reduce the credit limit for some Muslim New Yorkers. As a side-effect, implementing anti-terrorist measures has also made several specific techniques more publicly known.

Biometric technologies regard the body as information. The best known is probably fingerprinting, originally used on criminal offenders and suspects but today extended to migrants, welfare recipients and refugees and stored in electronic databases (Cole 2001). Any physiological or behavioural traits that seem stable may be used in biometrics, and they contribute to surveillance as categorization. Patterns of live individuals – from the face, iris, hand, finger, signature or voice – may be checked in real time against database records for all kinds of management and security purposes in workplaces, travel sites, such as airports, or consumer sites, such as bank machines. Their success depends on the quality of the original datum, the adequacy of the database and of course the level at which the system is used (see, e.g., Zureik and Hindle 2004).

Genetic technologies, or those relating to the Human Genome Project, rely on data actually taken from the human body – blood, body fluids, hair or human tissues. Although 'DNA evidence' has been in (often controversial) forensic use for some time, genetic methods of surveillance are becoming increasingly popular in health-care, in employment and in insurance calculations. If employers or insurance companies could have advance indications of possible health complications in some individual's future, these could be prejudicial for that individual. Although the film *Gattaca* (1997), provides a purely fictional account of how a 'genetic underclass' may develop, such fears are expressed by many analysts of genetic surveillance (see, e.g., Nelkin and Andrews 2003). Those carrying genetic markers for a disease that they may never develop could be unfairly discriminated against by insurers who assume that all such markers are likely signs of that disease developing.

In 1995 the UK set up the world's first national DNA database, promising to store details of the whole active criminal population. Ten years later it contained records of 3.45 million individuals. DNA evidence has a very spatial dimension to it in that specimens are collected from the scene of the crime to link the suspect with the location. Such DNA databases are believed to have widespread forensic utility, and other countries as well as the UK make extensive use of them (Norris and Wilson 2006). In addition to CCTV and electronic monitoring of offenders, each of which has an obvious resonance with space, DNA databanks are likely to expand within the surveillant arsenal of contemporary crime control.

A further spatial surveillance development is 'location technologies'. They are of various kinds, but they all refer to the tracking of items in space and time. Best-known examples are global positioning system (GPS)-enabled cell-phones that permit their holders to be tracked as they travel. In this case, the data refer to locations which, given the earlier discussion, are of great interest in many contexts, including law enforcement and marketing. Employers can check where their drivers are on the road, police may be able to locate suspect offenders, corporations may be able to pinpoint the position of consumers, such that they can be targeted for place-specific advertising, and, in non-systemic ways, parents may keep track of where their teenagers are in the borrowed family car. This is a relatively new development, consequent in the USA on the development of enhanced emergency services calls, but seems to be growing rapidly in some sectors (see Lyon et al. 2005).

Lastly, tracking technologies, using RFID, are a major component both of the new security arrangements in American airports and border crossings and of large-scale retail concerns attempting to follow the progress of goods in transit or passing from warehouses to customer outlets. These devices rely on small tags that may be read wirelessly from a tiny antenna as the tag passes near the sensor. Once again, they are a further means of classification and categorization whose data have to do with spatial location. Unlike location technologies, however, they have to be triggered by a sensor; they are not simply on and available at all times.

Plans are advanced for the widespread dissemination of RFID tags in passports, drivers' licences and medications as well as off-the-shelf supermarket products, and the benefits to certain groups are clear. Correct use of medications could be encouraged, for example, and if tags were on all store-bought products, human checkout could be eliminated in the supermarket, bringing new speed and efficiency to shopping. But some critics have become vociferous, arguing that RFID is destructive of privacy, citing examples such as the Procter & Gamble and Wal-Mart collaboration that had RFID trigger surveillance cameras on customers buying lipstick from an Oklahoma store, or the Sutter County grade school that attached RFID to students so that they could be tracked throughout each day. Consumer watchdogs Katherine Albrecht and Liz McIntyre produced a broadside, *Spychips* (2005), that immediately drew an angry rebuttal from the industry. Whether this kind of activity will escalate into a significant conflict between RFID-users and consumers remains to be seen.

The above discussion makes it clear not only that surveillance carried out in different sectors may be cross-referenced in some significant ways, but also that different kinds of surveillance data may be concatenated. These are both aspects of the surveillant assemblage, which captures flows emanating from bodies, bodies that have been fragmented into bits of data. Taken together these form constantly shifting versions of the 'data-double', which refers to individuals but simultaneously is only a kind of tool – useful or not to institutions wishing to distinguish between individuals and populations. The data-double is information. It can be recombined, in principle endlessly, for other purposes, and this may be seen in the commercial use of government information, police use of consumer information, and marketing use of emergency services information.

The surveillance assemblage seems to grow, as Deleuze says, not as a hierarchical structure but as a rhizome, a spreading plant-like organism that sends out shoots in different directions, each of which may take root in its own right. Under these circumstances it is hard to see how prohibiting parts of its operation or limiting institutions that tap into it will slow its overall growth. This does not mean, however, that participating in efforts to redirect and channel it in ethical and socially positive ways are futile. This is considered further in chapter 8.

One outcome of developments discussed here is that it becomes progressively more difficult to disappear. Anonymity seems impossible, and the gaze seems ubiquitous. However, this should not be taken as a counsel of despair, any more than the reminder that the assemblage grows 'like a weed' and cannot be countered merely by some legal measure, technical device or policy rule. Those so-called 'data subjects' to whom the data-double alludes, albeit fleetingly, are not incapable of noting the presence and effects of the assemblage and of negotiating and resisting their interactions with it at the points where they encounter it. The fact that we cannot disappear 'under the radar' of the assemblage does not mean that counter-measures are pointless. It means rather that the ensuing struggle is complex.

Challenges to democracy and to participation

The outcomes carry both deep dangers for democracy and potential for democratic involvement, ethical critique and alternative practices. Surveillance based on software coding is not the result of the 9/11 aftermath, although the 'war on terror' has contributed tremendously to the further digitizing and globalizing of surveillance. Nor can it be understood as a simple extension of, for example, class or bureaucratic power, even though these are still significant. Questions of risk and trust, of security and opportunity, are central. Today's surveillance is a peculiarly ambiguous process in which digital technologies and personal data are fundamentally implicated and meet in the software-coding nexus.

Firstly, existing regulation and legislation do not significantly reduce or mitigate the amount of potentially damaging social sorting that occurs. While the Fair Information Principles (see chapter 8) that lie behind data protection and privacy law include important items that, if complied with at all levels, could reduce social exclusion, unfair targeting and negative discrimination, on their own they do not go very far. The kinds of issues that are raised by urban data profiling, CRM and security operations go far beyond the narrow confines of 'privacy' and 'data protection' that were once raised in the context of debates over the 'information society'.

Secondly, the so-called 'personal information economy' that traffics very profitably in data derived from consumer and sometimes government transactions has grown up symbiotically with the global deregulatory regimes of the late twentieth and early twenty-first centuries in which markets were opened up and risk was transferred away from taxpayers to consumers and workers (Perri 6 2005: 36). The aim of liberalization is to reduce risk pools and eventually to individualize risk, transferring it to consumers. This raises questions of distribution and, ultimately, of human dignity, as opposed to the merely technical kinds of approaches that tend to prevail at present. The issues mentioned here include unfair exclusion (such as from bank services), unfair targeting (of credit risks, for instance) and unfair discrimination (by postcode or other geo-demographic category; see Hall 2005).

Although collective consumer power against some trends in corporate power is growing (Zureik and Moshowitz 2005), it is not clear that this aspect of consumer politics has become very significant yet. One reason for this is that powerful cultural currents run in the opposite direction, towards individualization. The idea of responsibilization, for example, which involves members of the community in solving or mitigating problems of social order, is based on some laudable instincts. But the more this leans towards offering information on others, or, conversely, seeking self-protection through devices such as PETs, the more it leaves the social dimension vulnerable to erosion. As Gary T. Marx comments, the 'idea of voluntary compliance and self-help valorizes increased individual choices, costs and risks. It simultaneously weakens many social protections and programs and pays less attention to the ways the social order may produce bad choices and collective problems' (Marx 2006: 49).

Thirdly, other levels of ethical critique and political involvement are required, in order to combat at least the most negative effects of these trends; above all, pressure on the accountability of organizations that process personal data (this is discussed in chapter 9). While data protection laws attempt to address this, with complex data-flows it is sometimes hard to determine who is the 'controller', which makes regulation problematic. But this also spells a willingness to engage the issues in conjunction with those who construct and understand code. There may be a role for a kind of 'counter-surveillance imagination' to combat those aspects of surveillance that invisibly and often unintentionally intrude on or invade people's lives, reinforce social divisions and reproduce social and economic disadvantage. A sociology of surveillance enables us to see 'personal troubles' as 'public issues' (Mills 1959), and perhaps even to act accordingly.

Lastly, these comments hint at the emergence of a new urban politics, one that is attuned to the ways in which the surveillant assemblage is using electronic systems to shape daily life in cities by mapping the configurations of personal data over the social geographies of the present. If the new urban politics is to be equal to the emerging task, it will have to be concerned not only about places of poverty and deprivation and how they relate to places of affluence and rule, but how those relations are themselves shaped by surveillance. New kinds of social classes are being created by the codes that classify and categorize populations, and the subtle ways in which they are created will have to be made visible before such a politics will start to make a difference.

6 Bodies, Borders, Biometrics

> The database is an instrument of selection, separation and exclusion. It keeps the globals in the sieve and washes out the locals.
>
> Zygmunt Bauman (1998: 51)

In the twenty-first century, surveillance is a global phenomenon. The capture, tracing and processing of personal data occur today not only within local organizational settings but also across national borders. Digital technologies permit the routine real-time transfer of such data, relating to citizenship, employment, travel and consumption, using far-flung networks that indirectly connect numerous agencies with the everyday lives of ordinary people. In particular, new biometric technologies make possible a growing array of systems for verifying identities, including upgraded passports and electronic national identity cards. This is the broad context that frames specific security and surveillance initiatives that are seen most prominently in airports, train stations, ports and subways.

However, it is not the new technologies that create this state of affairs. They merely enable it to happen. Certainly, the long-term trend towards using electronic technologies for surveillance purposes has to be borne in mind, and along with it the pressure from high-technology companies to deploy such systems on an increasingly large scale. Nor can the political commitment to adopting those techniques be discounted either. There is a deep vein of belief in the efficacy of new technologies to solve social and political problems, especially in North America. But the globalization of personal data and the surveillance capacities that this represents have to do with much more than mere technology.

The new links between bodies, borders and biometrics are forged by other kinds of forces as well: the development of what might be called the 'safety state', which also fosters predominant processes of risk management; the routinizing of 'states of emergency' and of 'exceptional circumstances' – a process that has been accentuated since the events and aftermath of 9/11; and the centrality of constant, accelerating mobility to global consumer-based capitalism. This last point may be made in relation to the now extensive work on the relationship between information and communication technologies (ICTs) and globalization. As Manuel Castells shows, data-flows are basic to emerging modes of organization (Castells 1996). Coordination is achieved through electronic flows that permit global real-time economic and other activity. Indeed, such data circulation is partly what constitutes globalization, as well as contributing to its growth.

Various kinds of issues are raised by these developments, some of which are more and some of which are less in focus in what follows. The main emphasis here is on personal data that may be used to impede or facilitate the actual movement of those persons to whom the data refer. Thus questions of immigration, international policing and citizenship feature prominently as global surveillance issues. But they also do so in terms of what kinds of persons are acceptable, and what kinds are not, in a world of consumer capitalism. As Zygmunt Bauman suggests, one of the basic (unspoken) categories is that distinguishing 'tourists' from 'vagabonds' (Bauman 1998: 77f.). Not everyone can be a tourist; indeed, their existence transforms others into vagabonds, who confront red rather than green lights in the form of immigration desks and nationality laws, 'clean streets' and 'zero tolerance'. Bodies, biometrics and borders are vitally related with each other. They are implicated in the growth of these barriers. So in a world of global traffic in personal information, what happens to those data as they travel? What are the general implications of cross-border data-flows, of which the movement of data and bodies is a special case?

If one considers the 'outsourcing' of data-processing, some significant issues come into view. Unprotected by the data privacy regimes of the originating country, personal information may be vulnerable to forms of fraud or other misuse among employees who handle the data. Equally, outsourcing may mean that data actually become subject to a data-handling regime of which customers may well disapprove, if they knew about it. Thus, for instance, in 2004 the British Columbia Privacy Commissioner publicly asked some important questions about the personal data of Canadian citizens as they migrate south into US jurisdictions (see Stoddart 2004). He observed that Canadian data in the hands of private corporations or US government departments may not only be out of reach of Canadian legal protection, it could also be subject to the US PATRIOT Act and available to the Department of Homeland Security.

Just to give a sense of the range of personal data that travel south of the Canadian border into the USA, consider the following. Canadian organizations transfer data to other organizations, including employment records, for example. Canadian organizations transfer data to foreign governments, such as airline manifests. Canadian government agencies transfer data to foreign governments for policing, intelligence, immigration and other purposes. Canadian government agencies transfer data to foreign companies for outsourcing. And Canadians hand over personal data by presenting passports, visas and drivers' licences when asked. In all these ways, personal data travel across national borders routinely, and they may be intercepted, diverted or in other ways used such that those to whom they refer may be affected, possibly negatively.

The cases that are referred to in what follows, however, are ones in which the personal data in question are used to ease or to block the movement of persons across borders. That is, they relate to physical as well as virtual mobility. First, we examine the arguments surrounding mobility or persons and data, in employment and law enforcement contexts; second, we look at the securitizing of identity in the contexts of passports, ID cards, biometrics and airlines; third, we discuss citizenship and identity management, with special reference to the 'exploitation of identity' and the 'ban'; and, finally, we consider the prospects and limiting factors for 'global surveillance'.

Global mobility

It is important to remember that the growth of global surveillance is not a conspiracy. The primary reason why surveillance is globalizing is that mobility is a fundamental feature of the flexible capitalism that now dominates the world of production, exchange and consumption. The personal information economy is an important aspect of this globalizing world, but so is mobile labour, which means that employment records also migrate. Travellers of all kinds are emblematic of these multiple mobilities, and their data are embedded in passports, visas and other identifying documents and read by machines and officials and passed from place to place the world over. One's identity as a citizen is checked by these means and others, such as national or category-specific ID cards, which also bring the 'border' to other locations than the 'edges' or territory, thus further virtualizing it (Lyon 2005).

It is worth commenting on one of these categories – labour – at this point, though I shall also return to it below. In a globalizing world, multiple mobilities include data (personal and other), goods, communications, wastes and persons such as tourists, businesspersons and casual and manual workers. While some workers are engaged remotely as outsourced labour, in data-entry, editorial work and customer service, for example, other labour from the global South or from poorer countries in a given region is still required to move to fulfil tasks for which insufficient willing workers can be obtained in the global North. Because such foreign labour is often needed, but not necessarily wanted, in the global North, the issue has become a central source of community tensions, whether of Hispanic fruit workers in the USA or Canada, North Africans in France, South Asian workers in the UK, or workers from Turkey in Germany. Nor is the problem confined to the North. Consider, for example, Indonesians in Malaysia or mainland Chinese in Hong Kong.

The desire to control the movement of such workers is central to a number of significant surveillance efforts, generally overseen by immigration departments, but also related to wider policy agreements. This also gives the lie to an early piece of one-dimensional 'globalization' nonsense, that borders would somehow be eliminated. Of course, borders do change, and new technologies are involved in this (Marx 1997). Surely, for tourists, businesspersons and trade relations, the world has never been as open. But simultaneously, borders are also becoming more tightly policed and patrolled, not least with regard to the category of 'illegal aliens' or 'illegal immigrants'. In fact, as Hélène Pellerin points out, they have become 'privileged places of regulation' (Pellerin 2005: 51). And in the two most powerful regions of the world, what Naomi Klein calls 'fortress continents' are under construction (Klein 2002). Europe and North America are being formed into sealed units to maintain a flow of trade and of cheap foreign labour without risking attack or infiltration from outside them. The desire to create these zones had been present for some time, but the key opportunity was provided by 9/11 (Lyon 2003a).

Global surveillance is also visible in policing and anti-terrorist activity. Although terrorism became an increasingly significant phenomenon during the twentieth century, stimulating the growth of surveillance, for example, in Israel following the Munich Olympics attack in 1972, in the UK during the British mainland campaign of the Irish Republican Army (IRA) from the 1970s, in Canada following the bombing of Air India flight 192 in 1985, or in Japan after the Tokyo subway attacks of 1995, it was not until the attacks on New York and Washington of 9/11 2001 that anti-terrorist security and surveillance were seriously globalized. It must also be recalled, however, that previous 'wars' before the 'war on terror' included the 'war on drugs', which operation also involved – and still involves – considerable cross-border surveillance (see Shields 2002).

Global surveillance was intensified following 9/11 as the USA took the lead not only in declaring the 'war on terrorism' but also in implementing measures that would inevitably affect other countries as well. The chief locus of these measures was at airports, given that the attacks on the symbolic power centres of New York and Washington were carried out using domestic aeroplanes and that these are the most obvious points of entry by potential enemies into any country.[1] And in the airports of the twenty-first century the dilemma of contemporary governments is writ large. Global flows through the airport are a vital component of a commitment to economic growth and 'free trade', and thus the airport must provide unimpeded conduits for those flows. But at the same time the airport is seen as a very vulnerable site of attack or of penetration by any unwanted persons of malign intent and thus must be guarded stringently in ways that would seem to contradict the first aim of free flows (see Andreas and Biersteker 2003).

In his exploration of the development of the passport, John Torpey comments on the ways in which state authorities have a monopoly of the 'means of movement' (Torpey 2000). Border controls encapsulate this with their capacity to determine who may enter and who may not. The analogy is, of course, with other monopolies, such as those over the means of production (Karl Marx) or of violence (Max Weber). But there is another possible monopoly – or at least an oligopoly – emerging in this context: that centred on the 'means of identification'. The ability to regulate the means of movement is clearly a strategic one, but it includes, prominently, the power to determine that people are who they say they are or, increasingly, to say who people are without hearing their own story at all. The question of identification has become central, and is now bolstered with the paraphernalia of biometrics and inclusion in networked searchable databases.

Airports are perhaps the most stringently surveilled sites in terms of the means of movement and of identification. And they are also places *par excellence* for social sorting. But the empirical and critical analytic literature on airports is still fairly thin as yet, partly because of the newness of the area and partly because of access difficulties. Although some treatments of airports romanticize them as points of departure for dream vacations and ultimate freedoms, or as 'non-places' of consumption (Augé 1995), in reality passage through the airport is highly uneven. Although most air travel is restricted to a well-heeled minority mainly from the global North, this applies to both matters of privileging 'preferred passengers' and of security checks and screening. Moreover, these two may also be linked.

In both cases, the airport acts as a 'data filter' (Lyon 2002c), sifting the travellers who pass through both as consuming opportunities and as threat risks. Major airlines pride themselves on the clear distinctions between different classes of passenger that enable some to board straight from the lounge without waiting at the gate and require others to remain patiently at the gate until the boarding call is given for their rows (read classes of ticket – who would choose the non-view window over the wing or the cramped corner by the rear washrooms?). And airports work with airlines and government authorities to ensure that some passengers with paid-for security clearance cards get through immigration and baggage checks rapidly while others wait their turn and may even miss flights in endless Disneyesque rat-maze queues. Those with 'dubious' backgrounds or appearance take longer to be processed and those on watch-lists never get to fly at all. Here again, the twin and apparently contradictory aims of the airport are writ large: to maximize but to regulate mobility (see Salter 2007).

Peter Adey's study of airports shows how from the early days of airport expansion (1960s) means were sought of 'visualizing' the flows of passengers through airports employing punched-card techniques (Adey 2004: 1368). This fairly abstract process was later augmented to enable the tracking of specific bodies through airport spaces, using scanning devices that use fingers, hands, eyes and faces. Passengers could thus be categorized, sometimes before they entered the space of the airport. This is where biometrics comes into the picture to provide what are claimed to be increasingly reliable means of verifying and identifying travellers (Zureik and Hindle 2004). The bodies that pass through the system are reconfigured as information (van der Ploeg 2003, 2006), which as such is readily sharable with other agencies in the quest of what in North America is called the 'smart border' (Salter 2004).

Not only does the 'informating' of bodies make the data sharable, it also facilitates sorting, categorizing and profiling. Peter Adey observes that this is supposed to speed up the mobility of those within the terminal, but the process is achieved by treating different categories of passenger differently, based on their threat and opportunity profiles. True, Colin Bennett's inquiry into 'what happens when you buy an airline ticket' found that in his own case the answer was 'not much that is negative' (paraphrasing Bennett 2005), but one wonders how different things might have been were his name Bin Yamin or Basheer. At any rate, Adey argues, rightly, that the airport is now a surveillance machine, an 'assemblage where webs of technology and information combine' (Adey 2004: 1375), for not only does profiling occur, simulations are also engaged – for instance dynamically to model the movement of passengers. Travellers are scanned like barcodes to be silently organized and processed through the airport, says Adey, a process that invites critical examination along with the underlying assumptions and concepts framing it.

Securitizing identity

Questions of identity and identification have become increasingly central to citizenship and indeed to ordinary everyday life in today's society. Manuel Castells used the title *The Power of Identity* for the third volume of his work on 'The Information Age' (Castells 1997) and today, as Richard Jenkins says, 'identity, it seems, is bound up with everything from political asylum to credit card theft' (Jenkins 2004: 8). But as Jenkins hints in this quote, and as the words I used above indicate, it is 'identity and identification' that are really important in this context. In the twenty-first century, identity questions cannot be answered without considering those of identification, and vice versa. To quote Jenkins again, '[T]he capacity of organizations to identify people – authoritatively or powerfully, as individuals or collectively – and to make those identifications "stick" through the allocation of rewards and penalties, should not be underestimated' (Jenkins 2004: 174).

It is worth rehearsing the background to this state of affairs. In a general sense, the means of communication developed mainly during the twentieth century were depopulated. That is to say, the interpersonal forms of communication predominant in earlier contexts were increasingly mediated by systems such as the telegraph, telephone and then radio, television and the internet. The bodies that were once involved directly in communication disappeared (even though images of bodies reappeared in photographs, television and latterly in various kinds of digital camera technology). Rising geographical mobility, plus the stretching of social relationships enabled by these new transport and communication technologies, meant the general decline of face-to-face relationships.

This does not necessarily mean that there are fewer such face-to-face relations today; rather, we simply communicate with many more people (and machines and systems) that we do not see. In fact, online relationships may help to increase rather than decrease the volume of offline contacts (see, e.g., Virnoche 2002). The upshot in any case is a demand for more and more 'tokens of trust' to stand in for the forms of trust that were previously sustained (or challenged) by the face-to-face relation. Seals and signatures have been supplemented with drivers' licences, social insurance numbers, PINs and bar-codes and photo IDs and biometrics.

From a governmentality viewpoint, Nikolas Rose sees contemporary shifts in terms of the 'securitization of identity' (Rose 1999: 240f.). As he says, in many contexts the exercise of freedom requires proof of legitimate identity. And this has to be done in ways that link individuation and control. To gain privileges or entitlement the ID holder must present a card that refers to a database record, and each time a transaction is made or access gained, the virtual identity (in the database) is modified. The virtual identity or data-double may also be enhanced by cross-checking with other agencies – banks with insurance companies, for instance – in a constantly spiralling search for further verification. Biometrics and DNA offer what many believe to be the most reliable ways of perfecting these tokens of trust. For Rose, the circuits of securitization are dispersed and disorganized and are best seen as 'conditional access to circuits of consumption and civility', especially in relation to work and consumption (Rose 1999: 243).

Rose also argues that citizenship is now primarily realized not in relation with the state or public sphere but rather in a variety of practices, in which work and shopping are paradigmatic. However, while it is important to bear this in mind, for as we see elsewhere their impact on life-chances and choices is enormous, the state does still have a very significant role to play, especially in relation to 'national identification' and citizenship. In his own work Rose comments on ways in which nation-states helped to develop a sense of 'national identity'; in the British case the 'colonial experience and the codes of race' were particularly significant for forming 'governable subjectivi-ties' (Rose 1999: 47). In the US case, census data were also important in giving a picture to 'foreigners' and 'our own people' of 'who we really are' (Rose 1999: 219). While census enumeration buttresses some freedoms of liberal democracy, it also helps to constitute and solidify social and racial divisions (see Zureik 2001).

Today, especially after 9/11 but also in relation to other trends such as fears of crime, especially identity theft, national identification is very much bound up with citizenship. This may be explored through the prisms of passports, national ID cards and biometrics, all of which are perhaps most evident in airports. These help to regulate popula-tion movements and sort out who belongs where as well as helping to protect and police state borders by these means. As Mark Salter adds, passports uniquely identify each individual that needs one, using a photo and number, indicating the country of origin and the state to which the bearer may be deported (Salter 2003).

Increasingly, however, interest in 'smart' national identification systems is expressed in countries of the global North (several countries in South East Asia such as Malaysia and Hong Kong already have them, and some in Europe, such as France and Italy, are developing electronic IDs). At the time of writing (2006), the British ID card is under development and the American 'Real ID' programme is simi-larly making strides towards reality (as it were). Each is underwritten by recent law. These go further than passports in the regulation of mobility, because they can be used internally to the nation-state, and in the securitization of identity, because unlike passports they are likely to become compulsory for all citizens, and because they depend more and more on standardized coding for inter-operability within regions.

While various rationales – from urgent felt needs for immigration control to the desire to demonstrate prowess in high technology (Lyon 2005) – have been forwarded for introducing electronic ID card systems in other contexts, recent global North initiatives gained their imperative character from 9/11. Indeed, the proposal for a national ID card system (from Larry Ellison of Oracle Corporation) was one of the first made following the attacks on America. Sometimes, of course, these rationales are combined. While Chinese and Indian authorities may not see 9/11 as a vital spur to ID card production, both are concerned with internal population movement, with migrant groups, and with developing electronics-based administration. Already existing systems in Hong Kong, Malaysia or Japan also have mixed rationales, which similarly have not a lot to do with 9/11. Conversely, it may turn out that even those countries using 9/11 as a reason for developing new ID card systems have other, perhaps more long-term concerns in mind, including the more general control of migration.

It is important to note that while various kinds of ID card systems have been in place for many decades, or have been installed for specific exigencies such as national war efforts, today's proposals and projects are of a somewhat different character. For example, they depend on electronic information infrastructures that support a variety of functions through networked databases. Indeed, the route to successful implementation of 'electronic government' (or 'e-government') is through the establishment of a single code, the 'Unique Personal Identifier'. The general-purpose card scheme, such as those in Singapore and Malaysia, that may be used for access to several government departments and as a means of verifying the identity of citizens is enabled by networked technologies (see Clarke 2006).

This also makes possible another new aspect of such ID cards: that they can be used for commercial as well as government administrative purposes. This means that conventional national interests in personal identification may be connected more directly with consumer ones (with consequences that are as yet unclear). Thirdly, the internal national purposes of ID cards may be linked with external ones through the passport. In the UK, the proposed ID card will be administered through both the drivers' licence and the Passport Office (in the USA, by contrast, the Real ID is a product of integrating state-based drivers' licensing). Thus conventional distinctions between government/commercial, domestic/international, territorial/ non- territorial and inside/outside are all challenged by new ID card schemes.

Crucially, ID card schemes are intended to categorize populations, distinguishing especially between insiders and outsiders or legitimate citizens and others. This is where the existence of the national registry database is so significant. The cards themselves raise questions about 'internal borders' and about unwarranted apprehension by police officers, but it is the database that facilitates automated forms of social sorting. Within the 'new penology' of which Malcolm Feely and Jonathan Simon wrote some time ago, 'techniques for identifying, classifying and managing groups sorted by levels of dangerousness' were sought (Feely and Simon 1994: 180). But this takes such governmentality to a more general level by connecting it to investigations of fraud (financial and self-representation) and to entitlement for benefits and services. It also assumes that the scheme in question is capable of reliably making such distinctions.

The reliability of new ID card systems across a range of stated purposes is linked with the fast-growing technologies of biometrics. At its simplest, biometrics relates to body-measurements, and may be defined as the automated use of physiological or behavioural characteristics for identifying or verifying the identity of a living person. As Zureik and Hindle say, biometrics relies on pattern recognition which converts images into a binary code by means of an algorithm (Zureik and Hindle 2004: 117). To be authenticated (or 'verified'), an individual must enrol by presenting some ID card, whose details are then linked with the biometric data from the eye, finger, hand or face. Once the linked details are stored, the individual's stated identity can be confirmed when the card and linked data are presented again. Identification occurs when an ID card (in this case) is submitted to, say, an airline or a welfare department to be checked against a no-fly list or a list of those who have already applied for the benefit in question.

The background to ID cards may be seen in various contexts in early modern times, not least in the pass laws introduced in Virginia in 1642, targeting people such as poor white Irish indentured servants trying to 'flee their obligations' (Parenti 2003: 19). By 1656 Native Americans entering the colony to trade had to carry 'tickets'. A few years later, as Christian Parenti has shown, slave-owners required slaves to carry passes in Barbados and by 1680 Virginia had a slave pass law. A hundred years later, tin tags, stamped with the slave's occupation, date and a number for recording annual slave taxes, were instituted in South Carolina. In time, analogous systems would also become the apparatus of criminal justice, and, together with military passes and schemes for the control of immigrant labour, would provide part of the genealogy of contemporary ID and biometric devices.

By the nineteenth century, the colonial inheritance and the 'codes of race' alluded to by Rose in respect of securitizing identity come into their own again, especially in the case of biometrics, for biometrics brings forward into the present certain practices that have been evident since the earliest fingerprinting of colonial subjects during the nineteenth century in countries such as India and Argentina (Sengupta 2003). William Herschel first used fingerprinting techniques in India in 1858, and these were systematized by Edward Henry and Azizul Haque of the Bengal Police in 1893. As Shuddhabrata Sengupta says, 'Anthropometrical data, in the form of cranial radii, nasal indexes and finger length, were tested for their utility in developing the science of criminology, often aided by an ethnographic discourse that constructed an elaborate taxonomy of criminal tribes, deviant populations, and martial races' (Sengupta 2003). In relation to this the Indian colonial state kept detailed political intelligence on 'subversive activities' that entered every domain of life. In the early twenty-first century, the 'war on terror' appears to be following a similar, but technologically upgraded, path.

Zureik and Hindle remind us that the use of biometrics 'has a direct bearing on racial and other types of profiling – welfare recipients, for example – and indeed on governance as a whole' (Zureik and Hindle 2004: 129). And yet at the same time their work, along with others', shows that biometrics also presents many difficulties in terms of accuracy. Unsubstantiated claims and persistent errors of matching tend not to be highlighted in the effort to promote these means of 'fighting terror'. As a general background to biometrics, it may be that the issue of FTEs (failures to enrol) will become peculiarly problematic. Although questions have been raised about specific kinds of difficulty experienced by some groups – those who have skin diseases, for example – no systematic research has yet been done on the general FTE rates among non-white groups such as Hispanics, Asians and Blacks. If, as initial evidence shows, fingerprint and facial scans seem to privilege whiteness, then at a very basic level the system itself could be thought of as prejudicial to other groups (see Pugliese 2005).

Combined with the quest of governments, especially the US Administration, to find new means of amassing personal information, and technology companies urgently seeking new markets, the prospects are poor for carefully assessing the promise of biometrics to increase national security. As Benjamin Muller observes in his description of a Canadian forum on biometrics, the event itself was framed by the 'common need for biometrics' (Muller 2005: 91). Such discourses make it hard to raise questions relating to privacy or civil liberties, despite the obvious problems associated with any reliable attempt to 'secure' spaces for 'legitimate' persons only, especially when the political climate is chilly for specific minority groups.

Airport security and screening

The processes of identity securitization are most intense in contemporary airports, although, as Michael Sorkin notes, these sites may also be seen as vanguards for organizing cities into spaces of heavily surveilled, highly managed flows. As a 'classification engine', he goes on, 'airport design is a distilled version of the segregated efficiencies of transportation planning in general in which the grail is the separation of means and, thereby, of people and privileges' (Sorkin 2003: 261–2). Identity securitization is a crucial aspect of this. Arriving at the airport, however, this is not the first hoop through which would-be entrants must pass. As Mark Salter shows, the airport as a 'transient institution' has three spheres: the arrivals hall, where newly landed passengers sort themselves into citizens, foreigners and refugees; the 'confessional', where the border agent inquires about your provenance and destination; and the passport check (also by the border agent). This last is the 'hyper-documentation' phase where the 'body-biometrics-file-profile' is central (Salter 2005).

If we look at the Anti-Terrorism Plan in Canada,[2] developed in the wake of 9/11, it is clear that it was intended to keep the Canada–USA border secure and open to legitimate trade, increase front-end screening for refugee claimants, improve both detention and deportation processes, increase security staff hiring and upgrade technology, integration and training practices. In fact, Canada had been pressing for a 'smart border' agreement for some time, but 9/11 seemed to offer the vital opportunity. The 'border' issues include both geographical and artificial border control sites such as airports. Almost immediately after 9/11, armed undercover police officers and state-of-the-art explosives detection systems were introduced. In the expectation that passengers would have to pay some of the bill for this, a CDN$12 per flight charge was levied at first, which was reduced to CDN$7 in 2003. Other initiatives included technical improvements, such as replacing cockpit doors and locking them from take-off to landing (May 2003), and installing 'dirty bomb' detectors in Ottawa Airport (November 2004; Pilieci 2004).

One significant border initiative that accents the reliance on new technologies is the Advanced Passenger Information/Passenger Name Record Program (API/PNR). Under the Immigration and Refugee Protection Act of 2002 commercial carriers are required to provide Citizenship and Immigration Canada (CIC) with passenger and crew information for analysis, so that any who appear to pose concerns may be identified and intercepted. Such data include five elements: the full legal name, gender, date of birth, nationality and travel document number. In a novel move, airlines have to provide CIC with such passenger and crew data before they arrive in Canada. Under joint Canada–USA agreements, various means such as CANPASS Air (or the Canada–USA harmonized, iris-scan-dependent, NEXUS Air scheme) have been implemented (November 2004) to expedite the travel of 'approved, low-risk travelers'.[3]

Another initiative, which comprises both technical and personnel skills, also followed the 9/11 attacks. The Canadian Air Transport Security Authority (CATSA) was created as a crown corporation in April 2002, initially with four training centres to teach effective pre-board screening to 3,000 new security personnel. By 2003 CATSA began building comprehensive datasets of all travellers plus 4,000 employees from all eighty-nine Canadian airports, in order to compile data reports. The idea was to improve seasonal travel warnings as well as to identify gaps in security training if a particular type of incident occurs more often in one airport than in others.

Despite these apparently stringent improvements in border security, critical questions have been raised (in Canada as in the USA and elsewhere) about the adequacy of the new measures. In December 2004 the Senate Committee on National Security and Defence reported on inadequate mail and cargo screening, unsatisfactory background checks on airport personnel, a lack of control over access to restricted areas and insufficient training of part-time customs staff. And in March 2005 Canada's Auditor General, Sheila Fraser, reported on lax Passport Office practices, including inadequate watch lists, outdated technology and poor record-checking to verify identification.

She argued that computer links were not in place to flag applicants ineligible for passports because they are on parole or charged with serious crimes. She also expressed concerns about passenger and baggage screening. Moreover, in 2005 a Senate report, entitled *Borderline Insecure*, argued that security is inadequate and should be the priority on borders (Senate Committee on National Security and Defence 2005). It seems, furthermore, that airport security initiatives south of the border have not been much more successful. A General Audit Office (GAO) report on the 'Secure Flight' programme in 2005 complained that the Transport Security Authority (TSA) was not effectively managing the program, to the extent that it risked failure (GAO 2005).

Borders, citizenship and exclusion

In a speeding and mobile world, the idea of borders as barriers to movement is an unacceptable irritation, but in a fearful and unsafe world such borders make a lot of sense. The post-9/11 world is both speeding and mobile and perceived as insecure and vulnerable, and thus borders have become the focus of political concern as well as academic attention. The dominant assumptions about the importance of mobility for economic growth in the global North hold sway even in so-called 'terrorist' times, so the urgent quest is for means of improving the sorting capacity of borders to ensure that approved movement is as fluid as possible while simultaneously ensuring that some fine-mesh devices prevent the passage of illegitimate entrants. Needless to say, those 'illegitimate entrants' include a cluster of national groups that have become 'suspect' since 9/11 (from Jordan, Saudi Arabia, Libya, Pakistan, and so on), along with those who have for a long time been lower priority for permission to enter.

This is why so much attention is currently paid to schemes for greater police cooperation, improved means of examining travellers, and technical means of checking, verifying and identifying persons who are in transit across physical and virtual borders, especially in airports (Salter 2004). From a surveillance perspective, personal information is under detailed scrutiny as never before at borders. And of course because the data are primarily digital, the 'border' is virtual not only in the sense that airports are seldom at the physical edge of territory but also in the sense that the processing often takes place 'upstream' of the actual location where documents may be checked. As well, it is worth recalling that not only personal data (or actual bodies) are under surveillance. Again, airports provide a prime example of locations where things – especially baggage but also physical documents like passports and the aeroplanes and other airport machines – are also surveilled (Adey 2003). Since 9/11, concern with 'things' such as small knives has been paramount, even to an obsessive degree. While stopping terrorists travelling by air may be an impossible task, ensuring that when they do they have no access to potential weapons may be the best one can hope for.

In so-called 'control societies', however, older means of determining who is 'innocent/guilty', 'approved/suspect', 'legal/illegal' seem to be at a lower premium. In an analogous way to that in which the 'categorical suspicion' of today's policing renders everyone if not guilty at least dubious until proven innocent, so 'identity management' seems to be encroaching on older definitions of citizenship (see, e.g., Muller 2004). The need for knowledge and visibility as management tools is clear here, which is why airports especially are dense surveillance sites. The key tool for identity management is biometrics, and in this context the chief aim is to ensure that only eligible persons enter a country. Interestingly, the identity management model derives from online businesses' protocols and technologies for facilitating and controlling users' access to critical online applications and resources – while protecting confidential personal and business information from unauthorized users. These are 'integrated solutions' that administer user authentication, access rights, passwords, and the like.

In the offline world of border controls, however, bodies become passwords (as Ann Davis put it in reference to biometrics, 1997) and the 'access rights' have deeply consequential aspects. As Muller comments, the shift to identity management emphasizes the emerging distinctions between friend and foe (some of which were articulated by George W. Bush after 9/11) and also – again like 'categorical suspicion' – plays down the role of citizen subjectivity and agency in border practices. Identities and origins become less significant than what constitutes dis/qualified bodies, and authorized access to certain privileges, resources and places becomes the key process in question. There is something disturbing about this process, in which the protocols of online business practice start to displace conventional citizenship discourses, but after 9/11 it was justified as being part of a package of emergency measures. The difficulties deepened several years later, however, as it became clear, as noted in chapter 3, that what Giorgio Agamben calls the 'state of exception' had actually become 'business as usual' (Agamben 2005).

Global surveillance

To talk of global surveillance certainly sounds conspiratorial, but this is not the intention here. Surveillance has become globalized just because economic and political processes are themselves globalized, for better or worse (Lyon 2004). Both flexible employment and transnational consumer corporations contribute to global surveillance, just as the quest for security and safety does. Indeed, they do so in a symbiotic fashion. As Bauman puts it in the epigraph, '[T]he database is an instrument of selection, separation and exclusion'. But as he also says, '[T]he database is a vehicle of mobility, not the fetters keeping people in place' (Bauman 1998: 51). At one and the same time, databases of global corporations and international policing help to lubricate desirable planetary flows and also to slow or stop undesirable traffic.

In relation to the 'war on terror', one of the most obvious signs of global surveillance is the agreement of the (United Nations-sponsored) International Civil Aviation Organization (ICAO) for its 188 contracted states to use standard machine-readable passports (MRPs) by April 2010. About 110 of these already use such MRPs and forty of these upgraded to the biometrically enhanced version or e-passport by the end of 2006. Security, immigration and customs checkpoints world-wide accept these MRPs, which are also accessed by embassies and consulates for visas. The aim is inter-operability and global networking, although what is much less clear is how far fair information practices (FIPs) govern the ways that personal data obtained from MRPs are handled in all the countries using MRPs and e-passports. The 2001 Smart Border Agreement called for common biometric standards between Canada and the USA, for example, a process that was still underway in 2006. Since the start of 2007 Canadians crossing into the USA have been required to hold passports or other accepted documents (such as an ID card) all of which will eventually carry biometrics.

The globalization of surveillance, just as with all other globalizations, is both a phenomenon in its own right and something that takes place in different ways in different countries, producing situations of complex inter-relations. In some ways, surveillance is 'glocalized' as local circumstances make a real difference to general trends.[4] Surveillance in different countries is linked with many factors, including economic priorities, technological development levels, legal oversight, colonial pasts and present relations with the USA. It is not uniform or homogeneous and may be constrained or enabled by any or all of these factors. Moreover, surveillance is perceived differently in different countries, which also makes a difference to its actual operation.[5]

The globalization of surveillance may also call forth new responses such as Toshimaru Ogura's proposals for a new kind of identity politics based on opposition to what he calls (biometric) 'identity exploitation' (Ogura 2006). Arguing that the securitization of identity leads to both a biological reductionism in conceptions of human identity, and to the minimizing of trusting and 'hospitable' international relationships through the mounting 'suspicions' of nationality and citizenship tests, Ogura argues for a proliferation of usable identifiers rather than a quest for increasingly unique single identifiers. Similar suggestions have been made by privacy advocates and civil liberties groups elsewhere, but also by computing professionals.[6]

Surveillance does indeed have some global as well as international dimensions, but this should not be taken as a claim that a 'global conspiracy' is afoot. Rather, a number of processes are occurring in locations linked by information and communication networks that enable personal data to flow around the world for several purposes. These surveillance data are sensitive and could equally be used for malign as for benign goals. They circulate at the behest of corporations as well as government administration and policing and in general their mobility, and also that of those to whom they refer, is actively encouraged. However, as Bauman points out in the epigraph to this chapter, some database systems enable the 'globals' to move freely while others ensure that the 'sieve' 'washes out' the locals. The databases that protect some in Bauman's sieve while washing out others may be run by government departments, police and border authorities, or corporations that together sort out who may move. The surveillance assemblage has increasingly international dimensions. The sieving or sorting process is done on the basis of agreed legitimate identifiers – biometric passports and ID cards – produced by government, corporations and high-tech companies.

These modes of identification are likely to become an important arena of struggles over surveillance in coming years, on several fronts. The resurgence of 'states of emergency' reduces reliance on the rule of law at the same time as increasing dependence on digital means of determining 'who goes where' using smart IDs and passports. The question of whether or not biometrics represents a fundamentally flawed means of identification due to its apparent racialized character has yet to be resolved. And the issue of what sorts of power will accrue to nation-states, working in conjunction with other forms of governance, as a result of using unique identifiers also requires research and political action.

PART III

Visibility

The last part of this book is devoted to considering how visibility is vital to surveillance. It is emphatically not the case that surveillance is all about huge systems for automating an all-pervading vision machine like the most paranoid portrayals of the Panopticon. It includes visibility, which in this context has to do with how people are seen and how they respond to being seen. Of course, visibility is ambiguous, just as surveillance is; ordinary people may seek as well as shy away from visibility. What was examined in part II as 'vision' is mainly about surveillance making people visible to those who have some interest in regulating their activities.

By contrast, in chapter 7, we start with depictions of surveillance in mass media and popular culture to consider how visibility is articulated with pleasure and how it could be active as well as passive, even though here, too, it is Janus-faced. Visibility is a metaphor of knowledge but also a real social process (Brighenti 2007). Of course, much of our understanding of surveillance is subtly shaped by novels such as *Nineteen Eighty-Four* (1949) and films such as *The Conversation* (1974) or *Minority Report* (2002). More recently, the phenomenon of reality TV, especially the original *Big Brother*, has turned surveillance more decisively into an entertainment experience. 'Acting up' in front of surveillance cameras gives this another twist, too. Two key reasons could be given for considering surveillance in media and popular culture. One is that through imaginative depictions we may understand surveillance experiences and processes better, and the other is that some such media are themselves becoming a means of surveillance.

Chapter 8 turns decisively to the politics of visibility. While it is clearly the case that in popular culture some desire visibility – such as Hard-Fi's 2005 song, 'Stars of CCTV' – others are equally keen to be left alone. They might say they desire privacy rather than publicity. But there are many ways of asserting an objection to surveillance, from 'a right to be left alone', as American lawyer Warren Brandeis famously put it, to demands for anonymity, confidentiality or the right at least to know what is known about oneself by a surveillant organization. In fact people respond in a variety of ways to what surveillance they know about, often complying, sometimes negotiating an arrangement that seems more equitable or at least more beneficial or less harmful to the subject, and occasionally resisting. This can be institutionalized in legal remedies or may be actively expressed in a social or political movement. Either way, what happens to personal data is becoming more central to the politics of information.

Finally, in chapter 9, we return again to issues of what ought to be made visible, especially under the rubric of 'transparency'. Because today's technology-assisted surveillance context seems to have an insatiable appetite for personal data, and because those data may be used in invasive as well as supportive ways and for negative as well as positive social sorting and discrimination, every effort should be made at every level to ensure that people know what is happening. It is not merely a question of data-subjects claiming their 'privacy rights' but, more importantly, of surveillant organizations revealing how they use personal data and, where possible, obtaining consent for their use.

7 Surveillance, Visibility and Popular Culture

We're the stars of CCTV
Making movies out on the street
Flashing blue lights, camera, action
Watching my life, main attraction
We're the stars of CCTV
Can't you see the camera loves me?

Hard-Fi, 'Stars of CCTV' (2005)

How do we know what being under surveillance, or engaging in surveillance, is really like? Why do we experience surveillance in specific ways? It is possible that we have been deliberately watched or, worse, bugged or stalked, or that we have become aware of advertisements 'mysteriously' targeted at us. Equally it is possible that we have studied surveillance or taken advantage of privacy policies or data protection law to discover how we can find out what 'they' know about us or to contest some infringement of our 'information rights'. Far more likely, however, that we know about surveillance because we have read about it in a classic novel such as *Nineteen Eighty-Four* (1949) or that we have seen a film depicting surveillance such as *Enemy of the State* (1998). Such movies and novels help us get our bearings on what surveillance is all about and – because they are usually negative, dystopian – give us a sense of the kind of world we wish to avoid.

But this is already to fall into the trap of thinking that 'surveillance and popular culture' is all about undesirable circumstances and anxious, paranoid responses. While it is true that one strand of the surveillance genre is indeed alarmist, unsettling, haunting, conspiratorial, other strands of popular culture may not only reassure about the realities of surveillance or support the view that surveillance is a necessary dimension of life today but even encourage deliberate disclosure. So, far from fearing exposure, in some contemporary media exposure is relished, sought and celebrated. So, far from the terrifying prospect of losing one's freedom and dignity (in *Nineteen Eighty-Four*) or one's means of identification ('identity theft') (in the movie, *The Net*, 1995), police TV shows like *CSI* give uncritical credence to the view that CCTV cameras 'really work' and reality TV shows such as *Big Brother* make full, intimate visibility to watchers a commendable condition.

While many surveillance theorists have debated the Panopticon, until Thomas Mathiesen offered a parallel concept of 'synopticon' little had been made of the vast array of electronic media developing alongside surveillance technologies in the twentieth century (Mathiesen 1997). Mathiesen argues that the 'viewer society' in which we live is not merely a surveillance society, where the few watch the many, it is also a mass media society, where the many watch the few. And whatever panoptic effects may be found in contemporary culture, they have to be considered in relation to synoptic ones because the latter help to shape our experience of the former. Indeed, Mathiesen suggested, they work together. This may be seen, strikingly, in the TV footage of 9/11 (where the many watched the few), which helped to establish in public opinion the notion that more surveillance (where the few watch the many) is required if terrorism is to be combated successfully (Lyon 2003a: 19–20; 2006c). One might also add to Mathiesen's comments the thought that while some people may have read social science or philosophical work on surveillance, a much larger audience will have seen a surveillance movie, so knowing how surveillance is framed in popular cultural forms such as film should at least be a rough guide to public perceptions.

Another take on this question comments not so much on the parallel worlds of electronic media as on the ways in which the gaze is already implicated and explored in popular media, especially in film. For Norman Denzin, one way of understanding the 'cinematic society' is as a 'voyeur's gaze' (Denzin 1995). Starting with Foucault's comment that the 'voyeur's gaze' is 'an inspecting gaze' that each individual interiorizes until they exercise surveillance over themselves (Foucault 1980b: 155), Denzin argues that the 'voyeur is the iconic, postmodern self, a product of the cinematic gaze' (Denzin 1995: 1). Such 'voyeurism' is shared, of course, by cinema audiences. 'Voyeurism' is a social as well as an individual practice, implicating on-screen characters who view each other and who are in turn viewed by those in the audience.

Denzin asks several key questions about the gaze that has dominated some 1,200 Hollywood films from 1900 to 1995. Why are only certain individuals allowed to look at others? What motivates the gaze, whether perverse or socially valued? What purposes does the gaze serve in wider society? And what are the costs and consequences of the gaze for the individual and society? But like Foucault, who in somewhat cavalier fashion lumps together the peeping Tom with the spy, reporter, detective or sociologist, Denzin argues that the cinematic society constantly switches surveillance codes so that the person gazed upon is the person doing the gazing. So what, he asks, gives anyone – including social scientists – a licence to gaze?

A further perspective on popular culture and surveillance is provided by Gary T. Marx (1996), whose analysis of a number of media is very suggestive. He suggests that a kind of *verstehen* – or sympathetic understanding of intentions and contexts – of surveillance experiences can be gleaned from popular media. I shall not replicate his telling comments on song lyrics and cartoons here – except for one – but it is worth noting his overall approach to the topic. The one exception is Marx's parallel text on the song by The Police, 'Every Breath You Take', in which he sees the title line as breathalyser, 'every move you make' as motion detector, ' every bond you break' as polygraph, and 'every step you take' as electronic monitoring. His analysis continues to the end of the song.

Marx argues that cultural analysis can help us understand the *experience* of being watched, or being a watcher, and also what sorts of values inform our understandings of surveillance technologies. More particularly, he says that these media help us see and understand new surveillance developments; that they remind us about power relations and struggles over meaning; that in contexts where egalitarianism and democracy are valued, surveillance practices are viewed cautiously but that the same technologies may be viewed differently depending on whether they are involved in care or control; and that looking at popular culture suggests new fields for social research, because both are concerned with the need to go 'beneath surface realities and to question conventions' (Marx 1996: 231).

In what follows, we explore the place of surveillance in popular culture and the place of popular culture in surveillance. While surveillance offers popular culture some of its dominant themes, our experience of surveillance is itself shaped in part by popular culture.

Thus, on the one hand, we have to examine what sorts of surveillance are portrayed in novels, films, song lyrics and other media, and how these may interact with extraordinary or everyday kinds of surveillance, with what consequences; and, on the other, it is necessary to look at how popular culture influences surveillance. In some obvious ways, ideas may be gleaned from mass media, such as the perhaps classic case of how a Spiderman comic strip inspired the electronic tagging of offenders (Lyon 1994), but in less evident ways, long-running TV shows such as *Big Brother* may not only normalize exposure but also open the door to further commercial surveillance of kinds that are far from apparent to its subjects.

In order to survey the terrain of surveillance in popular media (and vice versa) I shall deal with different kinds of media, in order, even though there may be considerable overlap in some important respects. Novels may become films, for instance, and take on a life that they never had in, or a different kind of life from, the text version. The aim is to ask how surveillance is portrayed in popular culture and thus how this might be thought to affect public perceptions of and interactions with surveillance. I draw on the work of a number of writers who have discussed these themes, both social scientists who examine the media and specialists such as literary, film and cultural theorists.

Defining surveillance studies: the novel

Sociologists and other social scientists frequently use metaphors and similes borrowed from elsewhere as descriptive and explanatory concepts. The idea of social *stratification*, for example, comes from the geological notion of the layering of rocks, and social *mobility* is loaned from kinetics, where actual physical movement is in mind. In fact, in the work of James Rule, the whole novel *Nineteen Eighty-Four* functions as a kind of 'ideal type' situation, a worst-case scenario against which other, less dire, situations are measured (Rule 1973). The political nightmare depicted in that novel is seen as a 'total surveillance society' and its various constitutive features are explored in relation to actual social practices and processes of surveillance in the USA and Europe, such that the analyst can judge 'how far' these societies have progressed towards the 'ideal type'. It is a telling mode of analysis because it doubles as a political warning of 'what could happen' if certain trends are permitted to continue. However, like 'stratification' (which could imply a rock-like resistance to change), the use of the novel as a conceptual trope could be misleading.

There is little doubt that the overwhelmingly popular metaphors for surveillance in the twentieth century came from George Orwell. In Western democracies, *Nineteen Eighty-Four* is standard fare in high school and students have understood the novel variously as an attack on state socialism (especially during the Cold War years) or, as Orwell probably intended, as a warning about the totalitarian potentials of any modern bureaucratic nation-state. Orwell rightly foresaw that state power would be augmented by electronic means and depicted life under the looming, intrusive 'telescreen' to indicate this. He also connected this with ironic changes in language (the 'Ministry of Truth', or 'Minitrue', for example, deals with government propaganda) to show how cultural change, rather than mere subjection to the state, is pursued in Oceania.

The surveillance system of Oceania relies on both audio and visual data. As long as the novel's chief protagonist, Winston Smith, 'remained in the field of vision which the metal plaque [of the telescreen] commanded, he could be seen as well as heard' (Orwell 1954: 6). In many respects, Orwell was prescient. Data have become highly malleable; profiles are sought; new technologies make surveillance less and less perceptible; fear is engendered by uncertainty; human dignity (of which privacy may be one component) is threatened; and social division is fostered ('proles' are excluded; Party members are included; see Lyon 1994: 60).

At the same time, one has to go a long way beyond Orwell to understand surveillance today. Subtle dataveillance based on the body is more important than either visual or audio surveillance; many other agencies than the state are obviously involved in control (there were other agencies in Orwell's time, too, but their role is now palpable); and huge improvements have been made in the storage, transmission and retrieval of data. So Orwell's dystopic vision is valuable but dated in some respects. His work deserves ongoing attention because he discerned the ever-present possibility of totalitarian controls and because he countered it with a strong – ontological – view of human dignity. But more is needed today.

Some see in Franz Kafka a writer who intuited lucidly the realities of contemporary surveillance, despite the fact that he was writing well before Orwell (Kafka died in 1924; Orwell in 1950). For Daniel Solove, for example, 'Big Brother' has outlived his usefulness as a metaphor. Today, he avers, we are heading towards 'a more mindless process – of bureaucratic indifference, arbitrary errors, and dehumanization – a world that is beginning to resemble Kafka's vision in *The Trial*' (Solove 2004: 55). Kafka's novels contain shadowy figures who are 'in the know' because they have access to the files and whose enigmatic activities keep their suspects in a constant state of anxiety because they do not know the nature of the charges against them. Indeed, they don't know why they have been picked up, on the basis of what evidence, which department is detaining them, how long they will be kept in the dark, or what will be the consequences of making one or another kind of statement. There is clearly information on them, but they have no access to it, let alone to recourse or redress.

The advantage of the Kafkaesque metaphors, argues Solove, is that attention is deflected from the malign person of Big Brother and towards the sense of being in a maze. Solove's intention is broader than one of correctly discerning literary relevance. Legal scholars and legislators, he argues, should worry less about the wrongful disclosure of confidential information to a personified 'Big Brother'. Instead, they would do well to be more concerned with regulating what public and private information may be collected and processed by commercial or government databases, how they might be secured, and how successive transfer to other databases should be limited. If this could at least in part be achieved by rethinking surveillance metaphors, then, avers Solove, the effort would be worthwhile.

Other authors have provided metaphors, insights and also plausible literary treatments of totalitarian situations. Two such are Philip K. Dick and Margaret Atwood, and they are worth mentioning not only because they each deal with wider issues – of humanness, for example – but also because their work hints at important dimensions of surveillance not touched on by Orwell or Kafka. Dick's work has some of the 'maze' features of Kafka's, but also connects this with technological fantasies (not to mention hallucinogenic drugs) such as identification by eye-type in *Do Androids Dream of Electric Sheep?* (1968; turned into the film, *Bladerunner*, 1982). As for Atwood, her dystopia *The Handmaid's Tale* (1985) explores the gender dimensions of a totalitarian world. State control of the means of reproduction is chosen as the answer to falling birthrates, and thus men and medicine feature as the powerful surveillors in the novel. Indeed, as Pamela Cooper points out, in the 1990 film version the audience is also drawn in to the surveillance, which brings home the point even more poignantly (Cooper 1995).

Novels are an important source of metaphor and simile, then, and help to alert us to significant dimensions of surveillance as well as helping the reader imaginatively to get inside characters who are either the surveillors or, more frequently, the surveilled. However, in the twenty-first century it is probably true to say that the novel is being supplanted by the film as a means of understanding surveillance. But while the very medium of film may provide surveillance insights unavailable elsewhere, it is likely that the key question of the surveillance metaphor, rightly raised by Solove and others, will still have to be sought in literary contexts.

The surveillant turn: watching movies

The term 'watching movies' is perhaps a misnomer, especially as the classic surveillance movie – *The Conversation* (1974) – is actually about audio surveillance, primarily, and only secondarily about 'watching'. But this 'listening movie' is a classic in the sense that it explores some of the deepest psychology of surveillance and it does so through a striking role-reversal. The surveillance expert discovers that he himself is under surveillance, but despite his expertise he cannot find out how he is being bugged. Harry Caul, a San Francisco wiretapper, who is meticulous about keeping his work and his private life apart, is seen surreptitiously recording the conversation of a couple in Union Park. Starting to think that they're involved in a murder plot, he tries some sleuthing himself, only to get fully entangled in their drama and to find himself caught on the horns of dilemmas about 'public' and 'private' life. He can no longer imagine that surveillance is a mere clinical 'science'. He eventually takes his own apartment to pieces to try to find the bug, never dreaming that it is in his saxophone (or is it?).

This subtle interplay between the role of surveillor as detached technical expert and the role of the uncertain, unnerved subject who realizes he is under surveillance underscores the importance of considering both together in surveillance studies. The systems expert, who takes a classic bureaucratic position of seeking efficiency in the smoothly functioning machine, stands in stark contrast with the surveilled subject, who is coming apart at the seams by the end of the movie, for which the deliberate and systematic destruction of his home is a trope. The growing awareness of being surveilled is accompanied by an inner change of mood in which the first role – of a detached observer, just doing his job – is jettisoned for a judicious but spare moral critique of the very possibility that surveillance could be neutral.

As Thomas Levin points out, however, *The Conversation* also marks a turning point in films dealing with surveillance. Whereas previous films included surveillance as a theme, *The Conversation* engages surveillance structurally. It is 'the movie's primary narrative concern' (Levin 2002: 582). Surveillance makes the story possible. Levin also observes, however, that surveillance does not become generally central to a whole range of films until the 1990s. It starts to appear with several films that feature prominently the role of CCTV cameras – *Thelma and Louise* (1991), *Sliver* (1993), *Snake Eyes* (1998) – but emerges decisively with Peter Weir's *The Truman Show* (1998). Here the synopticon and the Panopticon are mixed again, as the (mass) viewers take the role of the surveillance operator – the audience is told exactly which device, 'button-cam', 'crane-cam', is in use at which moment – to watch the lone soul, Truman, gradually come to the realization that he is under 24/7 scrutiny. It might be terrifying were it not for the fact that we're also reassured that everything is occurring in a giant studio – it's not the 'real world' after all.

What does seem more like the real world, however, is Mike Figgis's *Time Code* (2000), which takes the surveillant imaginary even further into the cinema than is the case with some more celebrated movies (such as *Minority Report* [2002] or *Enemy of the State* [1998]). While others rely heavily on CCTV images as a feature of the plot, *Time Code* brings the typical category of TV (time) into the realm normally under the sign of space (cinema) (see Doane 2002). The screen is divided into four segments, each of which contains a ninety-minute tracking shot of one character, followed in 'real time'. Once again the viewer becomes a surveillance operator, although the only choice offered is which segment to focus on (rather than PTZ – pan, tilt, zoom – or single image tracking). Time, as Levin says, is the 'key, or the code' to following and to understanding this film (Levin 2002: 593), but it does help, in a general way, to comprehend how difficult it is to watch several screen segments simultaneously (cf. Dubbeld 2004; Norris and Armstrong 1999) and thus what this might mean for routine CCTV operatives.

If *The Conversation* marked a watershed in surveillance films, it did so in part because of its emphasis on surveillance technologies. Though they appear crude in the twenty-first century, the audio-bugs are a crucial component of the psychological probing of the movie. It is precisely because the bug in Caul's apartment is so tiny that it can be secreted in a place that frustrates his panicking search. Turning the technological tables on Caul prompts his rethinking the question of how far he can remain a clinically uncontaminated 'expert'. But by the time the surveillance movie has become a frequent offering, in the 1990s, technological questions are synonymous with the 'new surveillance'. While the obvious danger this raises is technological determinism – surveillance is technology-driven rather than being the product of socio-technical processes – some other, more subtle questions are also raised by this emphasis. There is a general issue – from *The Conversation*, among others – of how far technologies can ever be 'neutral' instruments, but also of how far new technologies *enable* cultural shifts, such as that towards pre-emptive rather than reactive surveillance (which features strongly in *Minority Report*).

The question of 'new surveillance' is picked up in Tony Scott's *Enemy of the State*, which not only updates *The Conversation* technologically but also uses the same actor (Gene Hackman) and includes some footage from the original 1974 movie. But as Light notes, the update is not accompanied by a greater concern with the nuances of technology, nor is the psychological depth of *The Conversation* matched in *Enemy* either (Light 2002: 32). In a sense the later movie is parasitic on the earlier, because the surveillor becomes the surveilled and because questions of 'privacy' are revisited once again (it may even be the case that the lead characters of the two movies are intended to be one and the same person).

Yet the apparent philosophical or sociological shallowness of *Enemy* may be telling for other reasons. The movie makes much of the technological sophistication of computer, database and advanced communication devices and networks, almost as if the presence of high technology speaks for itself, somehow guaranteeing its own effectiveness. This is actually a very significant attitude, especially in the American context, where belief in the efficacy of technological 'solutions' far outstrips any evidence that technical devices can be relied upon to provide 'security' (see, *inter alia*, Mosco 2004 and O'Harrow 2005 for a critique of technological dependence). And as

Light comments, the message of *Enemy* seems merely to be (the disingenuous one from the perspective of *The Conversation*) that surveillance technologies may be dangerous 'in the wrong hands'.

Light goes on to propose, and I concur, that considerably more depth may be found in the no less thorough technological update embodied in Wim Wenders' *The End of Violence* (1997). This film is pitted with irony and, like some other Wenders products, is also a complex mystery plot with many levels of meaning. There is, for instance, the irony that the state-of-the-art surveillance equipment is housed in a disused observatory (it now looks down on LA rather than up to the stars), an irony deepened by the fact that the equipment is not tidily contained. There is also synoptic-panoptic irony in the fact that the observatory is on Mt Hollywood. But the treatment offered in *End* is subtle, ambiguous and profound. Ray Bering (the surveillance expert played by Gabriel Byrne) is himself ambivalent about the efficacy of 'modern technology' and dubious about the capacities of some police camera systems because of their potential gratuitously to invade private or anonymous spaces. He also recoils, embarrassed, from the voyeuristic role offered to him when he sees on his screen a blonde woman crying in her apartment.

End foregrounds critical questions about surveillance technologies, as Ray Bering struggles (as Light puts it) 'with the potential for this technology to create amoral distance between himself and others' (Light 2002: 48). He wonders not only about his own involvement in setting up the system, but also about the possibilities of becoming inured to the ethical problems in later generations of the same software. The film also makes evident the fact of technical limitations; the systems cannot be perfect. Specifically, satellite images are distorted by cloud cover and human figures are not unambiguously recognizable. Lastly, Bering's father appears in the plot as someone for whom new technologies are superfluous, rather than indispensable. He sticks doggedly with his old typewriter rather than switching to a computer. But the film as a whole raises a further surveillance conundrum, discerned by Light: if we really could use surveillance to create a perfectly safe world, might it not do so at the cost of undermining the very personal autonomy and integrity that it was supposed to protect (Light 2002: 50)? Some of the moral and political as well as the technical limits of surveillance are seen clearly in this film.

The same cannot be said – at least in the same way – for *Minority Report* (2002), which returns us to the centre of the gee-whiz world of what Light calls 'techno-geeks'. This film relies on the rather unlikely characters of 'pre-cogs', three female figures whose apparent ESP permits their use by the 'Pre-Crime Department' to detect murders before they occur, in mid-twenty-first-century Chicago. (Perhaps the 'unlikeliness' of the characters is meant as a warning that such pre-emptive dreams are hollow, but the seriousness with which the rest of the surveillance technology panoply is taken suggests otherwise.) Steven Spielberg, the director, carefully researched the up-and-coming surveillance technologies, such as RFID, in order to create his 'state-of-the-art' film.

What was striking about *Minority Report*, however, was its timing. Like *The Conversation*, whose audiotape storyline coincided eerily with the early 1970s Watergate scandal – the air is heavy with suspicion and paranoia – one could be forgiven for concluding that *Minority Report* was made for the Homeland Security era following 9/11. Seeing surveillance as a means of predicting, pre-empting and preventing undesirable behaviour was not a new idea. But it gathered momentum as it gripped the anxious public imagination in the months directly after the attacks on America.

Minority Report certainly does critically question the ubiquity of surveillance devices, from CCTV cameras to internet surveillance and beyond. So despite the clichés, there are some interesting oblique comments on being constantly in the gaze. The very idea of pre-emptive surveillance, based in the early twentieth century on simulation (discussed effectively first by Baudrillard [1983] and then by Bogard [1996]), lies behind many justifications for establishing new systems (even though, following the London bombings of 2005, it was once again the forensic, after-the-event use of CCTV for identifying the perpetrators that produced popular fascination).

Two other features of the film are worthy of mention. One is the increasingly interactive character of surveillance. The more ubiquitous computing becomes a reality, the more human interaction with devices triggers checking, monitoring and recording. Thus 'Mr Matsumoto' is hailed by name as he passes an RFID-enabled manikin that invites him to purchase some product for which no doubt his socio-economic status and geo-demographic markers classify him. The other feature, related with this, is the product and brand placement littering the movie. What was parodied in *The Truman Show* is an unremarkable commonplace in *Minority Report*. Again, the connections between police and consumer surveillance in the film echo those burgeoning in the post-9/11 world.

If categorization is a minor theme in *Minority Report*, it shifts to a major dimension in *Gattaca* (1997). Written and directed by the screenwriter of *The Truman Show* (Andrew Niccol), *Gattaca* is about a society in which not class, caste or merit but genetics determines social outcomes. The corporation that gives the movie its name highlights the letters G, A, T, C as the four components of DNA; rule is achieved through this code. Vincent, whose 'faith birth' condemns him to life as an office cleaner, is determined to overcome his genetic classification as 'in-valid'. He finds Jerome, a member of the genetic elite of 'valids', who was so badly injured in a car crash that he is confined to a wheelchair. Vincent takes on Jerome's identity, for a price, and uses his genetic make-up to fake his way into his chosen career. This movie questions genetic engineering by reminding audiences that genetic futures are merely probabilities and predispositions, yet fate may hang on them.

Information is central to several of these films, but in the case of *Gattaca* the information is genetic. It is a true work of science fiction in the sense that it extrapolates from present trends, and contains none of the science fantasy elements such as the 'pre-cogs' in *Minority Report*. As Dorothy Nelkin and Lori Andrews warn, DNA samples are more than just a source of identification: 'Revealing information about health and predisposition, they can expose a person to workplace or insurance discrimination, creating categories of those "at risk." And they can be used to reinforce race or ethnic stereotypes' (Nelkin and Andrews 2003: 95). Nor is this an empty warning. The UK boasts the world's largest DNA database and police are steadily gaining more powers to retain DNA profiles as well as the biological samples themselves. In 2004 police were empowered to take samples from anyone arrested on suspicion of a 'recordable offence'. Fears are expressed that because the police have a disproportionate number of samples from minorities, this could produce skewed accounts of their activities, and negative discrimination against them (Gosline 2005).

In these and other movies, it is apparent that contemporary surveillance is already well understood, even though the social or political analyst may wish to ask further questions. As Peter Marks shows, current films go far beyond Orwell, and not just by taking account of new technologies. They also offer a 'variety of complex and nuanced accounts that range over entertainment, genetic scrutiny, new forms of access and exclusion and the use of social sorting to create social and cultural hierarchies' (Marks 2005: 236). In addition, they look at 'terrorism, body screening, government and corporate surveillance and the effect of surveillance on those undertaking surveillance, not only on those under scrutiny'. They examine complicity as well as resistance.

For Marks, there are illuminating and even emancipatory aspects to this. He concurs with the classic argument about dystopias, that they are intended to engender not despair but determination to ensure they are not fulfilled (and, similarly, that utopias are intended to prompt negative contrasts with the present such that aspects of the utopia are translated into political goals[1]). Marks maintains that films like those discussed here, so far from reducing audiences to passivity and pessimism, 'have a built in counter-narrative that can inspire us to question and resist negative trends while critically assessing any changes presented as positive' (Marks 2005: 236). He goes on: '[T]his informed skepticism is vital in a contemporary world where the reference points of acceptable and unacceptable surveillance are highly fluid.'

Part of the question about 'watching movies' or surveillance films, then, is how far they are really 'about' surveillance. The high-tech surveillance thriller may glory in state-of-the-art devices encountered by movie characters but give little sense of the huge growth in everyday life of social discrimination produced by their mundane counterparts. And even a classic like *The Conversation*, though admittedly structured by surveillance, could be said to explore the subtle and delicate psychology of surveillance, or even its ethics, rather than its large-scale social and political implications. Similarly, the Cannes and Toronto prize-winning *Red Road* (2006) is certainly structured by, but not necessarily 'about', surveillance. Although the central character, Jackie, is a Glasgow CCTV operator, and the plot hinges on how her personal life becomes entangled with someone she sees on one of her screens, it is hard to imagine that this movie will offer the 'informed scepticism' of an Orwell or a Kafka, or of more surveillance-evaluative films.

There may be oblique and subtle criticisms of mass surveillance here, as Mike Nellis suggests, but what it amounts to is that we should not take too seriously the technological apparatus: 'Far from being omniscient, the few who watch the many, unseen and from a distance, have in fact no real understanding of what is really, humanly, going on in front of their eyes.'[2] Scanned streetscapes show surfaces; most of what matters is missing. Although *Red Road* touches briefly on some possible but controversial benefits of CCTV – crime prevention – and some problems of the abuse of CCTV systems, this is not its main point. Indeed, Nellis suggests that Andrea Arnold's otherwise sophisticated and beautiful film could be read as a shrug towards surveillance, just because surveillance 'misses the point' about the deep and daily realities of life. True, CCTV is portrayed as a fact of life, which apparently is how many in the UK experience it. But it seems that audiences will have to wait for the movie that says more than 'get over it!'

Domesticating Big Brother

If the classic surveillance novels depict life under the oppressive gaze, and the 'cinematic society' unmasks the voyeuristic desire to watch, then the advent of 'reality TV' turns the lens once more to focus on the desire to be watched. The ironies here are manifold. As if it were not enough that the fearsome figure of Big Brother should become absorbing, escapist entertainment and that visibility should become an enjoyable 'trip' rather than a 'trap' (as Foucault's discussion of the Panopticon conceived it), reality TV also reverses the conventional notion that there are sacrosanct 'private' spaces in bathrooms and bedrooms; these are now 'public' in all their banal, mundane and earthy glory. But the irony is really only available to those with an historical sense of the sea-change from post-World War II worries to postmodern parody.

Although reality TV is by definition not part of *cinematic* society, Denzin's comments on the latter help frame the former (and in any case, the convergence and integration of 'new media' in the early twenty-first century cast doubt on the categories that contain only one *kind* of medium). Denzin suggests that 'primitive-realist' cinema of the early twentieth century introduced the screen voyeur in ways suited to the more local capitalism of the time; modernist cinema kept the gaze alive but distanced from everyday life, although the voyeur was parodied in 'late modern' times. But 'with the postmodern the gaze is openly acknowledged, and its presence everywhere, including in the living room, is treated as commonplace' (Denzin 1995: 9). These words were written before *Big Brother* made its debut, but their relevance to that genre is evident. Indeed, they are arguably so in ways that go beyond what Denzin explores, especially in relation to the postmodern affinity with the multinational-consumerist phase of capitalism.

For Vincent Pecora, 'reality TV elaborates surveillance as a sublime object of desire' rather than a means of social regulation and discipline (although he also distinguishes it – mistakenly, I think – from the 'ever deeper penetration of market research into our lives'; Pecora 2002: 348). Pecora discerns a connection between, on the one hand, the 1930s Collège de France experiments aimed at understanding through community participation in 'sociological experiment' and, on the other, the surveillance-driven game shows of reality TV. He claims, plausibly, that they simulate sociological 'laboratories', display the normative conditions of collective solidarity, explore nostalgically the rituals of social ostracism and see how far individuals will go in manipulating group loyalty to achieve success (Pecora 2002: 353). However, while Pecora sees in reality TV some strong strands of narcissism (echoing its 'orgy of capitalist self-promotion'), he goes beyond Christopher Lasch's critique by that name (Lasch 1991).

Pecora links the desires of reality TV with those of 'enlightened social theory': a consequence of the 'demand to make the socially hidden visible, to expose the secret workings of individual choice and group authority and to create the increasingly transparent life-world that philosophers from Jean-Jacques Rousseau to Jürgen Habermas have held up as an ideal' (Pecora 2002: 355). Moreover, what increasingly restrictive academic ethics reviews would prohibit is paraded as possible and desirable in reality TV. Pecora intriguingly suggests that while the desire for transparency will not necessarily drive the development of more surveillance, the desire for surveillance may have the paradoxical side-effect of turning us into real-time participants in a social psychology experiment where we are both test subjects and clinical observers. Foucault's Panopticon meets Baudrillard's hyperreality.

Such an elite perspective is brought down to earth by John McGrath, however, who argues that in contemporary societies we inhabit more and more a 'surveillance space' that is beyond 'public' and 'private' (McGrath 2004). Moreover, this space is one in which 'performative effects' (see Butler 1993) are produced that constitute identities. McGrath maintains that crime control is the key ideology justifying the use of surveillance technologies in public space, and that as such surveillance spaces have emerged, so they generate a variety of (performative) behaviours. But so, for that matter, do surveillance art works, the genre that has appeared since the 1990s in art galleries, installations and in street theatre (e.g. the work of David Rokeby or Julia Scher). McGrath also discusses counter-surveillance activities, suggesting that these show both what deliberate responses achieve (and their limits) and the ways in which responses to surveillance space are not controllable by any single surveillance source.

As for *Big Brother*, McGrath holds that the kinds of desires for surveillance expressed in and promoted by these reality TV shows are becoming more important than crime control ideologies for justifying surveillance expansion. The on-camera performances function as a kind of analogy with the ways in which everyone has increasingly to come to terms with surveillance space. In the end, however, McGrath insists that today's surveillance spaces are very different from those worst-case scenarios that so preoccupied Orwell. As he says, '[T]he trashiness, repetitiveness and the occasional unexpectedness of this game show reminds us that, unlike Orwell's totalitarian eye, the many Big Brothers of our society can be submitted to partially and conditionally, can be played with and perverted. Unlike Winston Smith, we are not necessarily conceding defeat or loss of self when we admit to loving Big Brother' (McGrath 2004: ix).

Perhaps something else may be lost, however, that is left unmentioned by McGrath? For neither he nor Vincent Pecora mention the rather obvious relevance of the ratings – and thus of advertising – to the success of the *Big Brother* shows and their numerous spin-offs. While the spontaneity and unpredictability of surveillance space performances is a handy antidote to the over-determined spectre of surveillance as control, the imbrication of TV participants (on screen or in front of it) in the world of multinational-consumerist capitalism can hardly be irrelevant. For Mark Andrejevic, reality TV glamorizes surveillance, presenting it as hip and cool, a way into the world of wealth and celebrity (Andrejevic 2004a). It feels good to be watched, evidently, and as *Big Brother*'s Josh says, 'everyone should have an audience'.

In a sense, warns Andrejevic, reality TV fulfils the democratic promise of the emerging interactive economy, turning passive cultural consumers into active ones who can star on shows or vote on their outcomes. To Andrejevic, the real winners on these shows are the marketers, the corporations who have a high level of interest in seeing surveillance sold as soft and benign. The shows encourage the idea that self-revelation is innocent, even as customer relationship marketing seeks new ways of inducing people to self-reveal to them. What passes as 'self-expression' is actually re-interpreted as a kind of work in which consumers are unwittingly recruited to 'being watched' in ways that are primarily of benefit to those who 'watch' them. Such a perspective certainly fits with Denzin's comments about entertainment genres roughly paralleling economic developments, but it also could inspire objections based on the idea that those enamoured of reality TV are mere unwitting dupes of a capitalist conspiracy. While this debate is still open, it is worth recalling McGrath's comments about performativity. They hint that it is a mistake to think that all those involved in *Big Brother* either as participants or as viewers have similar motives. Or should one assume what Andrejevic implies: that the programme's aficionados simply 'love' Big Brother to their own loss?

Cultures of surveillance

Surveillance in modern times has become a phenomenon that affects everyday life and thus it has also become the stuff of popular culture, cropping up in novels, songs, films and other media and venues. As such, our understanding of surveillance is in part shaped by these popular media, from being sensitized by literary metaphors to vicariously sharing the vision of those who peep, snoop, observe and gaze. But because this is so, those popular media affect in turn the surveillance that they depict, as consumers of media are also subjects of surveillance.

Contemporary surveillance occurs in contexts that are already media-saturated. Electronic means of entertainment, leisure and even education operate alongside the media of surveillance and indeed are sometimes part of a two-way exchange. In film, novels and television, surveillance situations and processes are portrayed and analysed, and beyond those the internet provides games and spaces where surveillance may be explored as well as experienced. How they do this is worth examining carefully; as we have seen, some help us grapple with the 'gaze' more intelligently, some help the gaze drift out of focus. Some aid critique, some, complacency. In the worlds of theme parks, shopping malls and for that matter online computer games, too, surveillance is not merely an external process but something participatory.

The overlapping and cross-cutting cultures of surveillance may be reinforced and normalized by their interactions with entertainment media.

While the interactivity of TV may have important surveillance repercussions, as yet only at an early stage of analysis, interactivity takes on other dimensions in the world of surveillance games. No doubt other leisure sites exist that are marked by high surveillance levels, such that the experience of enjoyment and fun comes to be associated with monitoring and control. But this is certainly explicit in the case of games. As Anders Albrechtslund and Lynsey Dubbeld remark: 'In many computer and video games, surveillance, i.e. the tracking and tracing of people through data-processing technologies, became an intrinsic part of the gameplay' (Albrechtslund and Dubbeld 2005: 218).

Albrechtslund and Dubbeld comment on internet games such as the *Guardian*'s 'Blair Watch Project', which gave prizes for photos of UK Prime Minister Tony Blair that would be displayed online, and on the online *Monopoly Live* game. Players imagine a 'real' London in which the game takes place, but it also involves 18 real London cabs as movers. Earlier games include *The Sentinel* (1986), which is a power struggle about controlling 'synthoids' that are under the Sentinel's gaze, or *Sims* (2000), in which a virtual doll house is controlled and cared for by the all-seeing player. Albrechtslund and Dubbeld note that so far from these games questioning the legitimacy of surveillance practices, surveillance is never even problematized. Rather, the games simply make surveillance fun. That it can be such ought at least to be acknowledged by serious surveillance scholars, even if it is lamented for other reasons.

As we have seen, the domestication of the dreaded Big Brother in reality TV thus has surveillance consequences well beyond what 'domestication' initially suggests. As Mathiesen argues, the TV 'synopticon' where the many watch the few parallels and reproduces the 'Panopticon' where the few watch the many (Mathiesen 1997). The spectacle that Foucault thought had been superseded is actually crucial to the effectiveness of some of its supposed disciplinary replacements. And as Andrejevic shows, not only do many 'expressive' TV shows encourage display and visibility, but also all kinds of 'interactivity' (such as voting on reality TV) help to expand the consumption of goods and services as well as TV itself (Andrejevic 2004a).

This point is underscored by Serra Tinic (2006), who offers a timely reminder that the TV audience – media consumption – is itself highly monitored and likely to become more so. Interactive television (ITV), currently represented by companies such as TiVo and Replay, promises to circumvent all the timing inconveniences of conventional television and also to give opportunities to delete commercials. What seems to be audience empowerment and the personalization of tele-visual worlds has another side, argues Tinic. This theme is picked up as well in the more recent work of Mark Andrejevic (2007), who high-lights the ways in which the interactivity of emerging computer- and TV-based entertainment technologies has increasingly significant sur-veillance dimensions.

The personalization of interactive television works both ways, as data from viewing preferences are fed right back to the TV companies, without having to be aggregated, as in the traditional ratings. It is a difference machine, a panoptic sort – all the more so in the integrated future when, using the same equipment, subscribers will watch their chosen shows, surf the Web, message friends and bank online. Synergy and Claritas are already providing psychographic audience profiles to complement data gleaned from enhanced ITV (Tinic 2006: 315). Whether this is exactly what will emerge in this volatile field is unclear, but Tinic's work surely indicates a likely path, given present trends in consumer surveillance.

Surveillance and entertainment media all depend today on elec-tronic infrastructures in which the many 'watch' the few and the few 'watch' the many, both literally and literarily, but always in ways medi-ated by technologies. This is yet another reason why the outcomes of surveillance cannot simply be extrapolated from the supposed capa-cities of new surveillance technologies or from the apparent power of the agency deploying them, even if this is the mighty Department of Homeland Security.

Studying popular culture may help us learn about surveillance in more than one sense. On the one hand, insights into the inner work-ings of surveillance may be gleaned from popular culture. Today's media are subtly aware of ways in which surveillance has moved on a long way from *Nineteen Eighty-Four*. On the other, it is worth investi-gating how popular culture may facilitate further surveillance. It is clearly a mistake to assume that the imaginative world of film or TV exists in an entirely separate realm from everyday reality. They feed off and inform each other increasingly in a media-saturated environ-ment. In the end, the efficacy of surveillance measures themselves may depend in part on how they are understood by their subjects, which by any measure must relate in some ways to popular culture.

While it would be a mistake to ignore the contribution of popular culture to understanding surveillance, there are decided limits to what can be said. Much work remains to be done in exploring the connections, some of which may turn out to be important in ways that we cannot guess at today. The growth rate of new systems for blogging and interactive sharing of ideas and images on the internet – systems such as YouTube and its cognates – alone means that this field of study is likely to be a growth area. Beyond this, of course, questions of how to interpret audience interest and ratings will always be in dispute. And just as it is risky to rely on the technical limits of surveillance systems to protect people from their potentially negative effects, so it would be foolish to imagine that anything definitive let alone optimistic could be said about the chances of popular media contributing to a thoroughgoing assessment of contemporary surveillance. This is why we turn next to an analysis of modes of questioning and resisting surveillance and then to some ethical resources for offering some fresh ways forward. Issues of surveillance are too significant merely to be confronted indirectly.

8 Struggles over Surveillance

Humans are wonderfully inventive at finding ways to beat control systems and to avoid observation.

Gary T. Marx (2003: 372)

Surveillance may serve various purposes, from entitlement and easing entry to coercion and control. It may even serve more than one purpose at once. Entitlements, for instance, require registration, a process that is equally used to limit and control access. This applies to everything from registering for an email account to registering as a refugee at a national border. In order to work, however, many surveillance processes depend on the involvement, witting or not, of those who are surveilled. In the example given, registration represents one moment of such involvement. The persons surveilled are not merely subject to surveillance but subjects of surveillance. They will approach situations as diverse as email or refugee registration with expectations, hopes, fears and caution. In those contexts where surveillance is perceived as or has the effect of control, the fact that its subjects interact and react with surveillance means that its effects are mitigated or magnified in part in relation to their involvement.

Another way of putting this is that ordinary people find myriad ways of coping with surveillance – resigning themselves to it, finding modes of settlement that retain some dignity or freedom, or, on occasion, openly objecting to the gaze in whatever shape it takes. Some of these struggles over surveillance are carried out in isolation as individuals switch off devices, falsify identifying information, hide their faces from the camera or otherwise dissimulate. (One of the earliest uses of the word 'dissimulation', in the mid-fifteenth century, refers to the tactics used by small birds to evade the sight of their larger predators.) Other struggles are undertaken in concert with others, either directly against

159

surveillance or against the institution or process that inspires or under-writes it. Such larger movements may betoken a social movement proper, although it would be difficult to claim this at present.

Is it worth having a separate chapter on 'struggles', given that in every sphere where surveillance operates, some sort of friction, if not full-blown countervailing force, also appears? Just as the chapter on popular cultures of surveillance highlights media immersion as a key dimension of contemporary life, sometimes omitted in other studies, so this focus on struggle is intended as an antidote to studies that stress merely the potential of new surveillance technologies, and thus produce a sense of powerlessness or pessimism, or that analyse the relations of surveillance without offering studies of how specific groups may be disadvantaged or privileged and what might be done about it. This chapter deliberately focuses attention on the perceived troubles with surveillance and the tensions and turmoil that may ensue as they become political concerns.

In the twenty-first century, surveillance issues are increasingly sig-nificant for large-scale power and politics as well as in the processes of everyday life. Many government, commercial and military pres-sures push the politics of surveillance front and centre. Not a day passes without surveillance being in the news, from ever-expanding border controls (especially in the USA) to cases of identity theft and wrongful disclosure and right down to who has access to high school records and CCTV footage. It touches the largest matters of interna-tional concern – how did US authorities obtain information in Canada that led to the detention and year-long torture of Canadian engineer Maher Arar? – to mundane decisions about whether or not to use the internet to buy train tickets, due to uncertainty about what might happen to those sensitive data.

All surveillance is nuanced and varies immensely in intensity. Some is beneficial or relatively innocuous, and yet some is disturbing and dangerous. All surveillance invites careful assessment; some calls for critique and possibly more. Gary T. Marx's comment, quoted at the head of this chapter, may safely be taken as an accurate statement, in this case based on many years of research. But it has to be said that some surveillance systems present considerable challenges to human inventiveness at opposing oppressive control or evading the gaze. As is clear from other chapters in this book, this, too, depends on cultural contexts, prior conditions, power differentials, subject-knowledge and many other factors. Post-9/11 conditions alone are thrusting numerous challenges into the foreground, from how asylum-seekers may be criminalized at borders by association with terrorism, to how academic freedom is threatened by demands to teach, research and publish within limits prescribed by a 'state of exception'. In the one case, surveillant categories have the power to free captives or crush hope at borders, while in the other stringent steps are taken to find out who is on the 'wrong side' in a climate not seen in the USA since the McCarthy years of intolerance and repression.

For Anthony Giddens, theorizing modern conditions, a 'dialectic of control' is set up whereby the growing power of institutions calls forth countervailing responses, and this may be seen in the case of surveillance, in workplace, political and other contexts. For much of the time, and for a variety of reasons, people comply with surveillance, but they may also variously negotiate and resist, and these circumstances and processes deserve exploration. This chapter looks at some of these circumstances and processes and tries to make some sociological sense of them. At certain junctures, the dialectic of control – if that is the best word – produces regulatory and legislative change, for instance around the concept of privacy. However, in policy realms, privacy has largely lost whatever social dimensions it once possessed and today's issues are better thought of in social justice terms, to do with distribution and civil liberties.

The 'fair information practices' (see below) embodied in privacy and data protection law do speak at least obliquely to issues beyond mere privacy, but surveillance, I shall argue, is best seen within a broader terrain of today's politics of information. That is, struggles over surveillance may as frequently be seen as struggles over some other conditions or processes of which surveillance is a symptom or an effect. Either way, surveillance is once again shown to be a dynamic and fluid process, a far cry from the rigidly menacing machinery of some latter-day Orwellian dystopias. After all, it should be recalled, these dystopias themselves at least hint at system breakdown or some vindication or even victory for victims.

A dialectic of control?

It is one thing for social scientists to demonstrate that we live in surveillance societies as employers, government departments, credit card companies, banks, police, insurance companies and marketers gather and process more and more personal data. It is another to explain how this situation is understood by those supposedly 'under surveillance' and how ordinary people respond to the growth of surveillance societies. To get this in perspective, though, some important reminders are in order.

First, to reiterate, surveillance is ambiguous. It patently does not make sense to consider surveillance simply as a sinister or socially negative phenomenon. The garnering of personal data by institutions frequently facilitates entitlement, efficiency, convenience or security. The fact that it may have sinister or suspect sides does not negate this. Second, surveillance processes are subtle and complex. The processing of personal data may be carried out similarly by different institutions – say, a bank and a welfare department – but with very different effects. Moreover, the same surveillance technology, such as CCTV cameras, may be seen in a quite different light by different people, such as women and men. Indeed, the same people may see cameras differently at the same time. Some drug-users in Greenwich Village, New York, for instance, see cameras both as a means of spotting illegal behaviours and as ensuring their safety. Although they know that the cameras are intended to check illegal drug activity in a public park, they also look to them for protection should a fight break out (Yesil 2006).

Another point to be borne in mind is that the hardware and software of surveillance are not infallible, despite their promoters' hype. This does not necessarily mean that there is 'safety in the machine' in the sense that it is reasonable to assume that surveillance systems have much more limited capacities than their official specifications might suggest (see Bogard 2006). But it is worth remembering that the techniques used to process personal data are intrinsically limited and subject to failure or error, quite apart from how they may be overridden or subverted by operators or users. At the same time, anyone who doubts the wisdom of establishing a new surveillance system or of enhancing an existing one cannot afford to relax their vigilance on the grounds that the technology is less effective than advertised by designers and marketers.

Given these caveats, we can examine the ways in which people comply with surveillance as well as negotiate with it, which help to place in clearer focus the circumstances under which surveillance may actively be resisted. Even within the realm of 'active resistance', of course, many variations occur. For some, active resistance entails exerting political pressure to obtain legal limits on how personal data are collected and stored or who may obtain access to them and under what circumstances. But for others it may mean evasion or dissimulation, or perhaps direct action, such as burning passbooks, as anti-apartheid activists did in pre-1991 South Africa, or spraypainting CCTV camera lenses, as indignant Athenians did when the Olympic security machine invaded their city.

In his careful attempt to explain surveillance as an institutional dimension of modernity, Anthony Giddens, as noted above, invokes a 'dialectic of control' in which the presence of a negatively perceived surveillance generates opposition. The analogy is with capitalism, whose exploitative character provokes counter-tendencies in labour unions and socialist action, or with modern forms of patriarchy, which seem to call forth liberation and feminist movements that try to undermine them. Giddens' proposal is that 'free speech movements' constitute the countervailing power to modern surveillance, and this could be updated by considering the role of freedom of information as an antidote to excessive or secretive forms of surveillance.

Leaving on one side the question of how this proposal could be taken up positively in further ways not conceived by Giddens,[1] I want to suggest that the whole institutional approach is only a part of the story of power and control. Giddens' analysis relies on a model of surveillance in which the nation-state has a predominant role. But not only have corporations outstripped the capacity of state administration to undertake mass surveillance in the twenty-first century, the surveillance activities of many corporations themselves have now become part of a large ensemble of governance alongside and intertwined with government administration. This does not so much negate Giddens' work as demand more subtle ways of approaching the topic of resistance to surveillance.

Compliance

The term 'struggles of surveillance' suggests that surveillance is always perceived negatively, as something to be questioned, if not combated. But surveillance may also be welcomed as an ally, an alibi or an ark, or at least accepted with resignation or reluctance. Indeed, for most of the time, surveillance is met with compliance.

Today's social and economic world is so deeply permeated by surveillance practices and processes that it is simply impossible to know about all that happens using our personal data, let alone respond intelligently or imaginatively to it. Apart from anything else, we tend to take for granted certain kinds of surveillance, such as CCTV cameras or PINs for bank transactions, so that we think nothing of their presence.

Knowledge of surveillance is another issue affecting compliance. Checking dietary preferences when you book an airline ticket may seem a sensible and necessary bit of surveillance – no one wants to be hungry on a long flight because they failed to specify what food they could eat – but if you knew that these details could be used for racial or religious profiling, your attitude may well be different. As well, in contexts where 'privacy' is emphasized as a cultural good, it might never occur to you that other issues might attend the gathering of personal data. Young people in Canada who use instant messaging, for example, are mainly concerned about the local context of their activities and the content of the messages on their screens. They feel safer at their computers in their own rooms than in a public access library, and while they will guard their messages from the prying eyes of parents or roommates, they show little evidence of concern about what the messaging service might do with the data they collected in order to register. There is always the risk of lack of security with messaging services, such that data could end up in inappropriate hands. Moreover, there is constant pressure to share personal data (use-levels and usages rather than content) for commercial gain.

For most of the time, and in most contexts, people comply with surveillance. If the system is accepted as legitimate and necessary, then it is unlikely that anyone will question it – assuming that so-called 'data-subjects' know exactly what is going on. People key in their PINs, use their passes, scan their RFID entry-cards, give out their Social Insurance numbers, swipe their loyalty cards, make cell-phone calls, present their passports, surf the internet, take breathalyser tests, submit to face or iris scans and walk openly past CCTV cameras in routine ways. Few stop to think what the surveillance might mean or where the data go. They simply acquiesce with the system. Indeed, if people did hesitate, let alone withdraw willing cooperation, everyday social life as we know it today would break down.

Negotiation

If compliance is questioned, however, some sort of negotiation takes place. Whether relating to some sense of space ('this area is private') or dignity ('why exactly do you need a urine sample?') or control ('I have a right to control the circulation of information about me'), surveillance may not be refused or blocked so much as queried with a view to finding agreement. This approach also underscores the ways in which surveillance is not a static, relentless or unyielding process. Rather, in many contexts it is dynamic and amenable to modification. It is malleable, flexible, and the product of game-like processes in which, though the overall rules may stay the same, the outcomes are far from determined in advance.

Good examples may be found in the realm of information-processing organizations such as banks or call centres, those information age workspaces of outsourced business that have sprung up in many countries around the world since the mid-1990s. Because electronic communications and information transfer are central to their operations, they invite various applications of electronic monitoring. For this reason, computer-based performance monitoring (CBPM) has been the source of some controversy in the industrial relations field and provoked the response that this kind of surveillance simply leads to greater management control over workers at their terminals. It would hardly be surprising if this were so, given that in the case of call centres, flexible production is central, and labour costs are cut dramatically by shifting them offshore. CBPM enables management to observe workers without being seen in what seems like a classic panoptic sense.

Yet Kirstie Ball and David Wilson show that this simple conclusion is unwarranted (Ball and Wilson 2000). Their studies of actual banking and call centre practices, including the roles played by the employees, demonstrate that the outcomes may not be straightforwardly 'read off' the technologies or the managerial intentions. While not denying that CBPM is a technology of power intended to appraise, evaluate, provide feedback on workers and broadcast these data back into the workplace, they show that each local situation exhibits differences that produce varying outcomes. While management may seek to constitute the 'productive worker' using CBPM, employees themselves are only *relatively* normalized to this as they, and management, develop different 'interpretive repertoires' (or 'discourses') to construct their accounts of what goes on and to create practices in relation to them.

Ball and Wilson studied a British building society (trust company) call centre and a bank cheque-processing centre and discovered several distinct interpretive repertoires in operation, such as 'life-in-work', 'legitimate authority', 'power-through-experience' and 'empowerment'. These repertoires enabled employees and managers to see themselves in relation to others in a variety of different ways that generated a range of outcomes. For instance, a manager who presents himself as someone with whom employees can talk differs from one who distances himself by emphasizing the rules, and this affects the ways in which consent and compliance are obtained using CBPM. The 'objective' panoptic 'unseen observer' actually appears differently depending on the repertoires in use, such that, as Ball and Wilson conclude, 'the arguably panoptic technologies of power – CBPM and appraisal – are enmeshed within discourses which produce and reproduce relations of power and resistance in the workplace' (Ball and Wilson 2000: 562). It is within such discourses that surveillance power is negotiated.

Resistance

When the neighbour pulls down the blinds to prevent others seeing into her home, she is resisting surveillance. It is important to her to retain her privacy, and covering the window is a practical technique for evading any unwanted gaze. When workers complain to the labour union that they find the surveillance cameras in the rest area intrusive and unnecessary and the matter is taken up at an official level, surveillance is likewise resisted. Such complaints are often met with some compromise solution that allows employers to continue to use CCTV cameras in 'work' spaces but not where employees are relaxing. When whole municipalities or even states refuse to comply with some new regulations – for instance, the requirement to submit personal data to a central registry for an ID card, as has happened recently in both the USA and Japan – surveillance is resisted once more.

In each case, objections are raised and expressed to some surveillance process that is felt to cross some line, transgress some boundary. They range through the personal and domestic boundary of the home, the leisure-time boundary between monitored work spaces and rest areas over which workers feel the boss has no jurisdiction, and the administrative boundary protecting ordinary citizens from the incursions of state power. The first is not organized, although the latter two are. But a question that might be raised is whether resistance has to be organized to count as such. Clearly, the labour union organizes resistance, as does the activity of citizens concerned about invasive or liberty-denying regulation. But housewives who cover windows or teenagers who circumvent online systems designed to check their surfing are hardly organized, yet what they do is oppositional towards certain surveillance practices.

Ordinary, unremarkable resistance may take place involving only one or two individuals, and this type of resistance is *ad hoc* and spontaneous. And just as surveillance is normally yoked to some purpose beyond mere watching for its own sake, so resistance to surveillance may be a side-effect of some other intention. For instance, John Gilliom offers some rich interview materials from his studies of 'welfare mothers' in Ohio, discussed in chapter 4, who successfully evade and dissemble before the apparently indomitable 'CRIS-E' welfare surveillance system (Gilliom 2001). Aspects of their lives remain opaque to the authorities despite the highly intrusive activities of the caseworkers and the capacities of the computer system intended to make comprehensive inventories of their existence. But they do not see their activities as 'resisting surveillance', merely as ensuring that their children are adequately cared for, despite their straitened circumstances.

A useful taxonomy of everyday resistance modes has been compiled by Gary T. Marx (2003). He rightly reminds us that just because a surveillance system has been installed does not mean that it will have the effects desired by its installers, for both technical and human-social reasons. To quote him, 'The individual is often something more than a passive and compliant reed buffeted about by the imposing winds of the more powerful, or dependent only on protest organizations for ideas about resistance' (Marx 2003: 372). Creative responses to surveillance proliferate along with awareness that surveillance affects our everyday lives. Marx also cites Goffman's (1961) study of the underlife of organizations, saying that 'when individuals feel that surveillance is wrong, or that they are unfairly disadvantaged by it, it will often be challenged. Systems also may be challenged for reasons of self-interest' (Marx 2003: 372).

Marx offers eleven distinct (though sometimes linked) types of surveillance neutralization: discovery moves, avoidance moves, piggybacking moves, switching moves, distorting moves, blocking moves, masking (identification) moves, breaking moves, refusal moves, cooperative moves and counter-surveillance moves. Each constitutes a form of resistance or non-compliance.

Marx sees the'strategic actions' of both watchers and the watched as moves in a game, although, unlike other games, the rules may not be equally binding on all players. 'Discovery' involves the actor finding out that he or she is under surveillance, for example by using a device to warn of photo radar traps on the highway. 'Avoidance' is a passive kind of resistance where the subject evades surveillance, for instance by not using stores with loyalty cards or not filling out warranty forms. 'Piggybacking' can be achieved by acknowledging the surveillance but using another's identity, such as crossing a 'secure' threshold following someone with an electronic key. 'Switching' is similar but would entail actually using the ID of the other. Vincent does this in the movie *Gattaca* in order to simulate his 'validity' (see chapter 7). In the same family of moves, 'distortion' alters the evidence, as when a monitored keyboard worker holds down keys to give the impression of greater productivity or when someone taking a polygraph has a tack in his or her shoe to create 'stressful' results for baseline factual questions.

'Blocking' and 'masking' are similar strategies. The former might be wearing a low hat when in sight of CCTV cameras while the latter could be using an assumed name for a loyalty card or access to a website. 'Breaking' or 'refusing' are even more blatant. In the one instance, the surveillance device may be disabled (spraypainting a CCTV camera), and in the other, the subject will not part with the required data, such as the telephone number or postal code during a transaction in the store. The final two are of a different nature again. 'Cooperative moves' occur when a third party prevents or minimizes the surveillance. Again, *Gattaca* provides an illustration, as when a doctor testing urine results records a 'valid' rather than 'in-valid' out of sympathy, which is similar to some caseworkers in Gilliom's research sample who side with the 'welfare mothers', colluding with their evasion.

Marx does not suggest that this taxonomy proves that individual resistance is widespread, and indeed he sets out a research programme to test some of his hunches in a more sociological fashion.

But his point is well taken, that everyday examples of resistance do indeed occur frequently and examples can be culled from a number of already existing studies. Neither does Marx argue that his examples indicate anything about the general weakness or vulnerability of surveillance systems in the face of 'human ingenuity'. He freely acknowledges that power imbalances in most surveillance systems are considerable and that the moves he lists may seem trivial in light of the technical capacities of those systems and the fact that, once again, full knowledgeability on the part of the subjects is assumed. It is, of course, much harder to gauge situations where the subjects of surveillance remain in the dark about who knows, sees or hears what.

Again, it takes little imagination to see that in North America and Europe particularly, post-9/11 developments in 'national security' have tilted surveillance sharply towards control in a number of areas. Under such circumstances, resisting surveillance may well be perceived at least in some circles as a necessary, if risky, option. Such contexts make a big difference to how surveillance is perceived and thus to how efforts to combat its negative effects are mounted.

Privacy and anti-surveillance movements

Beyond spontaneous and *ad hoc* responses to surveillance, various groups are dedicated to querying surveillance or at least to improving the prospects for data protection and privacy. Some of these are direct and some indirect; some are concerned about specific limits to surveillance, others about more far-reaching prohibitions. Some are long-term institutions with a well-recognized existence and rationale, others are shorter-term, even single-issue campaigns that speak to the concerns of the day. If one assumes that social movements are organized efforts by significant numbers of people to change some aspect of contemporary social life, then the sorts of groups engaged in these 'personal data' issues probably do not count as 'social movements' *per se*. There is nothing like the 1990s movements against corporate globalization or against environmental degradation in the realm of personal data. On the other hand, the political power of some such groups is formidable.

If one considers resistance of organized types, there are a growing number of national and international organizations and movements dedicated to countering everyday surveillance. One thinks of Privacy

International (PI), based in the UK, or the Electronic Privacy Information Center (EPIC), based in Washington, DC, or consumer champions such as Consumers Against Supermarket Privacy Invasion and Numbering (CASPIAN), from Massachusetts, or international groups critical of marketing surveillance such as Adbusters. Civil liberties and human rights groups (American Civil Liberties Union or ACLU in the USA or Liberty in the UK) often oppose surveillance, as do groups concerned about international policing or the treatment of immigrants (such as Statewatch in Europe). And as I already mentioned, labour unions frequently represent their members in cases of excessive surveillance in the workplace (see, e.g., Kiss and Mosco 2005), and groups that question ethnic or racial profiling object to surveillance that contributes to such invidious classifications.

To put some flesh on the bones of the types of movement mentioned above, the most obvious candidate for a 'privacy' operation would be Privacy International (PI), based in London, England. It also finds expression in some ironic activities like the annual 'Big Brother' awards that mockingly celebrate companies or government departments that have signally failed to protect personal data or whose invasions of privacy or breaches of security have been striking. In the USA a large-scale organization devoted to maintaining privacy and attacking unwarranted surveillance is EPIC. Its activities overlap in style with PI in so far as it does serious research and produces reports, but it is less committed to headline-grabbing tactics. Its reports are well researched and hard-hitting, however, and its website is well used. In other countries, by contrast, some groups exist to counter government surveillance more generally. Japan's Network Against Surveillance Technology (NAST) is a case in point. NAST brings together lawyers, civil libertarians, journalists, academics and others to raise awareness and to catalyse opposition to surveillance measures deemed undemocratic or invasive.

There are also groups whose activities relate to broader aims, such as protecting consumers or promoting civil liberties. The ACLU is a clear example of the latter, and it often produces research reports on matters pertaining directly to personal data. Equally, Statewatch in Europe is concerned with democratic governance in general, and not just personal data, but this organization produces very useful work, such as the report *Arming Big Brother* on the EU's security research programme (Hayes 2006), which has strong surveillance aspects. In the former totalitarian-governed societies of Eastern Europe, organizations such as the Hungarian Civil Liberties Union maintain vigilance against the fresh growth of surveillance.[2] On another front, consumer groups such as Adbusters and CASPIAN also contribute to struggles over surveillance. CASPIAN, for instance, has some specific targets, but researches important areas such as the shift from 'savings' (using loyalty cards) to 'segmentation' in which prices are geared to different classes of consumer. These are good examples of 'indirect' action in relation to personal data.

Lastly, in this very brief survey, one might mention the short-term, single-issue campaigns relating to surveillance or to personal data. While opposition to something like the 2004 Athens Olympics was concerted, it is perceived threats such as the introduction of national ID cards that tend to provoke serious coalitions of protest. In Australia in the mid-1980s street demonstrations and newspaper advertising initiatives alongside some technical objections and the discovery of legal loopholes prevented the development of an ID card at that time (Graham 1988). In the UK in 2004–6, the national ID card proposal became law despite some well-orchestrated popular opposition such as the NO2ID campaign[3] and serious scientific and parliamentary misgivings and critique. Other examples of short-lived protest movements might be cited, such as the temporary tactics of Copwatch in Toronto and Montreal, whereby ordinary citizens follow police cruisers in unmarked cars carrying video cameras to record their activities. It is unlikely that we have seen the end of short-term protests such as this, and while it is true that they hardly count as social movements proper, their temporary power is considerable.

Much more research needs to be done before an accurate picture may be constructed of why, how and where anti-surveillance groups are obtaining a voice or making a demonstrable difference.

Legislating privacy and data protection

One of the most important ways in which struggles over surveillance have been expressed since at least the early part of the twentieth century is through legislation. However, it was the computerization of records from the 1960s onwards that threw up the peculiar problems of information privacy and what came to be known as 'data protection' (mainly in Europe) that were addressed by law. Interestingly enough, the challenge of new technologies produced responses in a number of different countries that were both very similar to one another and addressed in a single piece of legislation (Bennett 1992; Flaherty 1989). Those early laws have had to be revised since the 1970s, when they started to appear, mainly because of the rapidity with which the social-technical situations have changed. In some cases, the issues have come to be seen in human rights terms, rather than in terms of 'privacy' alone (e.g. EPIC-PI 2006).

Since the advent of personal data-handling by computers, in the 1970s, many attempts have been made to legislate privacy and data protection. This was initially a country-by-country process, but the globalization of commerce and of law enforcement means that international standards are now sought. Indeed, Jean-Philippe Walter of the Swiss federal data protection authority argued to a meeting of data protection and privacy commissioners at Montreux in September 2005 that such global harmonization of privacy and data protection laws, especially in commercial and banking sectors, is an urgent priority. This became explicit in a declaration issued after the event.

In the USA, privacy law has existed since 1974, and within the EU, data protection activities have included law-making and policy since roughly the same time. In both cases there is a longer history that has to be borne in mind. Nonetheless, it was the sense that computer power was being used in ways that hastened the coming of 'surveillance societies' that prompted all these developments (Flaherty 1989). More recently, academic experts have called for standardization of these personal data-handling regimes, on a global level (Bennett and Raab 2006).

The laws enacted nearly all make reference to or are generative of 'fair information practices' (FIPs), which once again developed in both the USA and Europe in the early 1970s (Bennett 1992: 95–111). In the USA, these grew out of labour and trade law and did not make explicit reference to new technologies, whereas in the UK they were the original product of the British Computer Society, taken up by the *Report of the Committee on Privacy* (1972), better known as the 'Younger Committee' after its chair, Sir Kenneth Younger (Bennett 1992: 86). These principles, starting with 'Information should be regarded as held for a specific purpose and not to be used, without appropriate authorization, for other purposes', now inform most national and international activities in this area.

There is a spectrum of views on how effectual such privacy and data protection laws are in ensuring that people are fairly treated with respect to the circulation of data pertaining to them. Some take the cynical view that such legislation actually enables the most egregious activities of 'fishing expeditions' or sharing data across agencies to occur; the devil, they will say, is in the details such as fine-print 'routine use' clauses. In other words, legal requirements serve simply to give the impression that care is taken with personal data, while in fact all kinds of data-mining and social sorting occur unimpeded. And those legal requirements may not be worth much in practice, either, given the difficulties attending compliance in a field where few laws really have teeth.

Others take a more sanguine view, that legislation is relevant (though it does need constant updating) and that it does oblige those processing personal data to take steps – such as registration of databases in the UK – to demonstrate that their practices are in line with generally agreed FIPs. More generally, those supporting the idea of legislation would argue – as I do myself – that the presence of law helps to create a culture of care regarding personal data. It shows that some have taken this seriously enough to ensure that the law of the land places expectations on both data-processors and data-subjects, who have certain rights and responsibilities. Neither sheer cynicism nor optimistic reassurance seems the right approach, however. Legal measures do have some effects, but they certainly may not be expected to 'protect' personal data in the absence of cooperation from other agencies and in a climate where there is a constant willingness to upgrade the measures as needed.

In order to achieve some victory in the legal domain, struggles are often necessary. And even when laws have been established and are later revised or added to, some struggle may be needed to persuade parliaments and congresses that such measures really are vital to the well-being of citizens. Pressure groups and advocacy organizations working on the margins of the actual legal processes usually play a part in obtaining the eventual legislative change. But such groups also make a contribution to the 'struggles over surveillance' in their own right. Although these have not yet been studied systematically, it is worth examining the activities of such groups. While they may not count as a fully fledged 'social movement', they are undoubtedly influential in the field.

Varieties of privacy and the loss of the social

Struggles over surveillance frequently refer to the idea of privacy. This is seen in many contexts as the embattled terrain where surveillance is encountered. Yet questions of what is 'public' and 'private' are complex, and culturally and historically relative. In Western societies specific kinds of 'privacy' are thought to be important – bathroom activities or salary details, for example. In other countries, however, 'bathroom' activities may be less sequestered (there are no bathrooms in parts of rural India, for instance) and in countries like Japan salaries are more 'public' than in the West. Definitions of 'privacy' vary, even in the West, such that 'the right to be left alone' or 'the ability to control communications about oneself' may each count. The latter 'informational self-determination' position is similar to the 'my home is my castle' view, where each has an inviolable space – an information bubble.

In the West, privacy has some important connections with print culture and liberal democracy – each of which is in some difficulties in the early twenty-first century – and with 'possessive individualism' (Lyon 1994). The latter means that privacy is often construed as something we 'own' – hence the analogous idea of 'identity theft' – and as something that is primarily individual, as distinct from personal, common, social or shared (see Regan 1995).

Arguably the best-known writer on privacy, Alan Westin, originally entertained quite a broad view of privacy in his book on *Privacy and Freedom* (1967), in which privacy functions to provide and protect personal autonomy, emotional release, self-evaluation and limited and personal communication. But in the process of translating these ideas into legal and practical terms, and with the rapid growth of new surveillance technologies, some of the original social force of Westin's ideas has been lost. Valerie Steeves shows how the social dimension has slipped away from Westin's work, especially as it has been translated into technical and consumer contexts (Steeves 2005). It could be argued that this 'loss of the social' within a predominantly individualistic 'privacy' culture also deflects attention from the 'social sorting' aspects of surveillance.

Before turning to that question, however, it is helpful to distinguish several different dimensions of privacy, although it should be stressed that all these are affected by electronic data-processing capabilities.

Bodily privacy refers to data that may be extracted from or observed in connection with the physical body. In the West especially there is a common-sense assumption regarding the inviolability of the body. Communication privacy emerges from the democratic ideal of freedom of speech – or silence. Information privacy has to do with any kinds of textual or numerical data pertaining to an identifiable individual. Territorial privacy captures the idea that there may be spaces in which tracing, tracking or observing a person is inappropriate. Image privacy refers to control over the circulation of images or visual representations of the person (EPIC/PI 2006).

It also helps to understand that people have different perceptions of privacy, which vary across a broad spectrum of contexts, situations, historical moments and personal and group circumstances. In 2006 the Surveillance Project undertook a comparative nine-country survey of attitudes that looks at issues of surveillance – including issues such as airline passenger profiling after 9/11 – as well as privacy and control over personal information, in order to go beyond conventional treatments of these themes. Privacy is both understood and valued differently in different countries and is hard to stretch over the whole range of issues that are raised by concerns over surveillance. It continues to have some important salience, but at the end of the day, privacy is simply not the sole solution for surveillance.

Today's surveillance is multi-faceted, continuous, networked, and it may well appear or actually be beneficial to the individual. For example, if you want to rent a car in a foreign country, you seldom need a passport (a relatively stable, national, twentieth-century document), but rather require a credit card and a drivers' licence (dynamic, fluid, partial documents). As Felix Stalder points out, the conceptual framework has altered in the networked twenty-first century. We need means of confronting surveillance appropriate to such generally desirable connectivity and yet which address issues raised by the potential for unprecedented data-flows between organizations and countries (Stalder 2002: 124).

The real issue, from the point of view of rapidly proliferating and intensifying surveillance systems, is not how individuals should find the means to protect themselves and their data. For reasons of lack of technological information, or lack of knowledge of what is known about us, or because we may well benefit from some organization holding data about us, this emphasis is inappropriate. The real onus should be on those who have the power to process personal data to demonstrate that they do so in ways that are not negatively prejudicial to the individual or to certain groups. In democratic contexts, this seems entirely appropriate, especially in an era when power is enhanced by integration and thus the inter-operability of databases.

Legal measures do need overhaul from time to time, and everyone concerned about surveillance would do well to see this as an arena of 'surveillance struggle'. In Canada at the time of writing, a review of the federal Personal Information Protection and Electronic Documents Act (PIPEDA) is under way, and many hope that the review will give teeth to legislation about personal data. At present, too little is known about the law, and too frequently care with personal data – or 'privacy' – is seen more as an organizational or business risk than as a moral and social obligation. Violators, if they are ever confronted, face only small penalties. At the same time, much more transparency is needed in the processes of law enforcement. Whose data are passed to whom should be publicly known, along with the criteria that place them in certain crucial categories.

Globally, there should be agreements on the appropriate handling of personal data, not just to ensure higher levels of security or to increase the speed of commercial transactions, but because the issues are intrinsically important. These are not mere 'business risks' or 'casualties of the war on terror', but matters of democratic practice, social justice and moral obligation. Personal data pertain to human beings whose life-chances and choices are affected for good or ill. As I see it, this is where the debate on surveillance should begin: outside the box of common assumptions about privacy as an individual matter, the zero-sum game of security and liberty and the pernicious *non sequitur* that if you have nothing to hide you have nothing to fear.

Social sorting, civil liberties and the politics of information

For some, the advent of ubiquitous everyday surveillance means that we have reached the 'end of privacy'. In the sense that there are fewer and fewer 'places to hide' from networked, algorithmic surveillance, this is probably true. The term 'privacy' is also stretched almost to breaking point across a growing number of situations that relate to new conditions of restructuring and post-9/11 developments. It may be 'ending' in that sense, too. The fact that appropriate responses to issues raised by contemporary surveillance cannot be encapsulated in the single concept also suggests we have reached the 'end of privacy'. But these three senses of the 'end of privacy' are not good grounds for pessimism. They are a challenge to think about contemporary issues in contemporary ways (without abandoning ancient wisdom, of course, aspects of which inform FIPs).

The growth of surveillance in today's world is an outgrowth of the processes of modernity, particularly high-technology systems applied to the problems of bureaucratic control, efficiency, productivity and speed. Surveillance is an unavoidable aspect of living in twenty-first-century societies. But at the same time it is far from a neutral process, dependent as it is on modes of categorizing populations and treating people differently according to socio-economic status, ethnicity, gender, region, age, and so on. Social sorting raises a whole series of different issues beyond privacy. The challenge is one of democratic practice in the information age: to oblige organizations to handle personal data responsibly and fairly, to ensure that the highly consequential coding of databases is a transparent process, and thus not only to reduce the risks to the most vulnerable of further social exclusion and marginalization but also to maximize the potential of networked technologies in ways that benefit all.

In the twenty-first century surveillance is multi-faceted, and this seems to suggest that multi-faceted responses would be appropriate. One can consider both theoretical and practical resources for resistance (and of course this distinction is itself dubious; the two are mutually informing). Among the theoretical resources would be the recognition that as bodies and identities are centrally involved in surveillance, so these are strategic sites for critique. As Kirstie Ball suggests, the use of biometrics in an increasing number of contexts means that the body is a contested site and as such may be considered as a terrain of struggle (Ball 2006). This also invites forms of feminist analysis as allies. Closely linked with biometrics are processes of identification and verification, and these, too, are sites for struggle.

Finally, the ambiguity of identity in the real world may be a source of oppositional culture for surveillance as well, as Toshimaru Ogura points out (Ogura 2006). When there is pressure towards finding single unique identifiers (such as national ID cards and their related registry systems), the existence of multiple identities, both those produced bureaucratically and those generated by ordinary people

making transactions, is a constant challenge to the would-be hege-
monic system. Gary Genosko and Scott Thompson show how this has
been true historically, too (Genosko and Thompson 2006). When regulatory bodies such as the Liquor Control Board of Ontario attempted
to create identification systems to exclude certain 'deviants' from purchasing alcohol, individual consumers regularly found ways around
the exclusion. Using false IDs is one route; sending an authorized
substitute is another. Either way, the surveillance struggle centres on
identity and identification.

At the start of this chapter I suggested that while Giddens' notion
of the 'dialectic of control' offers some helpful insights into the
processes whereby modern social institutions generate their own
oppositional movements, it is a limited perspective. It does not
account for the ways in which governance is multi-faceted and spills
well over the edges of government administrative control, such that it
permeates the social body like veins or muscles. Also, it fails to see
surveillance as something that may be carried out in a peer-to-peer
fashion or in contexts where it might be viewed as desirable or even
fun (see chapter 7 on this). And although it is worth rethinking in an
informational context Giddens' own proposal that 'free speech movements' be considered as the cockpit of struggles over surveillance, the
field is actually much broader, as I hope I have shown.

The struggles over surveillance are manifold and appear everywhere. If one assumes that only the obtaining of legal limits on surveillance counts as a victory for oppositional groups who wish to curb
the profligate processing of personal data, then this may not be
obvious. Equally, if only organized groups with a public face – and
probably a website – count as legitimate countervailing forces to over-
expanded surveillance, then the struggles will again appear to be more
constrained (though this seems to be changing; new groups spring up
quite frequently, and effectively). But if we take account of the myriad
forms of spontaneous, *ad hoc* and secondary-level opposition to and
negotiation of surveillance, pursued within the warp and woof of
everyday life, for which I have argued in this chapter, then a much
more nuanced and subtle picture of the struggles of surveillance will
emerge.

9 Data, Discrimination, Dignity

If one doesn't ask the question, *'What are the data going to be used for?'*, the powerless cannot defend themselves.

Ursula Franklin (1996)

'Light and liquid' late modern societies (Bauman 2000) differ in some significant ways from the early modern worlds in which the Panopticon first appeared. From those days to Big Brother and beyond, there was a sense of 'mutual engagement' between supervisor and supervised, watcher and watched (Bauman 2000: 11). Now, by contrast, mobile and fluid electronically mediated relations mean that the many operators of today's manifold levers of power have replaced the single-handed 'inspector' of Bentham's building design, and they can slip away from view much more readily than even their elusive predecessor. Far more is known about individual details than Bentham's inspector could have dreamed, but far less is known about the surveillance among those who are watched than in the panoptic spaces of prisons and production lines.

Contemporary societies are marked by their individuation and individualism. Roughly speaking, individuation is what institutions do to us and individualism is our response, though it is a chicken-and-egg issue. Once, we may have thought of our identity as a given. Now, it is much more of a project, or so it seems. We are expected to 'make' our identities, self-consciously in the CV, or less so in our car and clothing choices. Such individualizing tendencies are bad news for citizens and for citizenship, because they encourage the sense that self-interest is paramount, rather than considering how the common good – the welfare of the city – may be the context for discovering personal welfare too. Indeed, many have wryly observed how citizenship is very often redefined as a 'consumer' or a 'client' relation. Individuation and individualism have, like cuckoos, pushed the legitimate offspring of citizenship out of the nest.

What does all this have to do with surveillance in the twenty-first century? Everything. Bauman's 'liquid society' is the context in which the new surveillance occurs. It is 'light' and mobile the more electronic technologies are involved. Unlike the fixed spaces of the Panopticon, surveillance now shifts and undulates, expands and contracts like the swell and tides of the ocean. Though much surveillance deals in large numbers, and often in aggregates, such as in health or consumer data, there's a constant thrust towards greater customization and thus individualization of data. Geo-demographics, for instance, may note that birds of a feather flock together in handily post-codable neighbourhoods, but marketers seek relentlessly for ways of combining those data with identifiable ones, not to mention mining them for yet more 'relationships'. And since the same electronic networks permit sharing data through increasingly porous institutional boundaries – Homeland Security covets those consumer data for instance, and not only from Americans either (Millward 2007) – ordinary people know less and less about how our data are used.

Yet as we have seen, how those data are used has consequences, some beneficial and benign, others prejudicial and even perverse. How those 'individuals' are categorized by surveillance systems makes a difference. Thus as Ursula Franklin notes in the speech from which this chapter's epigraph is drawn, while protecting 'individuals' is important, it is equally important to look at 'the sectors among the population who will need protection . . . vis-à-vis the new technologies, the data-mining' (Franklin 1996). She has in mind categories such as the poor, Alzheimer's sufferers or certain ethnic minorities. Now, problems raised by surveillance are often thought to be best addressed in the language of privacy. Yet privacy is very easily construed as an individual matter when in fact it both has profound social aspects (Regan 1995) and is limited in the extent to which it can deal with the social questions posed by surveillance today. All too often, surveillance is seen in 'individual' terms rather than in terms of 'citizenship'. So although it is common to see problems associated with surveillance addressed in the language of privacy – and thus I discuss some aspects of privacy here – we also have to go beyond privacy discourses if the real challenges of surveillance are to be confronted adequately.

As this book has shown, systematic, routine, everyday surveillance has mushroomed in modern times. This is why it is no surprise that interest in surveillance studies has expanded rapidly as well. In its contemporary, computer-assisted forms, surveillance has become mobile and global as well as fine-grained and networked. The pace of development means that it is hard to keep up analytically, let alone politically, with what is happening. But it does seem clear that in addition to some troubling instances of 'privacy invasion' and of errors and frauds that expose personal data to public or unauthorized view, surveillance is closely articulated with some major modes of governance, through its capacity for social sorting. It is significant, sociologically speaking, to see the ways in which, for example, theories of 'class' and 'race' may have to be modified to take account of electronically enabled classifications (see Burrows and Gane 2006; Gandy 2006b). But such challenges as these also point up some urgent ethical and political questions to which we turn our attention in this final chapter.

Because many surveillance processes occur within technical, commercial or administrative spaces that draw a veil (intentionally or otherwise) over how surveillance actually works, and because these processes are at the same time so consequential for groups and individuals, it seems appropriate to focus on the problem of transparency or openness. By transparency I refer to a quality of 'seeing through', and by combining this with openness I suggest that the public should have access to information about the modes and purposes of surveillance. I do not mean 'seeing through' in a cynical way, even though some surveillance certainly invites cynicism and I do not infer by openness that every act of surveillance should be known to the surveilled. In some extreme cases, for instance those discussed classically by Gary T. Marx in *Undercover* (1988), good reasons may exist for not informing targets that they are being surveilled. In the context of the use of personal data in corporate and government settings, transparency raises questions of how open and accountable organizations are to those whose data they handle. This concluding chapter is intended to show why transparency is indeed of utmost significance in the twenty-first century and why it will increasingly be so.

Here are three reasons why transparency is vital: one, the surveillance society and the safety state have a growing appetite for personal data, and this has profound social and economic consequences; two, the issues of what happens to those data and especially how they are used for sorting, profiling and discrimination are becoming central to the politics of information; three, personal data refer to embodied persons in real places whose freedom and dignity are at stake. Transparency is vital for a healthy democracy and for human dignity.

Of course, qualifications must be made. There are no easy answers for the profound questions raised by this book. Transparency is vital to democracy, but this does not necessarily mean that there is no place at all for secrecy. Georg Simmel, for instance, argued that in a divided society where some socio-political oppression exists, secrecy has some positive value for the protection of persecuted groups (Simmel 1906). Transparency should not be read here as some overarching require-ment. Equally, in contexts where opportunities for media manipula-tion are rife, there may be an appearance of openness, transparency and communication, but no accountability worth the name. The sug-gestions I make here are simply ones that connect with the main themes of the book, now read as a spur to ethical engagement and political action.

The three reasons why transparency is so important relate to some of the key conclusions of this book. Firstly, the appetite for personal data and its social and economic consequences is seen, theoretically, in the desire for system integration, for the assemblage, as well as in the arguments for sharing personal data across agencies that had no access to them in the first place. As we have seen, Homeland Security offers some of the most far-reaching examples of this, seeking out data from employers, from educational establishments, from busi-nesses that deal in transactional data, and from airlines owned and operated in other countries than the USA. But other organizations, such as Google, also evidence an apparently insatiable desire for per-sonal data, seen in features such as their search engine cookies or their Gmail service. As CEO Eric Schmidt says, 'Google . . . knows more about you' (Orlowski 2006). The voracious appetite for personal data is unlikely to diminish in the near future, especially as ubiquitous computing and 'Ambient Intelligence' wrap our lives ever more com-pletely in wall-to-wall surveillance (see, e.g., Phillips 2004).

Secondly, transparency is vital because of the uses of those personal data to enable social sorting, profiling and discrimination. In some important senses, surveillance is social sorting and, in a sense, vision and visibility both enable this and are extended by it. The categories seen are the seen categories. Although, as I have argued, categories are necessary to the running of complex organizations, those categories always have politics, to use Lucy Suchman's telling phrase (Suchman 1994). Those politics come into focus more clearly in interrogating the kinds of profiling and discrimination that are enabled. All too often, it is already-existing categories of 'race', nationality, gender, socio-economic status or deviance that inform and are amplified by surveillance, which then enable differential treatment to be given to the 'different' groups.

Thirdly, transparency is vital because surveillance affects embodied persons in real places whose freedom and dignity are at stake. Following from the previous point, those statistical and algorithmic categories are far from abstract in their consequences. They affect workers, consumers, suspected offenders, children, women, travellers, citizens, refugees and audiences in different but very tangible ways. The distanciation permitted by electronic surveillance networks is not unconnected to the possibilities for exploitation, abandonment or even violence that they may feed, for such remote control by definition avoids seeing faces; it deals in data. Paradoxically, the more that is 'seen' by surveillance, the less is seen of embodied persons in everyday life. And this is consequential for justice, fairness, liberty, and even for life.

Social sorting in the surveillance society and safety state

Surveillance societies exist wherever personal data-capture is woven into the texture of everyday life and where the constant clustering and sorting of groups and individuals has become so commonplace that it is unremarkable. Information infrastructures with their increasingly ubiquitous networks, on which so much contemporary social life depends in the global, urban spaces of the present, are conduits for data-flows, including, crucially, personal and group aggregate data-flows.

Much popular and academic discourse in the 1980s and 1990s referred to the steady dismantling of the 'welfare state' then taking place under neo-conservative restructuring regimes. But until the early twenty-first century, the contours of what might be replacing the guiding notion of 'welfare' were unclear. Now, however, a good case can be made, not for the replacement of one idea by the other but at least of 'safety' as a leading motif of government policy in the global

North and in some countries beyond. The safety state may be eclipsing the welfare state. But as in all such transitional stages, there are plenty of ways in which the welfare state still works together with the safety state.

The safety state depends extensively on surveillance data. Indeed, it is interesting to note that certain kinds of data, such as census data or geo-demographic data, once produced primarily by government departments for policy purposes, are now of great commercial interest. But these commercially based data in turn are now sought in the quest of security or of law enforcement, which relocates them back in state-oriented domains. The safety state and the surveillance society have a common interest in personal data, often the same personal data.

So what, then, is the perceived problem with this situation? How might personal data also be construed as a 'public issue' (to paraphrase C. Wright Mills 1959)? Personal data are used in many contexts, and that is what helps to keep the wheels of commerce and administration turning. The problem is that all systems that use personal data have specific purposes, a number of which may place certain groups in a bad light, or reduce opportunities for some, or even exclude some from full social and political participation. The inequalities of power and access that have always dogged human societies, and that are institutionalized in specific ways in capitalist societies, reappear in new guises in the so-called 'information era'. At the same time, some public rhetoric suggests that things are otherwise: that there's a level playing field, that opportunities are equal, that free choices operate in the marketplace. Yet the software codes that classify us are designed to distinguish between one group and another to enable people to be treated differently depending on the category into which they fall.

So the major risk represented by today's all-pervasive surveillance is not the erosion of privacy. This latter fear is mainly a product of modern Western 'possessive individualism' (McPherson 1962). While there are important aspects of privacy that are worth defending (see Lyon 1994), especially its social dimensions (Regan 1995), and legislation based on this concept (and associated fair information practices) that contributes to minimizing of risks of negative discrimination, a more direct approach is also needed. What require direct attention are the classification and profiling processes (which resort to the techniques developed within the individualized marketing field) that, favouring and confirming the formation of social stereotypes, determine both the attribution of privileges and rights and social exclusion.

The events of 9/11 have exasperated even more this tendency, especially in that profiling has returned with a vengeance to controversial and unrefined ethnic-racial type of categories. The big question then becomes: who defines these categories? Are they located in technical knowledge, dreamed up by database management software programmers, promoted by governments – especially the current US Administration – or certain agencies like the federal Department of Homeland Security? As we have seen, the answer is all the above and more. Certainly, and dangerously for democracy, this process is all too frequently out of the arena of public debate and is not therefore accessible for examination in civil society. The big need, as I see it, is for fresh forms of transparency linked with accountability.

In the late 1980s and early 1990s, in studying emerging surveillance systems, I was struck by the similarity between the work of Gary T. Marx and Oscar Gandy (1993). What Marx said about 'categorical suspicion' in his classic work *Undercover: Police Surveillance in America* (1988) seemed also to be true of what Gandy wrote about in *The Panoptic Sort: A Political Economy of Personal Information* (1993) – only in the case of the 'panoptic sort', which is about discriminating between different classes of consumer on the basis of their purchasing patterns and preferences, it is not so much 'categorical suspicion' as 'categorical seduction'. Although these are not exactly equivalent, and are operating in quite different spheres, there are similarities in the persistent effort to target groups and individuals using personal data analysis and algorithms. The potential consumer, like the potential offender, is singled out for attention by virtue of being identified as part of a group with certain characteristics. In one case, the goal is to attach suspicion, perhaps leading to a criminal charge. In the other, the goal is to seduce the individual into making purchases. Since the early work of Marx and Gandy a number of important studies have underlined this fact – classification and profiling are the socially and politically significant signs of contemporary surveillance. Stephen Graham's work on 'software-sorted' pricing systems for urban infrastructure, Richard Jones' work on 'digital rule' in criminal justice systems and Clive Norris' work on CCTV discrimination in urban areas all speak to similar issues (Graham 2004a; Jones 2002; Norris 2003; Norris and Armstrong 1999).

Interestingly, there is a resonance between customer relationship management (CRM) and Homeland Security practices for attempting to identify potential 'terrorists'. CRM is a business tool software for sorting between customers who are worth pursuing and retaining for their business and others who are unprofitable to the corporation. Data-mining is done to discover a range of details about customers and profiles are built to characterize them in certain types (in ways that are now much more sophisticated than the old 'database marketing' methods). On this opportunity calculus a whole marketing technique has been erected and it is growing in sophistication all the time. After 9/11, however, CRM companies were among the first to advise what became the Department of Homeland Security, not of who might be potentially excellent consumers within an opportunity calculus, but who might be identified as potential terrorists within a risk calculus. Curiously, in view of the different domains in which they originated, the methods are essentially the same – in quite different surveillance spheres similar methods of surveillance are growing side by side. Not only this, the law enforcement type of surveillance is keen to utilize not only the methods but also the data obtained originally for customer profiles. Those transaction records and checks on choices and preferences may also reveal much about the potential terrorist.

Once, one could raise the question, *'quis custodiet ipsos custodes?'* – 'who's guarding the guards?' or in surveillance terms, 'who's watching the watchers?', but this has to be spelled out more precisely today. 'Who defines the categories?' might be a pertinent question. When people's life-chances depend upon what category they have been placed in, it is very important to know who designed the categories, who defines their significance and who decides the circumstances under which those categories will be decisive. In the marketing case, customers may be 'fired' from their banks, refused credit or insurance, or simply dropped from receiving certain kinds of consumer information just because the corporation has deemed them 'unprofitable' to the business. In the law enforcement context, and especially where 'terrorism' is concerned, travellers may be mistaken for bombers because of some data connecting them with a particular country or even a name that associates them with a known terrorist. Jose Padilla, the so-called 'dirty bomber', has been held since 2002 under US anti-terrorism laws, but the charges against him – largely dependent on phone-taps revealing he had contact with others in the 'terrorist' category – have altered significantly since the original 'terrorist' accusation (Sontag 2007). And US Senator Edward Kennedy was stopped and questioned on a regular internal US flight because his name tallied with the name of someone on a 'watch' or 'no-fly' list (Goo 2004).

In both these cases the criteria for making the profiles are opaque to the persons whose data have been used for this purpose. Without strong safeguards it is easy for negative discrimination, prejudice and stereotypes to enter the process whereby classifications are made. But automated social sorting depends by definition on processes that are technical and in which secrecy is likely to be the order of the day. Businesses do not like to reveal the means whereby they privilege one customer and cease to have dealings with another, and law enforcement agencies are also unlikely to jump at the chance to disclose how they plan to trace and track suspects. Both the technical and the social factors involved here point towards ongoing obfuscation of the means whereby surveillance systems do their social sorting. Items that ought to be the topic of debate within civil society and that ought to have some democratic oversight are obscured through their technical complexity and because the agencies concerned do not provide the information (which is sometimes a matter of the failure to enforce data protection or freedom of information regulations).

While some assume that it is the responsibility of customers, travellers and others to protect themselves from the consequences of the use, misuse or abuse of their data, it seems more reasonable to argue that the organizations that process the data should be held accountable for how they use them. After all, they have the technical expertise that few ordinary people could hope to gain, they are the ones who benefit from the processing of the data (frequently more than those whose data are processed), and they control the large-scale systems that carry out the surveillance in the first place. The imperative of transparency is ever more urgent. Self-protection may have its place, but the accountability of data-processing organizations is more to the point given the disparity of power between individuals and organizations. But even 'transparency' in the sense of giving notice that persons are under surveillance, while a good start, is insufficient. In employment situations, for example, this may be abused by an employer who insists that 'fair warning' was given. But fair warning is not consent. Transparency and openness hint at something further: the possibility of active involvement of those under surveillance in determining the conditions under which certain kinds of surveillance are appropriate. This may not work in all circumstances, but a commitment to the dignity of persons and the integrity of their relationships suggests it as a general aim.

Politics of information and governance

The fact that the way our lives are shaped depends heavily on the kinds of data available about us means that the politics of information is an increasingly important arena for debate. Alongside matters such as intellectual property rights, algorithmic surveillance using networked databases has become a crucial component of governance. At present, however, this is not seen as a major political issue, despite what is known about the processes and despite the fact that many members of the public are increasingly concerned about certain aspects of this. Although survey data in this field must be treated with considerable caution (and we sometimes know less than we might just because of the difficulties attending surveys of this kind of opinion; see Haggerty and Gazso 2005), one may at least get an impression of some issues from public opinion polling.

Various public opinion surveys, especially those done in the USA, show that people object to web tracking especially when their data are linked to a profile. A March 2000 *BusinessWeek*/Harris Poll found that 89% of respondents were uncomfortable with web tracking schemes where data were combined with an individual's identity, and 63% were uncomfortable with web tracking even where the clickstream data were not linked to personally identifiable information. An August 2000 study conducted by the Pew Internet and American Life Project found that 54% of internet users objected to tracking (Pew Internet and American Life Project 2000: 2).

Similarly, such surveys find that people do not trust companies with their data and fear that abuses may occur in both public and private sectors. An April 2001 study conducted by the American Society of Newspaper Editors found that 51% of respondents were 'very concerned' and 30% were 'somewhat concerned' that a company might violate their personal privacy, while 50% were 'very concerned' and 30% were 'somewhat' concerned that government might violate their personal privacy. In the same study 52% reported that they had 'very little confidence' or 'no confidence at all' that private companies use personal information exactly the way they said they would. A February 2002 Harris Poll found that a majority of American consumers do not trust businesses to handle their personal information properly. An August 2002 First Amendment Center study found that 60% of respondents thought that the government possessed too much personal information about individuals.

At the same time, it is significant that many internet users cannot identify the most basic tracking tool on the internet: the cookie. In the above-mentioned August 2000 study conducted by the Pew Internet and American Life Project, 56% of internet users could not identify a cookie (Pew Internet and American Life Project 2000: 3). It remains unknown whether individuals can identify more sophisticated tracking tools, such as 'web bugs' or 'spyware'. This is significant because it indicates, unsurprisingly to all but computer enthusiasts, it seems, that people interact with these technical devices not as knowledgeable operators but as non-technical users. Logging on to the internet is no more a 'technical' activity than driving a car or boiling a kettle of water on the stove.

As well, a report released by the US Annenberg Public Policy Center in June 2005 shows that American consumers are largely unaware of how their personal information is used by businesses, and that they object to behavioural profiling, price discrimination and the purchase of their personal information from database companies. The report, based on a phone survey of 1,500 internet-using adults, further found that the respondents believe incorrectly that 'laws prevent online and offline stores from selling their personal information', and that 'stores cannot charge them different prices based on what they know about them'.

The Annenberg Report also showed that most internet users believe falsely that the presence of a privacy policy on a website means the site cannot share their personal information with others. Only 34% of those polled could name one of the big three consumer reporting agencies, while 72% believed falsely that charities are barred by law from selling personal information without permission and 73% believed falsely that banks are barred by law from sharing information with other companies and affiliates. Users want notice of how their personal information is collected, used and with whom it is shared. In the March 2000

BusinessWeek/Harris Poll, 75% of respondents indicated that privacy notices were either 'absolutely essential' or 'very important' (the polls are summarized in EPIC 2005). These concerns have not gone unheeded. Indeed, in parts of the business world, there seems to be a growing acceptance of the fact that people care about what happens to their data. Information management today includes commitments to openness and transparency as a basis for customer trust.

So how do people respond to surveillance? Just as there is no single all-encompassing surveillance 'plan', so there is no one line of resistance. We noted earlier Anthony Giddens' argument that surveillance practices and citizenship rights grew hand in hand in the modern era. In his 'dialectic of control', developments in power seem to call forth countervailing strategies on the part of those who may be considered in subordinate or marginal positions. So policing could be seen as a form of surveillance, along with government administration and the management of production. In each case, a struggle for recognition and rights occurs that enables those in subordinate positions to answer back and to find means of protection and the promotion of their rights.

Today, the means of governance has expanded even more such that not only production but also consumption is managed (and thus surveilled), and the means of identification and of movement have also become sites of contestation. But at many levels the dialectic of control still seems to hold. In addition to ambivalent surveillance, the terrain of technology is also ambivalent. The same means of expanding surveillance capacity may also be used in – sometimes unexpected – countervailing ways. Indeed, as information technologies have facilitated the growth of the surveillance society and the safety state, with their large-scale surveillance assemblages, so too they facilitate new means of questioning existing power formations and of undermining existing authorities through the dissemination of alternative outlooks and practices. The politics of information, which, though not moving quite towards centre-stage, is rapidly becoming more significant, includes prominently the issues of surveillance.

Varieties of surveillance experience

Surveillance is experienced differently in different organizations, different regions and in different countries. People who may not worry for a moment about frequent-flyer card systems may be very concerned about biometrics in passports. People who do not care about (or may even welcome) CCTV in public streets may resent them in their work-places. Cultural differences also account for many variations. What is 'public' – personal financial details, bathroom activities – in one setting may be very 'private' in another. Some people have never experienced levels of surveillance that others routinely have to endure. Think of the South African passbooks under apartheid, or the invasive and demeaning activities of welfare bureaucrats dealing with single mothers obtaining government benefits. Or think of well-heeled Muslims in New York who after 9/11 found their banking and credit facilities curtailed, or university professors considered as 'security threats' because they discuss the real world of militarism or consumerism in their classes.

There is a culture of surveillance, however, not only in the sense that surveillance has become part of the currency of everyday life, and so-called 'peer-to-peer' surveillance (using cell-phones or internet checks) is accepted as 'normal' in some areas, but in the very way that social relations are shaped. Increasingly, the reinforcement of social divisions and differences by means of surveillance systems – social sorting – is recognized as it appears in some popular television and news media.[1] Members of the public are aware, if dimly, that their supermarket shopper's card and their bar-coded passport classify them in distinct and sometimes negative ways. As these matters start to appear in newspapers and TV documentaries, one may hope that broader awareness will result.

As the social sorting aspects of surveillance become clearer, it seems responses emerge at different levels. Many will resist in minor ways such as falsifying personal data or refusing to give out phone numbers or postcodes. Some will question the wider systems through freedom of information legislation or data protection rules. Others will urge their labour union to combat negative discrimination against workers that uses surveillance. Yet others will urge their political representatives to oppose developing surveillance measures at a national level, be it 'lawful access' or national ID cards.

Priority of persons: transparency and dignity

In this section I wish to indicate what seems to me to be the crucial reason why openness and transparency are vitally needed within systems that use personal data for whatever purpose. It may be simply stated: people are at risk. The risks are those of mistaken identity, or, more seriously, of correctly identified persons whose life-chances and choices and whose freedom to move about or to communicate are jeopardized by their being placed in categories that define them in specific ways. They are vulnerable to stereotyping, negative discrimination, marginalization or exclusion.

I should note that by emphasizing the 'priority of persons', I am not relapsing after all into some species of individualism. Quite the contrary. The 'person' is shorthand for the socially formed, embodied agent who is never ultimately reducible to an individual atom (see, e.g., Cahill 1998). Persons may be profiled as group members or as individuated entities; their data may be abstracted, fragmented and recombined in ways that make their 'data-doubles' scarcely recognizable as 'representations', but it is worth recalling their 'personhood' because this grounds any analysis once more in the material world of flesh-and-blood companions, neighbours, employees, fellow-citizens, and so on.

As the ultimate beneficiaries – and victims – of data regimes are not abstract categories but people, then transparency about the ways in which coded categories affect people's lives is of paramount importance. This can be illustrated by reference to no-fly lists, genetic screening and customer relationship management, each of which is a feature of the surveillance society and the safety state and each of which shows how automated social categorization affects ordinary people's choices and chances.

Before commenting on some specific measures that might be considered within the politics of information, however, some other threads may be drawn together to emphasize why 'persons' should have priority in debates over the potentially negative aspects of surveillance. A key dimension of contemporary surveillance is that it may be done at a distance, using proxies such as data-doubles and fragmentary data, from transaction records to fingerprints. Surveillance tends to be removed, that is, from the local, the proximate, the face-to-face. This is not to deny that much face-to-face surveillance still exists and nor is it to look back nostalgically to some supposed preferable past of mutual monitoring in the community (although it must be said that in many anecdotal accounts of 'village surveillance' the caring dimension features as much as does control).

It is easier to place personal data in categories of criminal suspicion or consumer seduction, or to ban at the border certain categories of ethnic or national origin, when the bodies and especially the faces of the persons represented are absent. On a broader scale, it is also easier to 'take out' targets in conflict situations using military surveillance when the faces of far distant victims are invisible. One way of thinking about this starts with the work of Emmanuel Levinas, on the significance of the face. Levinas maintains that ethics begins with the impossibility of being indifferent to the Other, and that when one encounters the Other, one immediately encounters the claims of the Other. Yet, as Lucas Introna observes, the screens through which we 'see' the Other, either visually or, more likely, in dataveillance, tend to hide as well as to re-present (Introna 2003). This is why 'screening' has such a deep level of ambiguity; it is a means of filtering, of hiding as well as revealing. The screen, suggests Introna, reveals the world in its image, according to its categories. The face remains hidden even, as Introna and Wood imply, in facial recognition systems (Introna and Wood 2004).

This is just a reorientation, however. The face is a reminder of the embodied person in real places with genuine needs, desires and hopes. But this starting point is the way in, for Levinas, to justice. As contemporary surveillance creates categories, it systematically shifts attention from the face, but if Levinas is correct, the face must be seen if justice is to be done. 'Justice is impossible without the one that renders it finding himself in proximity' (Levinas cited in Introna 2003: 12). As we have seen, justice is easily overturned or obscured in new surveillance systems. The presumption of innocence, as Gary T. Marx observed two decades ago, is compromised by categorical suspicion (Marx 1988). The opportunity to appear in a court of law may be denied to detainees at a border because they appear in a banned category (Bigo 2006). And the category into which a welfare claimant falls may prejudice her capacity to care for her children with dignity (Gilliom 2005).

Such a stress on the face and on embodied persons is indispensable if justice is to be sought. It is also vital for trust, forgiveness and acceptance – each of which is difficult to discover in the world of new surveillance, whose currency is suspicion, whose tendency is to amass and retain data long after they are needed (thus jeopardizing forgiveness), and whose logic, especially after 9/11, is increasingly exclusionary.

What is to be done?

If 'embodied persons' with faces are a priority, then how does this affect actual approaches to the politics of information on the ground? Professionals in the privacy and security sector argue that there must be a focus on responsible 'information management' that addresses – and redresses – the political, social and economic effects of weak accountability and poor control of expanding networks of information and converging technologies. They rightly observe that transparency does not stop at the policy practices or circumstances where information can be revealed, shared, sold and bought. No, transparency should also reveal how a person's personal information is managed and what tests and certifications have been used to protect personal information at all levels.

Canadian Federal Privacy Commissioner Jennifer Stoddart, addressing the review of the Canadian Anti-Terrorism Act in May 2005, said that her aim was to contain surveillance, increase oversight and promote transparency (Stoddart 2005). She made eighteen very pertinent recommendations to the government to that effect. Such interventions are to be welcomed, but the Privacy Commissioner of Canada – or anywhere else for that matter — cannot be expected to engage this struggle alone. A much broader coalition of interested persons and groups is needed if transparency is really to occur in a routine way. And other instruments, such as freedom of information policies and laws, will be needed to ensure that it is possible to demand transparency in an informed manner.

But how can this be achieved? Certainly, legal regimes can set guidelines for proper practice, and if they have teeth, they can impose penalties for failure. But privacy and data protection law may be fully in place and yet egregious cases of negative discrimination and social sorting still occur. What is needed beyond this is vigilance at every level, which ensures that accountability is demanded of organizations that process personal data. Whatever their data-mining, clustering and discriminatory practices involve, they should be transparent to the subjects of those data. The organizations that process the data have a built-in advantage of size, expertise and knowledge which tips the balance of power heavily in their direction. Only when the processes are exposed, strict limits on the potential for social harm are found and enforced, and ordinary people have the opportunity to participate in these processes will the politics of information really have begun to make its mark. This may be examined in relation to 9/11.

The fourth anniversary of 9/11 prompted a series of articles in Canada's national daily newspaper, *The Globe and Mail*, concerning border security and 'the social and technological changes that the attacks began' (Atkinson 2005). William Atkinson said that 'it's probably time for a thorough public debate on surveillance'. Not only in Canada, but in some other countries as well, such a debate is indeed long overdue. But what is the context of this debate, what should be its content, and what prevents it happening?

First, 9/11 did not introduce the surveillance society; it served to reinforce strongly some already existing trends. In some ways 9/11 operates as a very handy discursive construct for justifying developments especially in the USA – expanding wiretaps, shoring up border controls, using commercial data for criminal intelligence purposes, and so on – for which occasion has been sought for a long time. One of the most important socio-technical trends thus reinforced was noted a number of years ago by Lawrence Lessig in *Code and Other Laws of Cyberspace* (1999), namely that towards reliance on the use of searchable databases. This signalled a shift towards what was already starting to occur: the automated sorting by categories of personal data and the networking of these across organizations and the globe. You do not have to have done anything wrong to be captured within some category of suspicion. Since 9/11, detainees at Guantánamo Bay in Cuba and others have found this out the hard way.

Second, there are reasons why no serious surveillance debate has occurred (any more than there has been a debate over what positive steps could be taken to understand the roots of terrorism). The political economy of the war on terror is such that politicians and technology corporations are locked into mutually beneficial arrangements: politicians can be seen to be 'responding' to attacks by implementing high-technology 'solutions', and high-technology companies argue with little debate that their 'tools' are ideal for each arising situation (see, e.g., O'Harrow 2005). Moreover, the media-amplified view that obtaining 'security' involves curtailing 'liberty' deflects attention from arguments that both may be sought without compromise.

Third, all kinds of data are sought for 'national security' purposes. The item mentioned in the *Globe and Mail* article proposed internet controls that would require internet service providers to disclose subscriber information. While this is indeed significant, it is merely symptomatic of broader changes in which all kinds of authorities, especially in the USA, but also in the EU and to an extent in Canada, are expected to share personal data in the interests of 'security'. This applies to employers, libraries, universities, airlines, and so on. In Canada, the British Columbia government contracts health-care data to a US firm whose website announces that it is an 'outreach company for Homeland Security information-sharing' (FIPA 2004). In September 2005 then UK education minister Ruth Kelly announced to a meeting of university leaders in London that they should be on the look-out for 'suspicious characters' and 'extremists' on campus and report them to the authorities. On 16 September Governor Mitt Romney of Massachusetts declared to the Heritage Foundation that mosques should be wiretapped.

Fourth, 'privacy' has dominated the discourses of data-handling, at least in North America, and the ways that it has done so have tended to push the onus of careful data-handling back to the individual level (through courts in the USA and complaints in Canada, for instance). Even in many European countries, where data protection has expected more of data-handling organizations, data protection law, as privacy law, may be conceived as a means of lubricating the mechanisms of global personal data-flows. Privacy or data protection policies may be in place *even as* airlines pass data to authorities or as marketers profile customers in order to offer differential treatment to one group or another. This is not to say that such things happen without a struggle: the European Parliament and what might be called a privacy advocates coalition fought hard against the American demand for airline pas-senger data in 2006, for example, and Green Members of the European Parliament vowed to maintain pressure to protect civil liberties in the aftermath (Gow 2006).

Fifth, in any case, privacy and data protection laws and policies are in constant and chronic need of renewal and revision to 'catch up' with recent developments in technology and surveillance practices. The same goes, of course, for any kinds of policy or law to limit other aspects of surveillance. The debate must be about all kinds of surveil-lance, from supermarket loyalty cards to national ID cards, not least because consumer data are now accessible to law enforcement offi-cials. High-profile battles may on occasion be won by 'privacy' lobbies, but they do not seem to be winning the ongoing 'war'. Such 'catching up' becomes more elusive the more new systems – using biometrics, RFID, and so on – are deployed on a large scale, especially within the media-amplified cultures of fear following 9/11. One need only think of the proliferation of CCTV cameras in public places in cities – generally *with* the approval of the populace – to see that this is so.

Surveillance studies thus brings together the highest level of theoretical analysis of globally networked processes with the most mundane and quotidian concerns about the organization of everyday social existence. Its specific task is focusing a spotlight on the ways in which ordinary details of daily life are noted, watched, monitored, recorded, traced and tracked and asking how this happens, who does it to whom, why it is done, how its subjects respond and sometimes resist, what the consequences are and who and what are affected. At best, surveillance studies helps to dismantle and destabilize taken-for-granted understandings of the needs for, mechanisms and outcomes of contemporary surveillance, with a view to both empowering data-subjects and calling some new forms of categorical governance into serious question.

Those studying surveillance would do well to explore not only the psychological and policy dimensions under the rubric of privacy but also to investigate the social, cultural, political and democratic dimensions specified by social sorting. The simultaneous rise of the surveillance society and the safety state is no accident. They operate in tandem to create a culture of control within which surveillance is both a vital means and thus a central component of an emerging politics of personal information. And within that politics no priority is higher than providing protection to persons – especially those most at risk – by ensuring that those processing personal data do so responsibly, fairly and accountably.

Glossary

Ambient intelligence (AmI): Sometimes thought of as a step beyond 'ubiquitous computing', AmI is an emergent technology or system in which persons are surrounded by or immersed in computing and network technology that is unobtrusively embedded in their everyday surroundings. Although user-friendliness, empowerment and support for human activities is stressed, AmI raises surveillance and privacy questions as ongoing personal data exchanges may occur without explicit and specific sanction. The lack of physical markers denoting shifts from private to public cyberspaces creates new problems. *See also RFID.*

Biometrics: Physiological or behavioural characteristics to determine or verify identity. The physiological are based on measurements and data derived from a part of the human body such as fingerprints, iris recognition, hand geometry and facial recognition. The behavioural are based on an action taken by a person and include voice verification, keystroke dynamics and signature verification. Used in automated and remote identification and verification.

Categorical suspicion: Coined in relation to the 'new surveillance' by Gary T. Marx (1988: 219), categorical suspicion denotes attention paid to individuals by virtue of their inclusion in a social or behavioural category, rather than because of their actual actions or words. Policing conventionally deals more with specific suspects than categories, but newer forms of risk management, in policing and other domains, foster the widespread surveillance of groups with similar characteristics.

CCTV: The connection in a loop of several video cameras such that the images are sent to a central monitor or recorder. Primarily used for security purposes, CCTV may be found in public and private areas for purposes as diverse as traffic control, customer behaviour monitoring or checking on hospital patients. Systems may be enhanced with features such as tilt-pan-zoom or night vision capacities. With increased networking and digitizing of systems the systems are less 'closed' than previously, raising potential problems of migrating image data or footage.

Control society: Gilles Deleuze (1992) suggests that Foucault's 'disciplinary society' based on enclosed and specific places of surveillance gives way to 'societies of control' in which electronic technologies increasingly permit constant and mobile surveillance across the various spheres of everyday life. Old barriers and walls are replaced by computer systems that track people continually. A corresponding literary contrast is between Orwell's Big Brother (overseeing spaces) and Kafka's *The Trial*, marked by uncertainty about who is watching and why.

CRM: Customer relationship management is a business strategy to identify, cultivate and maintain long-term profitable customer relations. Methods are sought to select the most profitable customer relationships (or those with the most potential), to provide those customers with a high level of service, and to deselect others. CRM has also become an information technology (IT) tool as it depends on software systems such as data-mining and may thus be used as a means of surveillance in non-business as well as business contexts. *See also Dataveillance.*

Cybernetics: The study of communication and control, typically involving regulatory feedback loops, especially in its computer-based forms. Derived from a Greek word for steersman (*kubernetes*), it is also associated with forms of government as effective organization. Popularly, the term 'cyberspace' suggests contexts in which relationships are mediated by computers and communication networks, but in surveillance studies the accent is on how such mediation is always marked by control through feedback loops (see Andrejevic 2007).

Data-double: This refers to the electronic profile, compiled from personal data fragments, of an individual person and it takes on increasing social significance as assessments and judgments are made in various contexts based upon it. Also referred to variously as the software self or digital persona, the data-double becomes part of the make-up of the individual, a component of his or her identification, even though the data-subject may question its accuracy.

Data-mining: The process of sorting through data to identify patterns and establish relationships. Data-mining parameters include patterns of connection; sequences, where one item leads to another; classification, seeking new patterns; clustering groups of data in new ways; and predictive analytics or forecasting. CRM uses web-mining techniques to analyse uses of websites and data available online, sometimes using 'spyware' software of which users are usually unaware.

Data protection: Generally understood, especially in Europe, as the implementation of administrative, technical or physical measures to guard against unauthorized access to personal data. Derived from the German *Datenschutz* in the early 1970s, data protection goes beyond data security but in practice may be used as a means of legitimating new surveillance technologies (Flaherty 1989). It tends to be used in relation to market models, featuring 'stakeholders' and 'contracts', as distinct from rights-based models, which highlight citizenship and obligation.

Dataveillance: Surveillance based on collecting and monitoring personal data and not involving direct watching or listening is often described by this hybrid term (coined by Roger Clarke [1988]). Clarke argues that the systematic use of personal data systems in investigating or monitoring actions or communications of one or more persons using IT is becoming the dominant form of surveillance. This is true of both personal dataveillance for specific purposes and mass dataveillance to identify individuals belonging to a group. *See also CRM.*

Disciplinary society: Michel Foucault's *Discipline and Punish* (1989) maintains that the basis of modern social control is the shift to discipline, from the preceding 'society of the spectacle'. The key, for him, was Jeremy Bentham's Panopticon prison diagram, in which control was achieved as inmates trained themselves to comply with organizational demands through fear of an unseen observer. Disciplinary power rules by structuring the parameters of thought and practice, defining what is 'normal' and 'deviant'.

Disclosure: The revealing of personal data to individuals or institutions that is either authorized by rules or laws or happens accidentally or intentionally. Privacy and data protection law and rules are intended to limit both the grounds and the opportunities for disclosure.

Fair information practices: As the circulation of personal data has grown exponentially since the 1980s, so attempts have increased to ensure that the practices by which data are collected and processed are fair. Much data protection and privacy law is based on (but usually goes well beyond) five principles of privacy protection: notice to ensure awareness by data-subjects; choice to permit consent; access to the data and participation in determining its use; the integrity and security of data systems; and opportunities for redress alongside the means of enforcement (Bennett and Raab 2006). Such practices are constantly challenged by new surveillance developments. *See also Data protection.*

Function creep: The addition of new features beyond the scope of the original project. In surveillance contexts the term is used to describe the expansion into new domains of software or a surveillance system, and the ways that new functions are constantly found for surveillance technologies and practices. Sometimes rendered simply as 'surveillance creep'.

Gaze, gendered and racialized: So far from being 'objective', focused surveillance attention carries connotations of asymmetrical power. Sympathetic critics of Michel Foucault's work often comment that while his understanding of the 'clinical' or 'observing' gaze throws critical light on the supposed superiority of medical practice, he pays little attention to the ways in which watching may be deeply affected by gendered and racialized criteria (see Gandy 2006a; Mulvey 1975). Contemporary surveillance intensifies and disembodies these familiar practices. An example of the former is cases of voyeurism in the operation of CCTV systems, and of the latter, dubious assumptions about 'race' or 'ethnicity' embedded in epidemiological surveillance or biometrics.

GPS: Global positioning systems comprise satellites, computers and receivers that are able to determine the latitude and longitude of a receiver on earth by calculating the time difference for signals from different satellites to reach the receiver. For example, a GPS-enabled cell-phone may be used by technical support personnel as a location-tracking technology to speed up response times to customer calls, but it may also serve as a surveillance device to check where such workers are at any given moment.

ID cards: Systems for identifying and verifying the identities of individuals in given populations, for example in public services, transport or the workplace. The use of searchable databases and networked communications also make such systems attractive for identification in passports and national ID cards. Their surveillance capacity is much enhanced over conventional paper-and-file systems by the use of electronic technologies along with biometrics.

Information technology (IT/ICT): Sometimes also referred to as 'information and communication technologies', or ICT, information technology refers to the use of electronic systems for processing and communicating information. More broadly, IT may refer to networking, hardware, software or to professionals working in these areas. These are the primary technologies that facilitate surveillance today as they provide the infrastructure on which other systems, such as video, genetic or biometric, depend.

Location technologies: Also thought of as mobile surveillance or movement-tracking technologies, this emerging cluster of systems enables the tracking and tracing of persons geographically. They can pinpoint coordinates, continuously and in real time, such that anyone using them may have their geographic location and travels tracked any time or all the time, and the records may be recorded, stored and shared (see Lyon et al. 2005). Originally developed in North America in relation to emergency telephoning, they are enhanced by use with global positioning systems, for example in vehicle navigation devices.

Panopticon: The Panopticon is the Greek-based neologism applied to Bentham's 1793 diagram for a new penitentiary whose architecture ensured the visibility of inmates to an unseen observer. The term became the focus for theoretical debates concerning surveillance due both to Foucault's focus on the Panopticon and the realization that electronic technologies apparently permit panoptic possibilities beyond

Bentham's dreams. Mark Poster (1996) called this the 'superpanopti-con', where databases are understood as 'discourses' but the idea also appears, for example, in Shoshana Zuboff's (1988) study of electronic surveillance in the workplace.

Privacy: A contested concept whose meaning varies historically and culturally, privacy ranges from 'the right to be left alone' to 'the capa-city to negotiate boundary conditions of social relations' or 'the right of individuals to control access to their information'. The private is often defined in contrast to that which is public, but even this fails to yield definitional leverage. Some see it as a human right; others as a strategic resource for human dignity, selfhood and sociality, ensuring that the right data are used by the right people for the right purposes. It may usefully be thought to have distinct dimensions: communica-tional, informational, bodily, territorial. Priscilla Regan (1995) demon-strates the social aspects of privacy.

Privacy-enhancing technologies: A range of software devices, devel-oped since the internet became a central site for surveillance, for lim-iting the capacity of third parties from tracking online activities and for giving the persons concerned greater control over the disclosure and circulation of their data. Given the difficulty of defining privacy, other terms dependent on 'privacy' are also hard to define.

RFID: Radio-frequency identification: an automated data collection technology that uses electronic tags for storing data and retrieving them remotely. The tags, or transponders, may be read by dedicated scanners that pick up the radio signals. Tags may be attached to or implanted in products (e.g. on supermarket shelves), animals (to prevent straying) or humans (such as Alzheimer's sufferers). Passive tags are activated by a scanner; active tags require a power source. Other uses for RFID include tags in identification and verification documents such as passports.

Risk management: The systematic application of management poli-cies, practices, and procedures to the task of identifying, analysing, assessing, treating and monitoring risk. In order to manage risks, however, organizations must develop risk communication systems, which, as Richard Ericson and Kevin Haggerty (1997) point out in relation to policing, requires surveillance, by which knowledge of risk is acquired.

Social sorting: Processes of selection, inclusion and exclusion are central to the operation of contemporary surveillance. IT enables what current politics prescribes, the classification and categorization of populations within regimes of risk management, in order that people from different groups may be treated differentially. In this view, surveillance is highly consequential for life-chances and -choices. This may have socially positive or negative outcomes, but as yet the means of social sorting are insufficiently understood by either analysts or data-subjects.

Synopticon: If the Panopticon is the device that enables the few to watch the many, for Thomas Mathiesen (1997) the synopticon – seen best in mass media – enables the many to watch the few. Mathiesen argues that surveillance today must be understood in relation to pervasive mass media, which both frame public understandings of surveillance and foster visibility as a desirable aim.

Transparency: The ideal of many seeking best practices for personal data-processing is to achieve transparency, such that data-subjects are as fully aware as possible about what personal data are collected, how they are gathered, for what purposes and with what consequences. This applies both in the public sphere of government and to commercial organizations where citizens, employees and consumers have a right of access to data pertaining to them. Legal measures including freedom of information, subject-access rights in data protection, and privacy legislation may be tools for transparency.

Visibility: The state of being seen is apparently trivial, but in cultures where surveillance increases the 'seeing' of populations both literally and metaphorically and where some people also deliberately expose themselves to sight, visibility becomes very important for social order and change. The epistemology of seeing is central to Western cultures and influential in others, which helps place in context the social significance of surveillance and visibility.

Notes

Introduction

1 ACLU animation available at www.aclu.org/standup/myspace_memb-conf/pizza_movie/pizza.mov.
2 Fair information practices are a set of principles that lie behind most privacy and data protection law and regulation around the world. They indicate ways in which care should be taken with personal data by insisting that organizations should be accountable for their handling of personal data, identify the purposes for which they are used, collect them only with the knowledge and consent of the individuals concerned, and so on. See the discussion in Bennett and Raab 2006 and chapter 8 below.

Chapter 1 The Watched World Today

1 For example, several Canadian public opinion polls were flawed through asking loaded questions, such as one in a survey carried out for *The National Post*: 'Do you see the terrorist threat from Islamic extremists as greater than most threats?' or another in a survey done on behalf of Citizenship and Immigration Canada that created an implicit connection between immigrants and terrorism (see Zureik 2004).

Chapter 4 Information, Identification, Inventory

1 The word 'inventory' comes from a Latin word meaning 'a list of things found'.
2 This idea of looping, according to Hacking, is a distinguishing feature of human from natural sciences. It is closely related to Anthony Giddens' remarks on 'reflexivity' (see Giddens 1990).

3 It comes as little surprise that Gary T. Marx, mentored by Goffman at Berkeley (Marx 1984) and now a leading figure in surveillance studies, also examines the minutiae of responses to surveillance, which often subvert the intentions of the surveillors (Marx 2003).

4 As I argue elsewhere in the book, there are some contradictions within Foucault's work, not least the impression he gives that power may be located in the panoptic 'inspection tower' and that 'docile bodies' find there that 'visibility is a trap'. These are aspects of the ongoing critical debates over Foucault's work.

Chapter 6 Bodies, Borders, Biometrics

1 Whether or not this made sense in terms of the imaginative strategies of potential terrorists or of other kinds of vulnerability is another question. Mine is merely an empirical observation.

2 See details available at *www.justice.gc.ca/en/news/nr/2001/doc_27785. html/.*

3 Details available at *www.dfait-maeci.gc.ca/anti-terrorism/actionplan-en. asp.*

4 'Glocalization' was first discussed in an English-speaking context by Roland Robertson (1995). A similar point about globalization occurring only through national circumstances is made by Sassen (2006).

5 An international survey of attitudes to surveillance and privacy is being undertaken by the Surveillance Project at Queen's University. Its earliest results were published late in 2006. See *www.queensu.ca/sociology/ Surveillance/.*

6 See, e.g., the statement by the Institute of Electrical and Electronic Engineers at *www.ieeeusa.org/policy/positions/universalidentifiers.html/.*

Chapter 7 Surveillance, Visibility and Popular Culture

1 On this point, see further the excellent work of Ruth Levitas (1990).

2 Mike Nellis, unpublished review of *Red Road*, personal communication.

Chapter 8 Struggles over Surveillance

1 The ways in which surveillance could be said to reduce reliance on personal narratives and to trust instead the data produced from behaviours, transactions or body information would be one way of extending Giddens' analysis.

2 See *www.friends-partners.org/CCSI/Hungary/hclu.thm/*.
3 See *www.no2id.net*.

Chaptyer 9 Data, Discrimination, Dignity

1 For example, the 2004 ABC documentary in the USA, *No Place to Hide*.

Further Reading

Chapter 1 The Watched World Today

Several general accounts of contemporary surveillance exist, including some that are paranoid and fear-mongering. Of the rest, a good, accessible treatment is B. Staples, *Everyday Surveillance: Vigilance and Visibility in Postmodern Life* (New York: Rowman and Littlefield, 1997). Another, which focuses more on 'privacy', is R. Whitaker, *The End of Privacy: How Total Surveillance is Becoming a Reality* (New York: New Press, 1999). My own *The Electronic Eye: The Rise of Surveillance Society* (Cambridge: Polity, 1994) and *Surveillance Society: Monitoring Everyday Life* (Buckingham: Open University Press, 2001) cover similar ground, although for the post-9/11 situation see my *Surveillance after September 11* (Cambridge: Polity, 2003), K. Ball and F. Webster (eds), *The Intensification of Surveillance: Crime, Warfare and Terrorism in the Information Age* (London: Pluto Press, 2003) and R. O'Harrow, *No Place to Hide* (New York: Free Press, 2005).

Chapter 2 Spreading Surveillance Sites

A comprehensive survey of the various domains of surveillance may be found in Surveillance Studies Network, *A Report on the Surveillance Society* (London: Information Commissioner's Office, 2006), available at: *http://www.ico.gov.uk/upload/documents/library/data_protection/practical_app lication/surveillance_society_full_report_2006.pdf*. A helpful historical perspective on administrative surveillance may be gained from E. Higgs, 'The rise of the information state: The development of central state surveillance of the citizen in England 1500–2000', *Journal of Historical Sociology*, 14 (2), 2001: 175–97. An early sociological treatment of contemporary surveillance is J.B. Rule, *Private Lives, Public Surveillance* (Harmondsworth and New York: Allen

Lane, 1974). The classic on 'new surveillance' is G.T. Marx, *Undercover: Police Surveillance in America* (Berkeley: University of California Press, 1988). This deals with the specific topic of police surveillance but also opens out to consider broader issues in the final chapter. C. Norris and G. Armstrong, *The Maximum Surveillance Society: The Rise of CCTV* (Oxford and New York: Berg, 1999) deals with video surveillance in the UK, where it is most prevalent, while O. Gandy, *The Panoptic Sort: A Political Economy of Personal Information* (Boulder, CO: Westview, 1993) examines consumer surveillance in its country of origin, the USA.

Chapter 3   Explaining Surveillance

A helpful starting point for thinking about surveillance theory is R. Boyne, 'Post-Panopticism', *Economy and Society*, 29 (2), 2000: 285–307. For a Weberian view, see C. Dandeker, *Surveillance, Power, and Modernity* (Cambridge: Polity, 1990) and to understand Foucault on surveillance there is no substitute for M. Foucault, *Discipline and Punish: The Birth of the Prison* (Harmondsworth: Penguin, 1979). Surveillance is placed in the very significant context of 'risk' in R. Ericson and K. Haggerty, *Policing the Risk Society* (Toronto: University of Toronto Press, 1997). For some insights from Jean Baudrillard, see W. Bogard, *The Simulation of Surveillance* (Cambridge and New York: Cambridge University Press, 1996). My *Surveillance Society* (see chapter 1) devotes a chapter to theory, while my edited collection *Theorizing Surveillance: The Panopticon and Beyond* (Cullompton, UK: Willan, 2006) offers a number of recent discussions of surveillance theory from leading authors.

Chapter 4   Information, Identification, Inventory

To understand the importance of classification as a background to surveillance studies, see G. Bowker and S.L. Star, *Sorting Things Out: Classification and its Consequences* (Cambridge, MA: MIT Press, 1999). Applied to the consumer surveillance field, a helpful approach is offered by Perri 6, 'The personal information economy: Trends and prospects for consumers', in S. Lace (ed.), *The Glass Consumer: Life in a Surveillance Society* (Bristol: Policy Press/National Consumer Council, 2005). Placing this more fully in a communication context is G. Elmer, *Profiling Machines: Mapping the Personal Information Economy* (Cambridge, MA: MIT Press, 2004). Examining different areas from the common theme of 'social sorting' are the essays in my edited collection *Surveillance as Social Sorting: Privacy, Risk and Digital Discrimination* (London and New York: Routledge, 2003).

Chapter 5 Security, Suspicion, Social Sorting

The background to contemporary issues of control is elegantly set out in D. Garland, *The Culture of Control: Crime and Social Order in Contemporary Society* (Chicago: University of Chicago Press, 2001). The technical argument is set out in plain language in L. Lessig, *Code and Other Laws of Cyberspace* (New York: Basic Books, 1999). At an urban level, S. Graham, 'The software-sorted city: Rethinking the digital divide', in S. Graham (ed.), *The Cybercities Reader* (New York: Routledge, 2004) is helpfully concise. This is taken further, in relation to consumer issues, in S. Lace (ed.), *The Glass Consumer* (see previous chapter). How this updates earlier theories of social class is shown in R. Burrows and N. Gane, 'Geodemographics, software and class', *Sociology*, 40 (5) 2006: 793–812.

Chapter 6 Bodies, Borders, Biometrics

A focused collection of papers is E. Zureik and M. Salter (eds), *Global Surveillance and Policing: Borders, Identity, Security* (Cullompton, UK: Willan, 2005). P. Adey, 'Secured and sorted mobilities: Examples from the airport', *Surveillance and Society*, 1 (4), 2003: 500–19 (available at: *www.surveillance-and-society.org/articles1(4)/sorted.pdf*) deals with one of the most common border-sorting contexts, airports. Other mobile surveillance methods are discussed in C. Bennett, C. Raab and P. Regan, 'People and place: Patterns of individual identification within intelligent transportation systems', in my *Surveillance as Social Sorting* (see chapter 4), and the passport is considered in J. Torpey, *The Invention of the Passport: Surveillance, Citizenship and the State* (Cambridge: Cambridge University Press, 2000). Biometrics is used increasingly, and a springboard for thought is E. Zureik and K. Hindle, 'Governance, security and technology: The case of biometrics', *Studies in Political Economy*, 73 (Spring/Summer), 2004: 113–37.

Chapter 7 Surveillance, Visibility and Popular Culture

The first paper seriously to tackle popular culture and surveillance was G.T. Marx, 'Electric eye in the sky: Some reflections on the new surveillance and popular culture', in D. Lyon and E. Zureik (eds), *Computers, Surveillance and*

Privacy (Minneapolis: University of Minnesota Press, 1996). Surveillance questions are raised about film in N. Denzin, *The Cinematic Society: The Voyeur's Gaze* (London and Thousand Oaks, CA: Sage, 1995) and further work on film is found in A. Light, (2002) 'Enemies of the state? Electronic surveillance and the neutrality of technology', in A. Light (ed.), *Reel Arguments: Film, Philosophy and Social Criticism* (Boulder, CO: Westview, 2002). T. Mathiesen, 'The viewer society: Michel Foucault's Panopticon revisited', *Theoretical Criminology*, 1 (2), 1997: 215–34 argues that surveillance should be considered in the context of the TV age, and M. Andrejevic, *Reality TV: The Work of Being Watched* (Lanham, MD: Rowman and Littlefield, 2004) underlines this from a different perspective.

Chapter 8   Struggles over Surveillance

A humane account of ordinary people struggling against a faceless bureaucratic surveillance is J. Gilliom, *Overseers of the Poor* (Chicago: University of Chicago Press, 2001) and an inventory of various resistance modes is available in G.T. Marx, 'A tack in the shoe: Neutralizing and resisting the new surveillance', *Journal of Social Issues*, 59 (2), 2003: 369–90. P. Regan, *Legislating Privacy: Technology, Social Values and Public Policy* (Chapel Hill: University of North Carolina Press, 1995) explores sensitively the social dimensions of privacy (in the course of addressing a larger theme), and a number of essays in K. Haggerty and R. Ericson, *The New Politics of Surveillance and Visibility* (Toronto: University of Toronto Press, 2006) raise some fresh questions about how surveillance and visibility are becoming political issues.

Chapter 9   Data, Discrimination, Dignity

Issues considered under the rubric of privacy protection are well addressed in C. Bennett and C. Raab, *The Governance of Privacy* (Cambridge, MA: MIT Press, 2006) and in relation to specific technologies in P.E. Agre and M. Rotenberg (eds), *Technology and Privacy: The New Landscape* (Cambridge, MA: MIT Press, 1997). Another take on privacy, from a legal and a literary perspective, is D. Solove, *The Digital Person: Technology and Privacy in the Information Age* (New York: New York University Press, 2004). A feisty approach to questions of discrimination is in O. Gandy, 'Quixotics unite! Engaging the pragmatists on rational discrimination', in my collection *Theorizing Surveillance* (see chapter 3).

Surveillance studies websites include *surveillance-and-society.org/* for the journal *Surveillance and Society* and other resources (find further details of the Surveillance Studies Network here too) and the Surveillance Project at Queen's University: *queensu.ca/sociology/Surveillance/*. Currently in German only is *surveillance-studies.org/*. Sites with parallel concerns include Privacy International (*privacyinternational.org/*), Electronic Privacy Information Center (*epic.org/*), Statewatch (*statewatch.org/*) and the American Civil Liberties Union (*aclu.org/privacy/index.html/*). Other data protection, privacy, civil liberties, freedom of information and human rights organizations also have helpful sites.

Bibliography

Abercrombie, N., Hill, S. and Turner, B.S. (1986) *Sovereign Individuals of Capitalism*, London: Allen and Unwin.

Adey, P. (2003) 'Secured and sorted mobilities: Examples from the airport', *Surveillance and Society*, 1 (4): 500–19. Available at: *www.surveillance-and-society.org/articles1(4)/sorted.pdf*

Adey, P. (2004) 'Surveillance at the airport: Surveilling mobility/mobilising surveillance', *Environment and Planning A*, 36 (8): 1365–80.

Agamben, G. (1998) *Homo Sacer: Sovereign Power and Bare Life*, Stanford, CA: Stanford University Press.

Agamben, G. (2005) *State of Exception*, Chicago: University of Chicago Press.

Agre, P. (1994) 'Surveillance and capture: Two models of privacy', *The Information Society*, 10 (2): 101–27.

Albrecht, K. and McIntyre, L. (2005) *Spychips: How Major Corporations and Government Plan to Track Your Every Move with RFID*, Nashville, TN: Thomas Nelson.

Albrechtslund, A and Dubbeld, L. (2005) 'The plays and arts of surveillance: Studying surveillance as entertainment', *Surveillance and Society*, 3 (2/3): 216–21. Available at: *www.surveillance-and-society.org/Articles3(2)/entertainment.pdf*

Amin, A. and Thrift, N. (2002) *Cities: Re-imagining the Urban*, Cambridge: Polity.

Amoore, L. and De Goede, M. (2005) 'Governance, risk and dataveillance in the war on terror', *Crime, Law and Social Change*, 43: 149–73.

Andreas, P. and Biersteker, T. (eds) (2003) *The Rebordering of North America: Integration and Exclusion in a New Security Context*, New York: Routledge.

Andrejevic, M. (2004a) *Reality TV: The Work of Being Watched*, Lanham, MD: Rowman and Littlefield.

Andrejevic, M. (2004b) 'Monitored mobility in an age of mass customization', *Space and Culture*, 6 (2): 132–50.

Andrejevic, M. (2007) *iSpy: Surveillance and Power in the Interactive Era*, Lawrence: University Press of Kansas.

Atkinson,W. (2005) 'They're watching you', *Globe and Mail* (Toronto), 13 September.

Augé, M. (1995) *Non-Places: Introduction to an Anthropology of Supermodernity*, London: Verso.

Ball, K. (2003) 'Power, control and computer-based performance monitoring: Repertoires, resistance, and subjectivities', in D. Lyon (ed.), *Surveillance as Social Sorting: Privacy, Risk and Digital Discrimination*, London and New York: Routledge.

Ball, K. (2006) 'Organization, surveillance and the body: Towards a politics of resistance', in D. Lyon (ed.), *Theorizing Surveillance: The Panopticon and Beyond*, Cullompton, UK: Willan.

Ball, K. and Carter, C. (2002) 'The charismatic gaze: Everyday leadership practices of the "new manager"', *Management Decision*, 40 (6): 552–65.

Ball, K. and Webster, F. (eds) (2003) *The Intensification of Surveillance: Crime, Warfare and Terrorism in the Information Age*, London: Pluto Press.

Ball, K. and Wilson, D. (2000) 'Power, control and computer-based performance monitoring: A subjectivist approach to repertoires and resistance', *Organization Studies*, 21 (3): 539–65.

Bartow, A. (2005) 'Women as targets: The gender-based implications of online consumer profiling', Online Profiling Project, Comment P994809, Available at: *www.ftc.gov/bcp/workshops/profiling/comments/bartow.htm*

Baudrillard, J. (2003) *Simulations*, New York: Semiotext(e).

Bauman, Z. (1998) *Globalization: The Human Consequences*, Cambridge: Polity; New York: Columbia University Press.

Bauman, Z. (2000) *Liquid Modernity*, Cambridge: Polity.

Bennett, C. (1992) *Regulating Privacy*, Ithaca, NY: Cornell University Press.

Bennett, C. (2005) 'What happens when you book an airline ticket? The collection and processing of passenger data post-9/11', in E. Zureik and M. Salter (eds), *Global Surveillance and Policing*, Cullompton, UK: Willan.

Bennett, C. and Raab, C. (2006) *The Governance of Privacy*, Cambridge, MA: MIT Press.

Bennett, C., Raab, C. and Regan, P. (2003) 'People and place: Patterns of individual identification within intelligent transportation systems', in D. Lyon (ed.), *Surveillance as Social Sorting*, London and New York: Routledge.

Bigo, D. (2005) 'Globalized (in)security: The field and the banopticon', in J. Solomon and N. Sakai (eds), *Traces: A Multilingual Series of Cultural Theory and Transition*, Hong Kong: University of Hong Kong Press.

Bigo, D. (2006) 'Security, exception, ban and surveillance', in D. Lyon (ed.), *Theorizing Surveillance: The Panopticon and Beyond*, Cullompton, UK: Willan.

Bilefsky, D. (2006) 'Data transfer broke rules, report says', *New York Times*, 28 September.

Black, E. (2001) *IBM and the Holocaust: The Strategic Alliance between Nazi Germany and America's Most Powerful Corporation*, New York: Crown Publishing.

Bogard, W. (1996) *The Simulation of Surveillance*, Cambridge and New York: Cambridge University Press.

Bogard, W. (2006) 'Welcome to the society of control: The simulation of surveillance revisited', in K. Haggerty and R. Ericson (eds), *The New Politics of Surveillance and Visibility*, Toronto: University of Toronto Press.

Bordo, S. (1993) *Unbearable Weight: Feminism, Western Culture and the Body*, Berkeley: University of California Press.

Borgmann, A. (1999) *Holding on to Reality*, Chicago: University of Chicago Press.

Bowker, G. and Star, S.L. (1999) *Sorting Things Out: Classification and Its Consequences*, Cambridge, MA: MIT Press.

Boyne, R. (2000) 'Post-Panopticism', *Economy and Society*, 29 (2): 285–307.

Breckenridge, K. (2005) 'Verwoerd's Bureau of Proof: Total information in the making of apartheid', *History Workshop Journal*, 59: 83–108.

Brighenti, A. (2007) 'Visibility', *Current Sociology*, 55 (3).

Brodeur, J.-P. and Leman-Langlois, S. (2006) 'Surveillance fiction or higher policing?', in K. Haggerty and R. Ericson (eds), *The New Politics of Surveillance and Visibility*, Toronto: University of Toronto Press.

Bryman, A. (2004) *The Disneyization of Society*, London and Thousand Oaks, CA: Sage.

Burkert, H. (1997) 'Privacy-enhancing technologies', in P. Agre and M. Rotenberg (eds), *Technology and Privacy: The New Landscape*, Cambridge, MA: MIT Press.

Burrows, R. and Ellison, N. (2004) 'Sorting places out: Towards a social politics of neighbourhood informatization', *Information, Communication and Society*, 7 (3): 321–36.

Burrows, R. and Gane, N. (2006) 'Geo-demographics, software and class', *Sociology*, 40 (5): 793–812.

Burson, P. (2005) 'Use of "nannycams" raises issues of ethics, parents' rights', *Fort Worth Star-Telegram*, 19 January. Available at: *www.azcentral.com/families/articles/0119videotaping19.html/*

Butler, J. (1993) *Bodies that Matter*, New York: Routledge.

Cahill, S.E. (1998) 'Towards a sociology of the person', *Sociological Theory*, 16 (2): 131–48.

Campbell, D. and Connor, S. (1986) *On the Record: Computers, Surveillance and Privacy*, London: Michael Joseph.

Castells, M. (1996) *The Rise of the Network Society*, Oxford and Malden, MA: Blackwell.

Castells, M. (1997) *The Power of Identity*, Oxford and Malden, MA: Blackwell.

Castells, M. (2001) *The Internet Galaxy*, Oxford and New York: Oxford University Press.

Clarke, R. (1988) 'Information technology and dataveillance', *Communications of the ACM*, 31 (5): 498–512.

Clarke, R. (1994) 'The digital persona and its application to data surveillance', *The Information Society*, 10 (2): 77–92.

Clarke, R. (1997) 'Introduction to dataveillance and information privacy, and definition of terms'. Available at: *www.anu.edu.au/people/Roger.Clarke/DV/Intro.html#DV* [revised 7 August 2006].

Clarke, R. (2006) 'National identity schemes: The elements'. Available at: *www.anu.edu.au/people/Roger.Clarke/DV/NatIDSchemeElms.html*

Cohen, S. (1985) *Visions of Social Control*, Cambridge: Polity.

Cole, M. (2006) 'The role of confession in reflective practice: Monitored continued professional development (CPD) in health care and the paradox of professional autonomy', in D. Lyon (ed.), *Theorizing Surveillance: The Panopticon and Beyond*, Cullompton, UK: Willan.

Cole, S. (2001) *Suspect Identities: A History of Fingerprinting and Criminal Identification*, Cambridge, MA: Harvard University Press.

Coleman, R. (2004) *Reclaiming the Streets: Surveillance, Social Control and the City*, Cullompton, UK: Willan.

Cooper, P. (1995) 'Sexual surveillance and medical authority in two versions of *The Handmaid's Tale*', *Journal of Popular Culture*, 28 (4): 49–66.

Cross, M. (2006) 'Why doesn't the government ask me how much of my data it can share?', *The Guardian*, 21 September. Available at: *technology.guardian.co.uk/weekly/story/0,,1876713,00.html*

Dandeker, C. (1990) *Surveillance, Power, and Modernity*, Cambridge: Polity.

Dandeker, C. (2006) 'Surveillance and military transformation: Organizational trends in twenty-first-century armed services', in K. Haggerty and R.

Ericson (eds), *The New Politics of Surveillance and Visibility*, Toronto: University of Toronto Press.

Davis, A. (1997) 'The body as password', *Wired*, 5 (07). Available at: *www.wired.com/wired/archive/5.07/biometrics.html/*

de Certeau, M. (1984) *Practice of Everyday Life*, Berkeley: University of California Press.

de Certeau, M. (1986) *Heterologies: Discourse on the Other*, Manchester: Manchester University Press.

Deleuze, G. (1992) 'Postcript on the societies of control', *October*, 59: 3–7.

Deleuze, G. (1995) *Negotiations 1972–1990*, New York: Columbia University Press.

Denzin, N. (1995) *The Cinematic Society: The Voyeur's Gaze*, London and Thousand Oaks, CA: Sage.

Doane, M.A. (2002) *The Emergence of Cinematic Time: Modernity, Contingency, the Archive*, Cambridge, MA: Harvard University Press.

Dodge, M. and Kitchen, R. (2005) 'Codes of life: Identification codes and the machine-readable world', *Environment and Planning D: Society and Space*, 23: 851–81.

Downey, J. and Murdoch, G. (2003) 'The counter-revolution in military affairs: The globalization of guerilla warfare', in D. Thussu and D. Freedman (eds), *War and the Media: Reporting Conflict*, London: Sage.

Dubbeld, L. (2004) *The Regulation of the Observing Gaze*, Enschede: Twente University.

Ellul, J. (1964) *The Technological Society*, New York: Vintage.

EPIC (2005) 'Public opinion on privacy', Electronic Privacy Information Center. Available at: *www.epic.org/privacy/survey*

EPIC/PI (2006) *Privacy and Human Rights 2005*, Washington, DC: Electronic Privacy Information Center.

Ericson, R. and Haggerty, K. (1997) *Policing the Risk Society*, Toronto: University of Toronto Press.

Evans, R. (1982) *The Fabrication of Virtue: English Prison Architecture 1750–1840*, Cambridge: Cambridge University Press.

Fay, B. (1976) *Social Theory and Practice*, London: Allen and Unwin.

Feeley, M. and Simon, J. (1992) 'The new penology: Notes on the emerging strategy of corrections and its implications', *Criminology*, 30 (4): 449–74.

Feeley, M. and Simon, J. (1994) 'Actuarial justice: The emerging new criminal law', in D. Nelken (ed.), *The Futures of Criminology*, London: Sage.

FIPA (2004) 'US corporation selected to manage BC medical records actively promotes sharing of personal information with FBI', BC Freedom of Information and Privacy Association. Available at: *fpa.bc.ca/home/news/ 93*

Flaherty, D. (1989) *Protecting Privacy in Surveillance Societies*, Chapel Hill: University of North Carolina Press.

Ford, R. (2004) 'Beware rise of Big Brother state', *The Times*, 16 August. Available at: *www.timesonline.co.uk/article/0,,2–1218615,00.html*

Foucault, M. (1976) *The History of Sexuality*, Volume 1, Harmondsworth: Penguin.

Foucault, M. (1979) *Discipline and Punish: The Birth of the Prison*, Harmondsworth: Penguin.

Foucault, M. (1980a) 'Prison talk', in C. Gordon (ed.), *Michel Foucault: Power/Knowledge: Selected Interviews and Other Writings 1972–1977*, Brighton: Harvester.

Foucault, M. (1980b) 'Power/Knowledge', in C. Gordon (ed.), *Michel Foucault: Power/Knowledge: Selected Interviews and Other Writings 1972–1977*, Brighton: Harvester.

Franklin, U. (1996) 'Stormy weather: Conflicting forces in the information society', speech, Office of the Privacy Commissioner of Canada, 19 September. Available at: *www.privcom.gc.ca/speech/archive/02_05_a_960918_05_e.asp*

Franklin, U. (1999) *The Real World of Technology*, Toronto: Anansi.

Fraser, N. (1989) *Unruly Practices: Power, Discourse and Gender in Contemporary Social Theory*, Minneapolis: University of Minnesota Press.

French, M. (2007) 'In the shadow of Canada's camps', Social and Legal Studies, 16: 49–68.

Galloway, A. (2004) *Protocol: How Control Exists after Decentralization*, Cambridge, MA: MIT Press.

Gambling Magazine (2005) 'Technology has spawned a dramatic improvement in casino surveillance'. Available at: *www.gamblingmagazine.com/articles/40/40-337.htm*

Gandy, O. (1993) *The Panoptic Sort: A Political Economy of Personal Information*, Boulder, CO: Westview.

Gandy, O. (1996) 'Coming to terms with the panoptic sort', in D. Lyon and E. Zureik (eds), *Computers, Surveillance and Privacy*. Minneapolis: University of Minnesota Press.

Gandy, O. (2006a) 'Data mining, surveillance and discrimination in the post-9/11 environment', in K. Haggerty and R. Ericson (eds), *The New Politics of Surveillance and Visibility*, Toronto: University of Toronto Press.

Gandy, O. (2006b) 'Quixotics unite! Engaging the pragmatists on rational discrimination', in D. Lyon (ed.), *Theorizing Surveillance: The Panopticon and Beyond*, Cullompton, UK: Willan.

GAO (2005) *Aviation Security: Secure Flight Development and Testing Under Way, but Risks Should be Managed as System is Further Developed*. A Report to Congressional Committees, the United States Government Accountability Office, GAO-05–356, March. Available at: *www.gao.gov/new.items/d05356.pdf#search=%22GAO%20(2005)%20Secure%20Flight%20report.%22*

Garland, D. (2001) *The Culture of Control: Crime and Social Order in Contemporary Society*, Chicago: University of Chicago Press.

Genosko, G. and Thompson, S. (2006) 'Tense theory: The temporalities of surveillance', in D. Lyon (ed.), *Theorizing Surveillance: The Panopticon and Beyond*, Cullompton, UK: Willan.

Giddens, A. (1985) *The Nation-State and Violence*, Cambridge: Polity.

Giddens, A. (1990) *The Consequences of Modernity*, Cambridge: Polity.

Gilliom, J. (2001) *Overseers of the Poor*, Chicago: University of Chicago Press.

Gilliom, J. (2005) 'Resisting surveillance', *Social Text*, 83: 71–83.

Goffman, E. (1961) *Asylums*, New York: Penguin.

Goo, S.K. (2004) 'Sen. Kennedy flagged by no-fly list', *Washington Post*, 20 August. Available at: *www.washingtonpost.com/wp-dyn/articles/A17073–2004Aug19.html*

Gosline, A. (2005) 'Will DNA profiling fuel prejudice?', *New Scientist*, 9 April.

Gow, D. (2006) 'EU strikes deal with US over passenger data', *The Guardian*, 7 October. Available at: *www.guardian.co.uk/eu/story/0,,1889560,00.html*

Graham, P. (1986) 'The Australia Card', *The Australian Quarterly*, Autumn: 4–14.

Graham, S. (2004a) 'The software-sorted city: Rethinking the digital divide', in S. Graham (ed.), *The Cybercities Reader*, New York: Routledge.

Graham, S. (ed.) (2004b) *Cities, War and Terrorism: Towards an Urban Geopolitics*, Oxford: Blackwell.

Graham, S. (2005) 'Software-sorted geographies', *Progress in Human Geography*, 29 (5): 562–80.

Graham, S. and Wood, D. (2003) 'Digitizing surveillance: Categorization, space, inequality', *Critical Social Policy*, 23: 227–48.

Hacking, I. (1990) *The Taming of Chance*, Cambridge and New York: Cambridge University Press.

Hacking, I. (2004) 'Between Michel Foucault and Erving Goffman: Between discourse in the abstract and face-to-face interaction', *Economy and Society*, 33 (3): 277–302.

Haggerty, K. (2006a) 'Tear down the walls! On demolishing the Panopticon', in D. Lyon (ed.), *Theorizing Surveillance: The Panopticon and Beyond*, Cullompton, UK: Willan.

Haggerty, K. (2006b) 'Visible war: Surveillance, speed and information war', in K. Haggerty and R. Ericson (eds), *The New Politics of Surveillance and Visibility*, Toronto: University of Toronto Press.

Haggerty, K. and Ericson, R. (2000) 'The surveillant assemblage', *British Journal of Sociology*, 51 (4): 605–22.

Haggerty, K. and Ericson, R. (2001) 'The military technostructures of policing', in P. Kraska (ed.), *Militarizing the American Criminal Justice System*, Boston: Northeastern University Press.

Haggerty, K. and Gazso, A. (2005) 'The public politics of opinion research on surveillance and privacy', *Surveillance and Society*, 3 (2/3): 173–80. Available at: *www.surveillance-and-society.org/Articles3(2)/opinion.pdf*

Hall, H. (2005) 'Data use in credit and insurance: Controlling unfair outcomes', in S. Lace (ed.), *The Glass Consumer: Life in a Surveillance Society*, Bristol: Policy Press/National Consumer Council.

Hardt, M. and Negri, A. (2000) *Empire*, Cambridge, MA: Harvard University Press.

Harmel, K. and Spadanuta, L. (2006) 'Mickey wants your prints', *The Globe and Mail* (Toronto), 9 September, T9.

Hayes, B. (2006) *Arming Big Brother: The EU's Security Research Programme*, Amsterdam: The Transnational Institute. Available at: *www.statewatch.org/news/2006/apr/bigbrother.pdf*

Helten, F. and Fischer, B. (2004) 'Reactive attention: Video surveillance in Berlin shopping malls', *Surveillance and Society*, 2 (2/3): 323–45. Available at: *www.surveillance-and-society.org/articles2(2)/berlin.pdf*

Hentschel, C. (2006) 'Making (in)visible: CCTV, 'living cameras' and their objects in a post-apartheid metropolis'. Paper presented at the International Sociological Association World Congress, Ad Hoc Session on Security, Surveillance and Social Sorting, Durban, SA, 26 July.

Hewitt, S. (2002) *Spying 101: The RCMP's Secret Activities at Canadian Universities 1917–1997*, Toronto: University of Toronto Press.

Higgs, E. (2001) 'The rise of the information state: The development of central state surveillance of the citizen in England 1500–2000', *Journal of Historical Sociology*, 14 (2): 175–97.

Higgs, E. (2004) *The Information State in England*, Basingstoke and New York: Palgrave Macmillan.

Introna, L. (2003) 'The face and the interface: Thinking with Levinas on ethics and justice in an electronically mediated world'. Lancaster University Management School Working Paper 2003/092.

Introna, L. and Wood, D. (2004) 'Picturing algorithmic surveillance: The politics of facial recognition systems', *Surveillance and Society*, 2 (2/3): 177–98. Available at: *www.surveillance-and-society.org/articles2(2)/algorithmic.pdf*

Jay, M. (1989) 'In the empire of the gaze: Foucault and the denigration of vision in twentieth-century thought', in L. Appignanesi (ed.), *Postmodernism*, London: Free Association Books.

Jenkins, R. (2000) 'Categorization: Identity, social process and epistemology', *Current Sociology*, 48 (3): 7–25.

Jenkins, R. (2004) *Social Identities*, London and New York: Routledge.

Jones, R. (2000) 'Digital rule: Punishment, control and technology', *Punishment and Society*, 2 (1): 5–22.

Keen, M.F. (2004) *Stalking Sociologists: J. Edgar Hoover's Surveillance of American Sociology*, New Brunswick, NJ: Transaction Books.

Kiss, S. and Mosco, V. (2005) 'Negotiating electronic surveillance in the workplace: A study of collective agreements in Canada', *Canadian Journal of Communication*, 30 (4): 549–64.

Klein, N. (2002) *No Logo: Taking Aim at the Brand Bullies*, New York: Knopf.

Koskela, H. (2003) '"Cam era": The contemporary urban panopticon', *Surveillance and Society*, 1 (3): 292–313. Available at: *www.surveillance-and-society.org/articles1(3)/camera.pdf*

Kumar, K. (1985) *Prophecy and Progress*, Harmondsworth: Penguin.

Lace, S. (2005a) 'Introduction', in S. Lace (ed.), *The Glass Consumer: Life in a Surveillance Society*, Bristol: Policy Press/National Consumer Council.

Lace, S. (2005b) 'The new personal information agenda', in S. Lace (ed.), *The Glass Consumer: Life in a Surveillance Society*, Bristol: Policy Press/National Consumer Council.

Larsen, E. (1992) *The Naked Consumer*, New York: Henry Holt.

Lasch, C. (1991) *The Culture of Narcissism: American Life in an Age of Diminishing Expectations*, New York: W.W. Norton.

Latour, B. (1993) *We Have Never Been Modern*, Cambridge, MA: Harvard University Press.

Le Roy Ladurie, E. (1979) *Montaillou: The Promised Land of Error*, New York: Vintage Books.

Leong, T. (2001) 'Ulterior spaces', in C.J. Chung, J. Inaba, R. Koolhaas and S.T. Leong (eds), *Harvard Design School Guide to Shopping*, Cologne: Taschen.

Lessig, L. (1999) *Code and Other Laws of Cyberspace*, New York: Basic Books.

Levin, T.Y. (2002) 'Rhetoric of the temporal index: Surveillant narration and the cinema of "real time"', in T.Y. Levin, U. Frohne and P. Weibel (eds), *CTRL [Space]: The Rhetorics of Surveillance from Bentham to Big Brother*, Cambridge, MA: MIT Press.

Levitas, R. (1990) *The Concept of Utopia*, Syracuse, NY: Syracuse University Press.

Lewis, T. (2006) 'Critical surveillance literacy', *Cultural Studies*, 6 (2): 263–81.

Light, A. (2002) 'Enemies of the state? Electronic surveillance and the neutrality of technology', in A. Light (ed.), *Reel Arguments: Film, Philosophy and Social Criticism*, Boulder, CO: Westview Press.

Light, J. (2003) *From Warfare to Welfare: Defense Intellectuals and Urban Problems in Cold War America*, Baltimore, MD and London: Johns Hopkins University Press.

Lyon, D. (1988) *The Information Society: Issues and Illusions*, Cambridge: Polity.

Lyon, D. (1994) *The Electronic Eye: The Rise of Surveillance Society*, Cambridge: Polity.

Lyon, D. (1999) *Postmodernity*, Buckingham: Open University Press.

Lyon, D. (2001) *Surveillance Society: Monitoring Everyday Life*, Buckingham: Open University Press.

Lyon , D. (2002a) 'Surveillance studies: Understanding visibility, mobility and the phenetic fix', *Surveillance and Society*, 1 (1): 1–7.

Lyon, D. (2002b) 'Surveillance in cyberspace: The internet, personal data and social control', *Queen's Quarterly*, 109 (3): 345–57.

Lyon, D. (2002c) 'Airports as data-filters: Converging surveillance systems after September 11th', *Information, Communication, and Ethics in Society*, 1 (1): 13–20.

Lyon, D. (2003a) *Surveillance after September 11*, Cambridge: Polity.

Lyon, D. (ed.) (2003b) *Surveillance as Social Sorting: Privacy, Risk and Digital Discrimination*, London and New York: Routledge.

Lyon, D. (2004) 'Globalizing surveillance: Comparative and sociological perspectives', *International Sociology*, 19 (2): 135–49.

Lyon, D. (2005) 'The border is everywhere: ID cards, surveillance and the other', in E. Zureik and M. Salter (eds), *Global Surveillance and Policing*, Cullompton, UK: Willan.

Lyon, D. (ed.) (2006a) *Theorizing Surveillance: The Panopticon and Beyond*, Cullompton, UK: Willan.

Lyon, D. (2006b) 'Why where you are matters: Mundane mobilities, technologies and digital discrimination', in T. Monahan (ed.), *Surveillance and Security: Technological Power and Politics in Everyday Life*, New York: Routledge.

Lyon, D. (2006c) '9/11, synopticon, scopophilia: Watching and being watched', in K. Haggerty and R. Ericson (eds), *The New Politics of Surveillance and Visibility*, Toronto: University of Toronto Press.

Lyon, D., Marmura, S. and Peroff, P. (2005) *Location Technologies: Mobility, Surveillance and Privacy*, Ottawa: Office of the Privacy Commissioner/ Kingston: The Surveillance Project.

McCahill, M. (2002) *The Surveillance Web: The Rise of Visual Surveillance in an English City*. Cullompton, UK: Willan.

McGrath, J. (2004) *Loving Big Brother: Performance, Privacy and Surveillance Space*, London and New York: Routledge.

Macintosh, N. (2003) *Accounting, Accountants and Accountability*, New York: Routledge.

McPherson, C. B. (1962) *The Political Theory of Possessive Individualism*, New York and Oxford: Oxford University Press.

Madon, S. (1998) 'Information-based global economy and socio-economic development: The case of Bangalore', *The Information Society*, 13 (3): 227–43.

Marks, P. (2005) 'Imagining surveillance: Utopian visions and surveillance studies', *Surveillance and Society*, 3 (2/3): 222–39. Available at: *www.sur-veillance-and-society.org/Articles3(2)/imagining.pdf*

Marx, G.T. (1984) 'Role models and role distance: A remembrance of Erving Goffman', *Theory and Society*, 13: 649–62.

Marx, G.T. (1988) *Undercover: Police Surveillance in America*, Berkeley: University of California Press.

Marx, G.T. (1996) 'Electric eye in the sky: Some reflections on the new surveillance and popular culture', in D. Lyon and E. Zureik (eds), *Computers, Surveillance and Privacy*, Minneapolis: University of Minnesota Press.

Marx, G.T. (1997) 'The declining significance of traditional borders (and the appearance of new borders) in an age of high technology', in P. Droege (ed.), *Intelligent Environments*, Amsterdam: Elsevier Science BV.

Marx, G.T. (1999) 'Measuring everything that moves: The new surveillance at work', in I. and R. Simpson (eds), *Deviance in the Workplace*, Stanford, CT: JAI Press.

Marx, G.T. (2003) 'A tack in the shoe: Neutralizing and resisting the new surveillance', *Journal of Social Issues*, 59 (2): 369–90.

Marx, G.T. (2006) 'Soft surveillance: The growth of mandatory volunteerism in collecting personal information – "Hey buddy can you spare a DNA?"', in T. Monahan (ed.), *Surveillance and Security: Technological Politics and Power in Everyday Life*, New York: Routledge

Mathiesen, T. (1997) 'The viewer society: Michel Foucault's Panopticon revisited', *Theoretical Criminology*, 1 (2): 215–34.

Milbank, J. (1990) *Theology and Social Theory: Beyond Secular Reason*, Oxford: Blackwell.

Mills, C.W. (1959) *The Sociological Imagination*, New York: Oxford University Press.

Millward, D. (2007) 'US "licence to snoop" on British air travellers', *Daily Telegraph*, 2 January.

Mosco, V. (1989) *The Pay-Per Society: Computers and Communications in the Information Age*, Toronto: Garamond.

Mosco, V. (2004) *The Technological Sublime: Myth, Power and Cyberspace*, Cambridge, MA: MIT Press.

Muller, B. (2004) '(Dis)qualified bodies: Securitization, citizenship and "identity management"', *Citizenship Studies*, 8 (3): 279–94.

Muller, B. (2005) 'Borders, bodies and biometrics: Towards identity management', in E. Zureik and M. Salter (eds), *Global Surveillance and Policing: Borders, Identity, Security*, Cullompton, UK: Willan.

Mulvey, L. (1975) 'Visual pleasure and narrative cinema', *Screen*, 16 (3): 6–18.

Murakami Wood, D. and Graham, S. (2006) 'Permeable boundaries in the software-sorted society: Surveillance and the differentiation of mobility', in M. Shelley and J. Urry (eds), *Mobile Technologies of the City*, London: Routledge.

Murakami Wood, D., Lyon, D. and Abe, K. (2007) 'Surveillance in urban Japan: An introduction', *Urban Studies*, 43 (4).

Nelkin, D. and Andrews, L. (2003) 'Surveillance creep in the genetic age', in D. Lyon (ed.), *Surveillance as Social Sorting: Privacy, Risk and Digital Discrimination*, London and New York: Routledge.

Nellis, M. (2006) 'Surveillance, rehabilitation and electronic monitoring: Getting the issues clear', *Criminology and Public Policy*, 5 (1): 103–8.

Norris, C. (2003) 'From personal to digital: CCTV, the panopticon, and the technological mediation of suspicion and social control', in D. Lyon (ed.), *Surveillance as Social Sorting*, London: Routledge.

Norris, C. and Armstrong, G. (1999) *The Maximum Surveillance Society: The Rise of CCTV*, Oxford and New York: Berg.

Norris, C. and McCahill, M. (2006) 'CCTV: Beyond penal modernism?', *British Journal of Criminology*, 46: 97–118.

Norris, C. and Wilson, D. (eds) (2006) *Surveillance, Crime and Social Control*, London: Ashgate.

Ogura, T. (2006) 'Electronic government and surveillance-oriented society', in D. Lyon (ed.), *Theorizing Surveillance: The Panopticon and Beyond*, Cullompton, UK: Willan.

O'Harrow, R. (2005) *No Place to Hide*, New York: Free Press.

Orlowski, A. (2006) '77% of Google users don't know it records personal data', *The Register*, 24 January. Available at: *www.theregister.co.uk/2006/01/24/google_privacy_poll/*

Orwell, G. (1954) *Nineteen Eighty-Four*. Harmondsworth: Penguin.

Parenti, C. (2003) *The Soft Cage: Surveillance in America from Slave Passes to the War on Terror*, New York: Basic Books.

Pecora, V.P. (2002) 'The culture of surveillance', *Qualitative Sociology*, 25 (3): 345–58.

Pellerin, H. (2005) 'Borders, migration and economic integration: Towards a new political economy of borders', in E. Zureik and M. Salter (eds), *Global Surveillance and Policing*, Cullompton, UK: Willan.

Perri 6 (2003) 'The governance of technology: Concepts, trends, theory, normative principles and research agenda'. Paper presented at the 'Human Choice and Technological Change' conference, Lisbon, Portugal, 24–5 February.

Perri 6 (2005) 'The personal information economy: Trends and prospects for consumers', in S. Lace (ed.), *The Glass Consumer: Life in a Surveillance Society*, Bristol: Policy Press/National Consumer Council.

Perri 6 and Jupp, B. (2001) *Divided by Information?* London: Demos.

Pew Internet and American Life Project (2000) 'Trust and privacy online: Why Americans want to rewrite the rules', 20 August. Available at: *www.pewinternet.org/pdfs/PIP_Trust_Privacy_Report.pdf*

Phillips, D. (2004) 'From privacy to visibility: Context, identity and power in ubiquitous computing environments', *Social Text*, 83: 95–108.

Pienaar, J. (2006) 'Olympics audio surveillance row'. Available at: *news.bbc.co.uk/1/hi/uk_politics/6186348.stm*

Pilieci, V. (2004) 'Airport gets dirty bomb detectors', *The Ottawa Citizen*, 8 December.

Porter, H. (2006) 'There's just no escape from these snoops', *The Observer*, 3 December. Available at: *observer.guardian.co.uk/comment/story/0,,1962937,00.html*

Poster, M. (1996) 'Databases as discourse or electronic interpellations', in D. Lyon and E. Zureik (eds), *Computers, Surveillance and Privacy*, Minneapolis: University of Minnesota Press.

Pressman, J.L. and Wildavsky, A. (1984) *Implementation: How Great*

Expectations in Washington are Dashed in Oakland, Berkeley: University of California Press.

Pridmore, J. and Lyon, D. (2005) 'Customer relationship management as surveillance', unpublished paper, Queen's University.

Pugliese, J. (2005) '*In silico* race and the heteronomy of biometric proxies: Biometrics in the context of civilian life, border security and counter-terrorism laws', *Australian Feminist Law Journal*, 23: 1–32.

Raab, C.D. (2005a) 'Governing the safety state'. Inaugural Lecture at the University of Edinburgh, 7 June.

Raab, C.D. (2005b) 'Perspectives on "personal identity"', *BT Technology Journal*, 23 (4): 15–24.

Regan, P. (1995) *Legislating Privacy: Technology, Social Values and Public Policy*, Chapel Hill: University of North Carolina Press.

Richtel, M. (2004) 'In Texas, 28,000 students test an electronic eye', *New York Times*, 17 November.

Ricoeur, P. (1992) *Oneself as Another*, Chicago: University of Chicago Press.

Rigakos, G. (2002) *The New Parapolice: Risk Markets and Commodified Social Control*, Toronto: University of Toronto Press.

Roberts, Y. (2006) 'Beware the parent trap', *The Guardian*, 26 June. Available at: *www.guardian.co.uk/commentisfree/story/0,,1808379,00.html*

Robertson, R. (1995) 'Glocalization: Time–space and homogeneity–heterogeneity', in M. Featherstone, S. Lash and R. Robertson (eds), *Global Modernities*, London: Sage.

Roethlisberger, F., Dickson, W. and Wright, H. (1939) *Management and the Worker*, New York: John Wiley.

Rose, N. (1999) *Powers of Freedom*, Cambridge: Cambridge University Press.

Roy, A. (2004) *An Ordinary Person's Guide to Empire*, Cambridge, MA: South End Press.

Rule, J.B. (1973) *Private Lives, Public Surveillance*, Harmondsworth and New York: Allen Lane.

Salter, M. (2003) *Rights of Passage: The Passport in International Relations*, Boulder, CO: Lynne Rienner.

Salter, M. (2004) 'Passports, mobility and security: How smart can the border be?', *International Studies Perspectives*, 5 (1): 71–91.

Salter, M. (2005) 'At the threshold of security: a theory of international borders', in E. Zureik and M. Salter (eds), *Global Surveillance and Policing: Borders, Identity, Security*, Cullompton, UK: Willan.

Salter, M. (2007) 'Governmentalities of an airport: heterotopia and confession', *International Political Sociology*, 1: 49–66.

Samatas, M. (2004) *Surveillance in Greece: From Anti-Communist to Consumer Surveillance*, New York: Pella Publishing Company.

Sassen, S. (2001) *The Global City*, Princeton, NJ: Princeton University Press.

Sassen, S. (2006) *Territory, Authority, Rights: From Medieval to Global Assemblages*, Princeton, NJ: Princeton University Press.

Seltzer, W. and Anderson, M. (2000) 'After Pearl Harbor: The proper use of population data systems in time of war'. Paper presented to the Population Association of America Annual Meeting, March.

Senate Committee on National Security and Defence (2005) *Borderline Insecure: Canada's Land Border Crossings are Key to Canada's Security and Prosperity*, An Interim Report by the Senate Committee on National Security and Defence, Canada, June. Available at: *www.parl.gc.ca/38/1/ parlbus/commbus/senate/com-e/defe-e/rep-e/repintjun05-e.pdf*

Sengupta, S. (2003) 'Signatures of the apocalypse', *MetaMute*, 26. Available at: *http://www.metamute.org/en/Signatures-of-the-Apocalypse*

Sennett, R. (1996) *Flesh and Stone*, London: Faber and Faber.

Sewell, G. (1999) 'On the possibility of a sociology of workplace surveillance', University of Melbourne Department of Management, working paper no. 4.

Shearing, C.D. and Stenning, P. (1985) 'From the Panopticon to Disneyworld: The development of discipline', in E. Doob and E.L. Greenspan (eds), *Perspectives in Criminal Law*, Toronto: Canada Law Books.

Shields, P. (2002) 'Beyond "loss of control": Telecommunications, surveillance, drugs and terrorism', *Info: The Journal of Policy, Regulation and Strategy for Telecommunications and Media*, 4 (2): 9–15.

Simmel, G. (1906) 'The sociology of secrets and of secret societies', *American Journal of Sociology*, 11: 441–98.

Simmel, G. (1950) 'The metropolis and mental life', in K.H. Wolff (ed.), *The Sociology of Georg Simmel*, Glencoe, IL: Free Press.

Smith, D. (1990) *Texts, Facts and Femininity: Exploring the Relations of Ruling*, London and New York: Routledge.

Smith, D. (2006) 'Mobile vigilantes snap sex pests in action', *Observer*, Sunday, 30 April. Available at: *observer.guardian.co.uk/world/story/0,,1764585,00.html*

Smith, G. (2004) 'Behind the screens: Examining constructions of deviance and informal practices among CCTV control room operators in the UK', *Surveillance and Society*, 2 (2/3): 376–95. Available at: *www.surveillance-and-society.org/articles2(2)/screens.pdf*

Solove, D. (2004) *The Digital Person: Technology and Privacy in the Information Age*, New York: New York University Press.

Sontag, D. (2007) 'In Padilla wiretaps, murky view of "jihad case"', *New York Times*, 4 January. Available at: *www.nytimes.com/2007/01/04/washington/04padilla.html?pagewanted=1&ei=5094&e/*

Sorkin, M. (2003) 'Urban warfare: A tour of the battlefield', in S. Graham (ed.), *Cities, War and Terrorism: Towards an Urban Geopolitics*, Malden, MA and Oxford: Blackwell.

Stalder, F. (2002) 'Privacy is not the antidote to surveillance', *Surveillance and Society*, 1 (1): 120–4. Available at: *www.surveillance-and-society.org/articles1/opinion/*

Staples, B. (1997) *Everyday Surveillance: Vigilance and Visibility in Postmodern Life*, New York: Rowman and Littlefield.

Staples, W. (2000) *Everyday Surveillance: Vigilance and Visibility in Postmodern Life*, New York: Rowman and Littlefield.

Steeves, V. (2006) 'It's not child's play: The online invasion of children's privacy', *University of Ottawa Law & Technology Journal*, 3 (1).

Stepanek, M. (2000) 'Weblining', *Business Week*, 3 April: 26–34.

Stoddart, J. (2004) 'Letter to BC and Alberta Privacy Commissioners'. Available at: *www.privcom.gc.ca/legislation/let_040312_e.asp/*

Stoddart, J. (2005) 'Anti-Terrorism Act: Opening statement', Senate Special Committee on the Anti-Terrorism Act, 9 May, Ottawa, Ontario, Available at: *www.privcom.gc.ca/speech/2005/sp-d_050509_e.asp*

Suchman, L. (1994) 'Do categories have politics? The language/action perspective reconsidered', *Computer-Supported Cooperative Work*, 2 (3): 177–90.

Surveillance Studies Network (2006) *A Report on the Surveillance Society*, London: Information Commissioners Office. Available at: *http://www.ico.gov.uk/upload/documents/library/data_protection/practical_application/surveillance_society_full_report_2006.pdf*

Thompson, E.P. (1963) *The Making of the English Working Class*, Harmondsworth: Penguin.

Tinic, S. (2006) '(En)visioning the television audience: Revisiting questions of power in an age of interactive television', in K. Haggerty and R. Ericson (eds), *The New Politics of Surveillance and Visibility*, Toronto: University of Toronto Press.

Torpey, J. (2000) *The Invention of the Passport: Surveillance, Citizenship and the State*, Cambridge: Cambridge University Press.

Townley, B. (1994) *Reframing Human Resource Management: Power, Ethics and the Subject at Work*, London: Sage.

van der Ploeg, I. (2003) 'Biometrics and the body as information: Normative issues of the socio-technical coding of the body', in D. Lyon (ed.), *Surveillance as Social Sorting: Privacy, Risk and Digital Discrimination*, London and New York: Routledge.

van der Ploeg, I. (2006) *The Machine-Readable Body*, Maastricht: Shaker.

Virilio, P. (1994) *The Vision Machine*. London: British Film Institute.

Virnoche, M. (2002) 'The stranger transformed: Conceptualizing on- and offline stranger disclosure', *Social Thought and Research*, 24 (1/2): 343–67.

Volf, M. (1996) *Exclusion and Embrace: Theological Exploration of Identity, Otherness and Reconciliation*, New York: Abingdon.

Webster, F. and Robins, K. (1986) *Information Technology: A Luddite Analysis*, Norwood, NJ: Ablex.

Westin, A. (1967) *Privacy and Freedom*. New York: Atheneum.

Whitaker, R. (1999) *The End of Privacy: How Total Surveillance is Becoming a Reality*, New York: New Press.

Winner, L. (1977) *Autonomous Technology: Technics Out-of-Control as a Theme in Political Thought*, Cambridge, MA: MIT Press.

Winseck, D. (2003) 'Netscapes of power: Convergence, network design, walled gardens and other strategies of control in the information age', in D. Lyon (ed.), *Surveillance as Social Sorting*, London and New York: Routledge.

Wolterstorff, N. (1976) *Reason within the Bounds of Religion*, Grand Rapids, MI: Eerdmans.

Yar, M. (2003) 'Panoptic power and the pathologisation of vision: Critical reflections on the Foucauldian thesis', *Surveillance and Society*, 1 (3): 254–71. Available at: *www.surveillance-and-society.org/articles1(3)/pathologisation.pdf*

Yates, J. (1989) *Control through Communication: The Rise of System in American Management*, Baltimore, MD: Johns Hopkins University Press.

Yekutiel, Y. (2006) 'Is somebody watching you? Ancient surveillance systems in the Southern Judean Desert', *Journal of Mediterranean Archaeology*, 19 (1): 65–89.

Yesil, B. (2006) 'Watching ourselves: Video surveillance, urban space and self-responsibilization', *Cultural Studies*, 20 (4–5): 400–16.

Zuboff, S. (1988) *In the Age of the Smart Machine*, New York: Basic Books.

Zureik, E. (2001) 'Constructing Palestine through surveillance practices', *British Journal of Middle Eastern Studies*, 28 (2): 205–27.

Zureik, E. (2003) 'Theorizing surveillance: The case of the workplace', in D. Lyon (ed.), *Surveillance as Social Sorting*, London and New York: Routledge.

Zureik, E. (2004) 'Globalization of Personal Data Project – International Survey Concept Paper'. Available at: *www.queensu.ca/sociology/Surveillance/files/concept_paper.pdf*

Zureik, E. and Hindle, K. (2004) 'Governance, security and technology: The case of biometrics', *Studies in Political Economy*, 73 (Spring/Summer): 113–37.

Zureik, E. and Mowshowitz, A. (2005) 'Consumer power in the digital society', *Communications of the ACM*, 48 (10): 47–51.

Index